Napoleon's Men
and Methods

Napoleon's Men and Methods

The Rise and Fall of the Emperor
and His Men Who Fought by His Side

Alexander L. Kielland

LEONAUR

Napoleon's Men and Methods
The Rise and Fall of the Emperor
and His Men Who Fought by His Side
by Alexander L. Kielland

First published under the title
Napoleon's Men and Methods

Leonaur is an imprint of Oakpast Ltd

Copyright in this form © 2010 Oakpast Ltd

ISBN: 978-0-85706-409-7 (hardcover)
ISBN: 978-0-85706-410-3 (softcover)

http://www.leonaur.com

Publisher's Notes

Contents

Preface

The history of Napoleon is of inexhaustible interest. When the English government decided to send him to St. Helena, after the Battle of Waterloo, Lord Liverpool wrote to the Duke of Wellington, that in that island he would soon be forgotten; he even repeated this remark in another letter. 'Yes,' he said, 'he will soon be forgotten.' Yet at the present time there is no individual about whom more is written in all languages and in all branches of literature. Histories, novels, plays, are never tired of his story, and a serious student finds that there is no personality about whom more discoveries are constantly being made and with regard to whom it is more necessary to reconsider his judgment.

At the dawn of the 19th century, two great names, one in literature and one in the world of action arrest the attention of mankind: Goethe and Napoleon. Their careers have been so minutely studied that we are acquainted with, what they did every day, almost every hour of their lives. Yet subjected to this fierce light of publicity, which few could endure, they both gain by it, and Napoleon not the less. The more we know about him the more we admire him, the more reasonable do his actions appear, the less well founded the stories which are told to his discredit.

Napoleon was born a French subject, in Corsica, of a noble family of Italian descent. He received an excellent education in military colleges, distinguished himself by his diligence and regularity, entered the artillery, and was made a general at the age of twenty-three. During this time he had been the prop and guardian of his family, which had been left in a sad condition by the early death of his father. He had gained the highest credit for his conduct at the siege of Toulon, where he had been the means of driving the English fleet out of the harbour, and delivering the town into the hands of the French. His next service of importance was in Italy, where, by a strategy which is still a model to soldiers, he defeated the allied armies of Piedmont and Austria, and subdued the whole of the Lombard plain.

In this he was acting as general of the Directory. It was not he, but they, who plundered the museums and libraries of the conquered country. But when the Directory wished to annex Italy to France, he withstood them, making Italy into a self-governing Republic, and giving to Austria the rotten oligarchy of Venice, a government so degenerate that it could neither endure its maladies nor the remedies which were necessary to cure them. To receive Belgium and Lombardy from Austria in exchange for Venice was a good bargain, although it cost Napoleon much to make the sacrifice. After this the young general was sent to Egypt, where he conducted a notable campaign, which, however, led to no permanent result.

The Directory was the worst government with which France was ever cursed. It had no dignity, authority, or power, it could not preserve order at home, and it lost abroad what more energetic rulers had acquired. Napoleon was justified in saying, when he returned from Egypt: 'What have you done with the country which I left so powerful?'

The French people were tired of the Directory, and they were tired of themselves. Bonaparte became First Consul by the wish of the nation, the fittest man, indeed, the only man, to repair the errors of the past and to restore France to its proper place in the family of nations. His first act was to offer peace to England and Austria, offers which were insultingly refused. He compelled Austria to make peace by the battle of Marengo, and England was soon obliged to follow her example. The Peace of Amiens ensued and Englishmen could again visit Paris, from which they had been excluded for a decade.

The Peace of Amiens was broken in May, 1803, and there can be no doubt but that it was broken by England. Such is the verdict of independent authorities, who are not favourable to Napoleon. It was the interest of England to make war, whereas peace was essential for the furtherance of Napoleon's plans. Then began for Napoleon the war with England, which did not cease till his defeat at Waterloo. We need not repeat, even in a summary, the well-known tale of the Emperor's victorious career, but the statement that he was insatiable of blood, and that peace was impossible for him will not bear examination. He made peace with his enemies when he could, forcing them on their knees and claiming the spoils of victory; but England was always im-

8

placable, always on the watch, and war was again stirred up and supported by English millions.

It is customary to condemn his action with regard to Spain and Russia, but Spain was a dependency of France, which it was absolutely necessary to preserve in a condition of tolerable government and of loyalty to the French alliance. To place Joseph on the throne of Spain was certainly not more reprehensible than to give the crown of that country to the Duke of Anjou. The expedition to Russia, which Napoleon afterwards regarded as a fatal mistake, has not yet been completely elucidated. We do not precisely know the causes of it, the plans of Napoleon in respect of it, or the proper apportionment of blame between Alexander and Napoleon for its having taken place. At any rate, it broke the power of Napoleon, which no other country in Europe had been able to destroy. It was fated that he should only be conquered by himself.

In his misfortunes, friends and enemies rose against him. Saxony alone remaining faithful. Austria made the great mistake of joining the coalition, and entered upon a course which delivered her, at a later period, an easy prey to Germany. It is commonly said that at this time Napoleon ought to have made peace, but historical research has shown that he could not have done so, and that every offer submitted to him was a trap which it was wisdom to avoid. He fell on the plains of France before his converging enemies. He abdicated at Fontainebleau and retired to Elba. It was impossible that he should stay there.

The pension promised to himself and his family was not paid, his wife and child were withheld from him, plans were formed for deporting him to the Azores. He took an heroic course, he landed on the coast of Provence with a thousand men, marched to Paris without firing a shot, and entered the Tuileries, decorated and crowded for his reception. Never in history was there a more emphatic plebiscite, never a clearer announcement of a nation's will. Deaf to this appeal and blind to the consequences of their action, the diplomats of Vienna, led by Talleyrand, and followed, alas! by the Duke of Wellington, made ruthless war against him, and in the battle of Waterloo he suffered irreparable defeat. What followed is not pleasant for an Englishman to relate. We denied him the hospitality he asked for, and sent him to perish by a slow but inevitable death on the rook of St. Helena.

Such was, in brief, his marvellous history. How are we to judge his character and his career? The dominant passion of Napoleon was that nothing within his grasp should be done badly if it might be done well. There were two principles at work in the French Revolution, often mingled, sometimes undistinguishable, reform and anarchy. Napoleon was a friend of reform, but he was a bitter enemy of anarchy. No man living ever possessed a better ordered mind, and he desired that everywhere should reign the order which he felt within himself. England made the great mistake of regarding him as the continuator of the Revolution.

He was the negation of the Revolution, the repairer of its errors, the rebuilder of its ruins. Consequently the most enlightened men of Europe were on his side. Italy owes to him its creation, Bavaria her civilization. Examine where you will, the Napoleonic governments were everywhere good, until they were spoilt by the exigencies of the war which was forced upon him by the hostility of England. If France does not admire him today, she is supremely ungrateful. Without him, she would not exist. When ten years of anarchy had destroyed in that country not only all government, but all the elements out of which a Government could be formed. Napoleon appeared as the great restorer, and the most stable elements in France at this moment owe their origin to him.

This is the story which you are about to study in the present volume. It is written by a Norwegian, and is therefore more impartial than if it had been written by an Englishman, a Frenchman, or a German. It has had a large circulation on the Continent. It is brilliantly composed, and will doubtless have many readers in this country who will be induced by its perusal to explore, from a less insular point of view, the most marvellous, the most fascinating, the most instructive, career of any individual of modern times.

Oscar Browning

King's College
Cambridge
1907

Introduction

The following study of Napoleon is an incidental outcome of research that I undertook for a different theme. I had an idea of mastering the reaction which, as I believe, settled over the whole of Europe, after a brief period of advance, at the close of the eighteenth century. For this purpose I proposed to make a thorough study of the Congress of Vienna, and this occupied me from 1895 to 1898.

But as the inquiry proceeded I found it more and more difficult to interpret the story of the reaction from the Congress of Vienna to our own time. It seemed as if everything turned on a point that lay further back. I could not advance a single step, but was drawn, against my will, into the circle in which men and ideas moved. I made every effort to advance from the standpoint I had chosen, but I was forced to turn my eyes in the direction in which they all looked. Then I caught sight of the little man with the folded arms and the hat set crosswise on his head.

I flung everything else aside and fastened on Napoleon, whom, at first, I had deliberately excluded from my historical inquiry.

In thinking of the Congress of Vienna, I am always reminded of two caricatures of the time. The first represents all the sovereigns of Europe as children, sitting, with paper crowns on their heads, at a long table and playing with guns and tin soldiers. Then enters the officer with the announcement from the Consul at Livorno that Napoleon has left Elba. He brings a new toy, a box, which he flings on the table amongst the eagerly expectant children.

Suddenly a little man with folded arms and crossed hat leaps out of the box; and the second caricature shows all the sovereigns scrambling to get under the table, and the little man standing alone amongst the scattered toys. I have such a vivid impression of these caricatures that I cannot really say whether I saw them, or only read of them, or, in fact, invented the whole thing myself. But that was what actually took place.

They were so pitifully small, these princes and courtiers, parading in the venerable chambers at Vienna, and strutting about before each other and the ladies, much like the cocks in the barnyard when the hawk has flown away. The most brazen of them all is Metternich's private secretary, Gentz. He has all the refined vices of the time together with an unblushing vulgarity that shrinks from nothing. He crawls in the dust, and is ready to lend himself to any petty manoeuvre.

But at the same time he sees the threads of the intrigues and plots better than any other, and he jots down in his diary for his own edification:

As I have nothing in the least to reproach myself with, I am far from being depressed by my intimate knowledge of the miserable business that was done here and of the mean creatures who rule the world. On the contrary, it amuses me, and I enjoy the whole thing as a sort of play that is enacted for my express entertainment.'

With this eel-like slipperiness he came in the end to attain an enormous influence, although his official position in so important an assembly was inconsiderable. But he was not duped. After one of the dinners that he gave, he writes in his diary:

I took hardly any part in the conversation. The talk was all between Metternich and Talleyrand, on the usual lines. But I felt more keenly than ever how vapid life is, and how frail the men are who have the fate of the world in their hands; while I enjoyed my ascendancy without pressing it. The frivolous chatter of the princes had drawn a sort of mist over my mind.

There was little to choose between them. After all the years of anxiety and humiliation, when everything in Europe had been turned upside down, they had lost all feeling of restraint. All the leading families in Europe had suffered heavily, in the loss of wealth and property, and in sorrow over the bright young generation that had fallen in the field, or returned from it wounded and crippled, with no result but defeat and humiliation. And the most frightful circumstance of all was that they had had to entertain in their castles the man whose name they could not bring themselves to utter, or had been forced to come and do him homage. Then there was all the deception that had been practised when the ladies at the older courts crowded about the dust-covered adjutants who brought the first news from the field of battle in the usual terms:

The French, with 20,000 men, attacked a Russian corps of 5,000 under Prince Bagration. Bonaparte himself was present. The Russians bore down on them, cut down the French like mushrooms, killed Marshal Soult, and after a brilliant fight, reached the main body.

And, after two or three dances, there is a rush to the stairs, shrieking and consternation, and a general flight down the corridors and to the back doors. The French have reached the city. Marshal Soult, Duke of Dalmatia, may be at the castle before the sun goes down.

That was all over when they came together again at Vienna—kings and emperors and great nobles, Metternich, Schwartzenberg, Hardenberg, Castlereagh, Nesselrode, and, above all, Talleyrand with the lame foot and the thirteen oaths of loyalty. Which of them could fling the first stone at him? Even we, today, despise rather the prince who received his thirteenth oath, and the contemporaries who looked on all his successive promises of allegiance with complacency.

The ability of Talleyrand, in its cold falseness, scattered the politics of his time to right and left like heaps of snow, and marked out the way for them all with such grace and amenity, such clearness and acuteness, that it has the air of the most rigorous probity. After the second restoration a distinguished French *émigré* came to Talleyrand and asked for his influence in securing a suitable position in the new court.

'Certainly. But what services do you rely on in pleading your case?'

'I went with the king to Ghent during the Hundred Days.'

'Are you quite sure? Did you really go with him to Ghent, or were you only one of those who came back with him? Because, you see, there were only seven or eight hundred that went with him to Ghent, but when we reached France we numbered about five thousand.'

In his shrewdness he overlooked no current of feeling. But in whatever direction the new current set, it always ended in the direction that Talleyrand wished. In 1807, when he signed the Peace of Tilsit, after the Battle of Friedland, and when Napoleon's star seemed to be at the first magnitude, Talleyrand said to himself:

There is nothing decisive in the victory of Jena, in all the blood that has been spilt at Eylau, or in the triumph of Friedland. Poland has not been restored. Prussia, bleeding and bruised, is still

13

alive and thinking of revenge. The *Tsar*, who has been beaten and has lost his army, has received a million fresh subjects in Finland.

Talleyrand saw from this moment that Napoleon was really sinking. He turned to other masters, and at once set afoot his intrigues with the Bourbons.

At the Congress of Vienna he had so great an ascendancy that no one dared even to hint his astonishment at seeing him there at all, to say nothing of his being the first envoy of the Bourbons. His presence harmonised with the general feeling of security. When they heard his lame foot trailing over the floor of the Viennese palace, they felt that it was all over with the muddy boots that used to break in at the middle of a ball. But in spite of all came the sudden shock that ran through the city. He was here again. Napoleon had left Elba. all the old terror broke out afresh, and they scrambled under the table, or hurried home—each one thinking only of himself and his own.

I too left the Vienna Congress and began at the beginning. Napoleon Bonaparte was born on August 15th, 1769. As I read the story of his life, I noticed numbers of small traits that I now present in my own fashion.

CHAPTER 1

General & Consul

Napoleon did not enter the service of any of the political sections in France, and it was not until the later years of the Republic that he began, purely in his capacity as officer, to take any notice of politics. After the retaking of Toulon under his direction, his talent was so far recognised in military circles, that the war in Italy was really conducted according to his plans, though he was then only a general of a division. In 1796 he was appointed to the supreme command of the Republican troops in Italy. He was then in his twenty-seventh year, and it was in the same year that he married Josephine.

On April 12th he fought the Battle of Montenotte, one of the first in the series of eighteen great pitched battles that he won before the peace of Campo Formio in 1797, and the names of which still reflect his early glory—Millesimo, Mondovi, Lodi, Arcole, Rivoli, etc.

The day after the battle of Montenotte, as the different divisions of the French army, which had hitherto fought independently and had seen little of each other, marched all together over the plain in the bright sunshine, and took their places along the shimmering Bormida, without any confusion or disorder, it flashed on the old soldiers at once that a new spirit had taken the lead. On that day were born the confidence in and enthusiasm for the young commander that grew stronger and stronger. All of them, generals and soldiers, devoted themselves to him for life and death. From that came the blind unwavering obedience and trust that brought success to Bonaparte's carefully planned and able combinations.

While, not merely the whole of France, but the whole of fighting Europe, now began to listen to his name, it was not less remarkable how quickly the veterans of the Republic discovered the great leader. They were accustomed to having their commanders sent down by each succeeding government at Paris, sometimes genuine officers, at others men who had pushed their way to the front in the troublous times of the Revolution. After the battle of Lodi a deputation of old grenadiers came to Napoleon's tent and told him that he had been appointed corporal by the army! After Castiglione he was made sergeant. Bonaparte was shrewd enough to understand and appreciate these things; and ever afterwards, in all his campaigns, even in the days of misfortune, a smile passed over his features when some old grenadier in the ranks called him 'the little corporal.'

The love and regard of the army for this leader who never spared himself led in 1797, when he barely escaped falling into the hands of the Austrians, to the formation of a guard of honour for him. Napoleon afterwards made his corps of Guards out of this famous troop of guides, and the uniform of an officer of the Guards—green with red facings—was his favourite one. Bessières, head of a squadron, who had taken two Austrian cannon at Roveredo with six men, was entrusted with the command of the bodyguard and made responsible for the life of the general. As Marshal and Count of Istria, he commanded the Guard until 1812.

At once the men came into prominence who were to share Napoleon's glory afterwards. But not one of his later wars has so much brilliancy— one might almost say, so much festive cheerfulness—about it as the first two campaigns in Italy. It was, of course, a matter of life and death; the balls were as merciless as ever, when they did strike. But the operations went on more smoothly there. One saw the enemy working away with his ramrods, biting off the end of his cartridges, shaking his powder on the pan, and then the long aim and the shot so often miscarrying, especially in bad weather. The artillery did not hold off at a distance; you were not apt to be scattered with a hail of shells as happens today.

During a fight near Frankfort in 1791, Frederic William sat on his horse and watched a republican grenadier holding a small bridge alone against the troops. The king had him taken alive, and said to him: 'You are a brave lad, 'it's a pity you fight for a bad cause.'

'Citizen William,' the soldier answered, 'we should not agree on that point. We had better change the subject.'

It was especially in Italy that the war had peculiar features, because the French officers were young and fearless. They bewildered and bluffed the methodical Austrians, and frightened the more timid Italians to death. Bonaparte himself, the chief general, set them an example. Once, accompanied by only a few soldiers, in addition to his general staff and a number of officers, he rode through a small town named Lonato, on the day before the battle of Castiglione. The town was suddenly surrounded by a strong division of the Austrians, whose leader sent an officer to demand the surrender of the French.

Bonaparte had the man blindfolded, as was customary, and brought into the circle of high officers. When the bandage was taken from his eyes, and he looked round on the brilliant company, Bonaparte thundered at him:

'Ride back to your chief, and tell him that I give him eight minutes to lay down his arms! He has got into the midst of the French army, and he may give up all hope once that time is up.'

The officer hurried away, and the Austrian general was so terrified that he surrendered with 2,000 men and four guns.

Another time, in the year 1796, Lannes, then a young chief of a battalion, came upon a division of the papal cavalry, 300 strong, in the course of a reconnaissance. Lannes himself had only two or three officers and a dozen orderlies with him. Lannes rode at once to the papal officer, who had already ordered his men to fire and attack.

'What are you doing?' Lannes shouted. 'Put up your sabre at once.'

'Certainly,' said the officer.

'Tell your men to dismount and lead their horses to my headquarters.'

'Quite so,' answered the officer, and he obeyed.

It reminds one of Tordenskjold, when he was tired of lying before Marstrand and waiting for the Swedish fleet to come out. At last he went into the town and reached the house where the Swedish admirals were chatting and drinking.

'What the devil are you waiting for?' he shouted through the window.

So the Swedish fleet came out and received its punishment.

The Duke of Montebello resembled Tordenskjold in many ways. He was recklessly brave, always in the line of fire, yet a cool and diligent commander, and kept his head in the most desperate situations. It was in the first Italian campaign that Bonaparte noticed how Lannes, who was then chief of a battalion, led his men into action at Dego. From that day they were never separated until Lannes fell in 1809 at Esslingen, a marshal of France and Duke of Montebello. He was the last of all generals to maintain the old terms of intercourse with the Emperor, and addressed him as 'thou' to the end. He died in the height of his and Napoleon's glory, and escaped the evil days that tried so many of his comrades and found them wanting, or at least leave a good deal of obscurity about Napoleon in the end,

Lannes was one of the officers who were always wounded, which is hardly surprising when we remember the boldness with which he exposed himself. There were others equally daring, however, who were said by the soldiers to be invulnerable, such as Masséna. It was said of Lannes that balls flattened themselves against his bones. During the campaign in Syria he received a ball in the temple and fell to the ground. They thought he was dead. But it was found that the bullet had passed round the skull and remained under the skin at the back of the head, so that it was easily extracted. During the Battle of Aboukir, where he still suffered from the wound in his head, he got a bullet at short range in the shin. It was flattened, and ran round the leg and buried itself in the calf. He received many other wounds in the course of time, until a cannon ball smashed both his knees at Esslingen in 1809.

Lannes was also one of those who were wounded when they ran on the bridge with the general at Lodi, and covered him. The brave officer, Muiron, fell dead at Napoleon's feet on the bridge. Muiron was one of the officers that Bonaparte had discovered, and who was likely to accomplish great things under him. To the end the only way of advancement in Napoleon's army, however large it became, was for the general himself to pick out the best officers; and of that they were well aware. His knowledge of men, extending over all his armies, was so great and accurate that he was as well acquainted with his officers as the leader of a small troop usually is with his men. He had, moreover, an eye for the characteristics of each individual, and he was rarely wrong in his estimate.

During one of the Italian campaigns, on the eve of a great battle, a common soldier stepped out of the line, as they often did, with the old republican liberty, and said: 'Citizen general, I know how you will beat them tomorrow,' and he began to describe a plan of operations.

Napoleon swiftly interrupted him: 'Be quiet, you scoundrel.' The soldier was describing, word for word, Napoleon's own plan of battle, which he thought was utterly unsuspected by anybody else. The day after the battle he sent for the soldier—he had noted his regiment—but found that the great talent had perished in the simple uniform of a soldier, and he had probably lost a marshal.

When the supreme command was entrusted to the twenty-seven year old officer there were old and experienced generals and officers who had little disposition to bow to their new leader. Augereau, who was twelve years older, made a great noise, and said he was not going to have this raw lad from Corsica put over him. He soon changed his mind, and, although Augereau was never anything else in Napoleon's opinion than a brave and noisy swaggerer and incorrigible plunderer, he became a marshal and Duke of Castiglione, and was always with Napoleon until he finally deserted him.

Napoleon never had favourites that he would put in high positions in spite of their incompetence; and he was just as careful to appreciate and use men he did not like and whose treachery was fully known to him through his spies.

Others of Napoleon's men came into prominence in 1796. Berthier, who had been in America and Jamaica with Lafayette, and had received a command under the aged Kellermann, the victor of Valmy, was one of Napoleon's generals, and a particularly intimate friend. He was with Napoleon in the Egyptian campaign, but was allowed to return home on the ground of illness; though the real reason was his infatuation for Mme.Visconti. The indefatigable and fearless Oudinot, also, who lived until 1847, was with him in Italy. Under Napoleon he became marshal and Duke of Reggio. He always led the grenadiers who marched close to the Emperor; and he led the infantry in the early bayonet fights. The soldiers were accustomed to seeing him amongst them. He was one of those who were always wounded; he had in the end, I believe, twenty-three wounds.

Besides the unfortunate Muiron, General la Harpe also fell in the first Italian campaign, being shot in mistake by his own men. Another loss was that of General Steingel, an Alsatian, whom Bonaparte always quoted afterwards as an incomparable leader of the advanced posts, Steingel was short-sighted, and rushed into the fight at Mondovi so furiously with his hussars that he was slain by a sabre-cut, fighting in the front line like a common soldier.

The aged General Causse saved the Battle at Dego, but fell mortally wounded. He called for Bonaparte and learned that the battle was won. The old general nodded to the young one, and died with the words: 'Long live the Republic'

When Napoleon lay dying at St. Helena, they heard him call out, just before the end: 'Steingel! Desaix! Masséna! On them! We have them now.' He saw once more the forms of the generals of his young days.

The brave and neatly-equipped Austrians, retreating from point to point in their white uniforms, and looking so handsome in their powder and pigtails, deserved a better fate. But their antiquated methods could not resist the new French ones, and they had too many leaders who were too aged for effective service. Beaulieu was eighty years old. Wurmser, who had beaten the republican forces at Weissenburg, Heidelberg, and in the Palatinate, was an old man; so was Melas. Their best general was Alvinczy. In these stiff troops with their aged generals, swept out of the field by the fiery French armies, we see involuntarily something of the ridiculous, as generally happens when the older fall before the younger.

At the same time there was a certain politeness maintained between the enemies, something of the chivalry that always moderates the horrors of war, though in the new and terrible forms of warfare we see less of it every century. When the aged Wurmser was compelled at length by famine to surrender Mantua, Bonaparte, who was in command, sent the comparatively aged General Serrurier to receive the capitulation, so as to spare Wurmser the shame of giving up his sword to a young man of twenty-seven.

Before the peace of Campo Formio, Bonaparte and Josephine held a sort of small court in the *château* of Montebello. From the moment when he first set foot on the soil of Austria his whole being instinctively assumed a character that made it plain that he had a far higher aim in view than any other French general had ever had. His companions noticed with regret the departure from the easy ways that had hitherto prevailed in the armies of the Republic.

The *château* of Montebello received ministers from Vienna and from the king of Naples, envoys from the papacy, the Republics of Genoa and Venice, the Duke of Parma, the Swiss cantons, and a number of German princes. The house almost looked like a royal residence. Apparently without any change in his manner the young Bonaparte took his place with his usual seriousness and coldness, and the whole of those present—probably without noticing it—fell into the position that was to be taken up for many years to come; Napoleon alone in the centre and all the others in a circle round him. The finest diplomatists of Vienna came and tried their hand on him. There was nothing that he did not understand, not a manoeuvre that he did not see through, and certainly nothing under the sun that could daunt him.

On the other hand—not in anger, but quite coolly and deliberately, aiming to make an impression on the elderly diplomats—he took up the costly Chinese tea-service that the envoy Cobentzl had received from Catherine II, and threw it on the ground. 'That's how I'll smash Austria,' he said, and swept out of the room like a hurricane. They hurried after him, and brought the treaty ready signed, just as he had wanted them to do.

It was at this time he began to issue his grandiose proclamations to his soldiers. They are said to have had a considerable effect. For my part I have always found them too lengthy and affected, and I cannot endure the style of them.

Bonaparte himself delivered the abstract of the peace of Campo Formio to the *Directorate*, and Paris gave him and Josephine a series of estivities. The finest was, of course, that given by Talleyrand, who was foreign minister of the Republic at the time. Art and science came to do him homage. David painted him, and the famous artist, Grassini, whom he had brought from Italy, sang before him.

But France soon learned that there were 30,000 men and 10,000 sailors gathered in the Mediterranean harbours, and that vast preparations were in progress at Toulon. The best generals and a number of scholars were to take part in the mysterious campaign. It was the celebrated adventure in Egypt, of which, to be quite candid, I have never really understood the meaning. If it had succeeded, we might have seen how deadly a blow it would have been to England. As things were, it has remained quite obscure, in my opinion, and the campaign failed altogether.

On June 9th, 1798, the French fleet lay before Malta. Five hundred vessels came in sight, and so terrified the Grand Master, that, after a few days negotiations and a few harmless cannon-shots, he surrendered the island to the French. What had happened was that the Grand Master of the Knights of Malta, a German named Hompesch, received 600,000 *francs* and the promise of a yearly pension of 300,000 *francs*. With that he retired into private life. The chief harbour of Malta, Valetta, had always been regarded as absolutely impregnable. When the French officers came on land after the capitulation and examined the fortifications, one of them said: 'It was lucky for us there were people in there to open it for us; otherwise we should never have got in.'

Bonaparte's rare good fortune went with him on his Mediterranean voyage and brought him safely home from Egypt. Nelson crossed his track below Malta. He was three days in Alexandria before the French fleet arrived, and then he had put to sea again in search of

Bonaparte. Hence the French army landed in safety, and the struggle began. After Napoleon's entry into Cairo on July 25th, he met his first mishap, the first and most decisive blow to his expedition. He heard that the French fleet was destroyed on August 1st in the Bay of Aboukir. Nelson had found them at last, and though the French admiral was brave and made a good fight, the fate of any fleet was sealed when it met Nelson, as surely as the fate of an army that encountered Bonaparte. It was the weakest point in the whole plan to suppose that a French fleet could hold its own in the Mediterranean as long as Nelson was about.

After the expedition into Syria and the failure of the storming of St. Jean d'Acre, Napoleon received the journals from home at Cairo, and decided to return to France. He left behind him a letter to General Kléber, in which he put him in supreme command of the army in Egypt with a mass of instructions. Then he rode down to the coast secretly with a chosen few. They embarked on two frigates, and by some means or other reached Fréjus, in the south of France, on October 9th, 1799, without meeting a single one of Nelson's ships, which were scouring the Mediterranean and descending on everything that passed.

The Egyptian campaign has a certain resemblance, on a much smaller scale, to the Russian campaign of 1812. Both of them failed, and this was partly due to the same lack of knowledge of the land, the people, and the climate. From both the leader returned home, and left his followers in distress. It was not surprising, therefore, that officers and soldiers thought, when they heard of the general's return, that he had shamefully betrayed them, and left them in the Egyptian desert; just as, on the morning of December 5th, 1812, the Emperor's generals murmured against him, when it was known that he had departed for France during the night, abandoning what remained of the grand army to the cold and the *Cossacks*.

The qualities and sentiments of solidarity and concern that engender in the good citizen the mutual feeling that sustains domestic and public life were quite foreign to Bonaparte's nature. He assuredly never made any personal sacrifice for others or for the common good. What he gave never had the character of a sacrifice, but came of the splendid generosity that distinguishes the lofty prince. Had anyone expected him to remain on the wreck when things had gone wrong, he would have called it the stupid notion of an idealist.

He never had any other scheme of action than completely to realise his aim; and this was so great that he had no time to think of others.

The campaign in Egypt was not lit by the sunshine of Italy. The heated air, the thirst, and the plague, followed it everywhere; and the shadow of such deeds as the massacre at Jaffa, where he had several thousand prisoners of war shot because there was no food for them, and of the charge of having given opium to a large number of pest-stricken French soldiers, so that they might not fall alive into the hand of the enemy when the army left Syria, was cast over the figure of the young general.

However, in the famous Battle of the Pyramids and in the land-battle at Aboukir, a fresh splendour was added to the names of many of Napoleon's greatest generals—Junot, Rapp, Lannes, Davoust, and especially Kléber and Desaix, who remained in Egypt. Kléber was a brave general, and a big, handsome man. He soon concluded that Napoleon's large and vague plan of holding and colonising Egypt could not be realised, and he opened negotiations with the English admiral. In these he succeeded in securing a free passage home for the French, but the English government insisted that the French troops should be considered prisoners of war. Kléber would not agree to this, and he reconquered the whole of Egypt.

Meantime General Desaix had, almost from the beginning of the expedition, penetrated to upper Egypt, where he had not only conquered the whole country with great heroism, but had conducted the administration so skilfully as to win the affection of the half-savage inhabitants, who called him 'the wise *Sultan.*' They called Bonaparte 'the lord of fire.'

On July 14th, 1800, Kléber was assassinated on the streets of Cairo by an Arabian fanatic, and Desaix was killed at the same time by a cannon ball on the plain of Marengo, where he just arrived in time to secure the victory of Napoleon. General Menou was appointed to the chief command in Egypt, but he was still less able to hold together the impossible colony, constantly assailed as it was by the English. Menou was in his fiftieth year, and therefore one of the oldest of Napoleon's generals. He quarrelled with his officers, and made himself ridiculous in the eyes of the army by wearing the dress of an Arab. He married a young Egyptian and lived on oriental lines. Napoleon always treated him well, and he died as governor of Venice in 1810, it is said, out of love of a young actress. In his hands the Egyptian expedition came to a disastrous close, and the last of the French troops were brought home in English ships, though not as prisoners of war.

During the year of Bonaparte's absence in Egypt, the French Republic and the French arms met with serious reverses. He learned this from the journals that the English allowed to reach him in Egypt. No sooner did he land on French soil than the cry went up that he alone could save the country, and he was hailed everywhere as the deliverer. His unfortunate expedition was at once forgotten. The moment he landed he was met with every sign of rejoicing, and the feeling ran to enthusiastic heights as he made his way from town to town, making a triumphal march of his journey to Paris. He vigorously thrust out of sight the failure of his late campaign, and made even larger plans than when he had returned from the subjugation of Italy. But the young and suspicious general was not yet the man to be led away by illusions.

At Paris, where the whole world sought him, he maintained a great reserve. He hardly showed himself at the magnificent official festivities or in the theatres. But he worked and intrigued secretly against the constitution of the country with no scruple, and firmly determined to introduce into politics the strongest element of the time—the army, which in turn meant himself.

The first person to be associated with him in his secret work was, of course. Citizen Talleyrand, who was not a minister at the time. He was quite ready to put himself at the disposal of the new rising force. In 1799 the Republican government consisted of five Directors, who were held in no esteem, and of the Legislative Assembly. Bonaparte did not want a revolution, but a *coup d'état*, without conflict or bloodshed. The Legislative Assembly was sent out to St. Cloud, far away from Paris, and Bonaparte coolly determined to dissolve it by force, and substitute for it other forms that would prepare the way for him.

His assistants and fellow-conspirators were a number of men that had gathered about him, and were to be the first generals and statesmen in Europe. Up to that time they had been merely young officers, and they took up the political manoeuvre, at the general's order, much as they would have done a cavalry attack. Chief amongst them were his near relative Murat, Leclerc (who was married to Pauline), Sébastiani of Corsica, Lannes, Berthier, and Moreau. Bernadotte held back, and only made his appearance when the manoeuvre had succeeded. Lucien, the President of the Council of the Five Hundred, made himself very useful; it was the only help Napoleon ever got from one of his brothers.

Early in the morning of November 9th, 1799—the famous '18 *Brumaire*' according to the Republican calendar—the troops began to stir in the barracks. General Lefebvre, in chief command at Paris, at once scented a conspiracy. He drove down to make an inquiry, met Colonel Sébastiani, and asked him sharply what he was doing at that hour with his men.

'General Bonaparte wants to speak to you,' Sébastiani answered.

The street was so narrow that Lefebvre's carriage could not turn round, and so he went on to Bonaparte's hotel. The general met him with the words: 'You are one of the props of the Republic, General Lefebvre! You and I will today deliver France from the hands of these miserable lawyers.'

'Down with the lawyers,' Lefebvre replied. 'I am with you.' And he forthwith allied himself to Napoleon.

When Bonaparte entered the chamber of the Five Hundred he was greeted with a loud outcry about tyrants. The members crowded about him with violent gestures, and the grenadiers began to be concerned for their little corporal. Murat then ordered the room to be cleared, and it was done so quickly that many of the delegates of the people had to leap out of the windows. They were meeting in the orangery, so that the leap was not very dangerous; but it was an act of political violence that many never forgave Napoleon.

In the first ministry that Napoleon formed as First Consul—there were three Consuls, but no one took any notice of the other two—Talleyrand was to be Foreign Minister, though the place was held for a time by a German, Count Reinhardt, who was often used by Napoleon in administrative and diplomatic capacities. The Minister of Police was Fouché, whom Napoleon seemed never able to dispense with, though he saw through his knavery and often had experience of his duplicity afterwards.

In spite of the resemblance it would be most unjust to put Talleyrand and Fouché on the same footing. Talleyrand was like the finest kid, while Fouché was common fox-skin. Talleyrand passed with some subtlety from one party to another, but Fouché sold and betrayed one to the other, and lived on and for deceit, hated and despised by all. Napoleon deposed and reinstated him; he made him Duke of Otranto, and was often in a rage with him; but he could not live without the network of spies that Fouché could best spread about him. Indeed, there was no one else that he could use so readily for the meanest offices.

In the four years of the Consulate, which were certainly the happiest years of Bonaparte's life, France recovered from the effects of the Revolution. The unquenchable vigour with which the nation always rises again when the storm is over brought out a new and energetic society; and certain forces at once became active in it that centred about the person of the one great man, under the very mantle of the new found liberty, and raised him high above the citizens of the Republic. And his immense plans developed and found embodiment with a gigantic power that created afresh everything that it touched. In these mighty hands France was transformed immediately.

The First Consul betook himself to the palace of the older kings, and the citizens were subdued. When he passed from the Luxembourg palace to the Tuileries and the Louvre on the other bank of the Seine, it was with all the pomp of a royal ceremony. The familiar tone of the Revolution disappeared in a few days. The republican forms of social life were chilled in the cold court atmosphere that at once began to fill the halls of the Tuileries. People ceased to call each other citizen and citizeness, and began to cut their hair and wear decorative costumes. No change ever proceeded so rapidly as this.

The Republic was recognised by all the European powers except England. Peace reigned in some sort, and it only remained to conciliate England. Bonaparte, who then and throughout his whole career was far from understanding England and English ways, wrote a personal letter to George the Third, in which he suggested a *rapprochement* between the two great nations. The answer came, drily enough, in the form of a declaration made by Pitt in Parliament: 'England will not subscribe to the peace until France has returned within its earlier frontiers.' It clung rigorously to this determination never to treat with Napoleon under any circumstances. This meant that there was to be war in Europe as long as Napoleon retained power.

In France there was great rejoicing at the termination of the terrors of the Revolution. Many of the emigrants returned, prisoners were set at liberty, and the sentence of banishment was annulled. Social and commercial life received an unprecedented' impulse under the wise legislation and practical aids that were now given.

England was the first to feel the fire of war that Bonaparte set aflame. Every time that a country was beaten, England came to it with fresh money and fresh proposals for a coalition. The first coalition was originally an alliance of Austria, Bavaria, Turkey, Russia, Sweden, Denmark, and England, the latter Power maintaining fleets both in the North Sea and the Mediterranean for the attack on France. But the First Consul found a means of drawing Russia out of the coalition. Since the wars of the Republic there were a number of Russian prisoners in France and in the frontier fortresses. Napoleon equipped them all with Russian uniforms, choosing the correct uniforms and ensigns according to the rank and regiment and arm of each prisoner.

Then he sent the whole of them—many hundreds in number—comfortably back to Russia with a greeting to the Emperor, Paul I, without saying a word about the return of French prisoners of war. This was, perhaps, the only occasion on which Napoleon's calculation was correct when he tried to treat the other European princes as comrades. The half-demented Paul was caught by the stratagem, and became a fanatical admirer of Napoleon. He recalled his troops from Germany, left the coalition, and expelled all Englishmen from St. Petersburg. The First Consul also sent his friend and confidant, Duroc, afterwards Duke of Friaul, as envoy to Berlin, and in a very brief time he succeeded in embroiling the coalition to such an extent that he could himself lead his troops across the Alps to the liberation of Italy, which had been taken again by the Austrians while he was in Egypt.

Austria, if not the whole of Europe, was astounded when Bonaparte's generals crossed the Alps with all their artillery and baggage, and marched down upon the plains in the north of Italy. He himself stood before the gates of Milan on June 2nd (1800) as Italy's deliverer. The Italians were beside themselves with joy at seeing him once more; he was reported to have died in Egypt. The second Italian campaign thus succeeded more brilliantly than the first. The same sun shone on the French troops; but they were now the finest soldiers that Europe had ever seen, not the ragged and shoeless bands of the Republic.

At the beginning of a campaign, Napoleon, especially in his earlier and more slender years, used to spread his maps on the ground, and crawl over them, and work his plans with coloured needles. The friend of his youth, Bourrienne, who was his private secretary in the early years, has related that Napoleon had fixed his needles round the plains of Marengo before he left Paris, and said that he would fight the Austrians there. With the divisions of Lannes, Victor, and Desaix, he marched on the village of Marengo on July 13th in search of the chief Austrian army under General Melas.

He had, however, commanded Desaix to take a different route on the following day, as he was uncertain where he would find the enemy.

Early the next morning, the famous July 14th, 1800, Bonaparte suddenly confronted the far superior numbers of the Austrian army, and the battle began at once. He sent most pressing messages to Desaix, but he knew that it would be several hours before Desaix's division could join him in the conflict.

The battle began with the taking of the village of Marengo by the Austrians and the scattering of Victor's division. Bonaparte, who knew well that the issue depended on Desaix's arrival, made strenuous efforts to hold his ground to some extent with the left wing; the right wing and the centre retreated during the whole morning, and were driven from one position to another by the more numerous Austrians. Napoleon followed them, and when the corps that he was with had retired some distance, he halted and cried to the general of the division: 'That will do, general. Now we'll fight again for a little.'

Thus matters went on until three in the afternoon, and everybody but Bonaparte looked upon the fight as hopelessly lost. The aged Melas, overcome with fatigue, and injured by a fall from his horse, was now so sure of victory that he left the field, and went back across the Bormida. He at once sent couriers from Allessandria to Vienna to say that he had gained a decisive victory at Marengo. He left it to General Zach to follow up the defeated Bonaparte. It was now five o'clock. Bonaparte did not give up hope. He led the retreat, and kept his fine troops together so well that the retreat nowhere degenerated into flight.

At last Desaix galloped up with several adjutants. He had just returned from Egypt, and hurried with all speed to his friend Bonaparte. They were the best leaders at the time, in the eyes of the troops. He had impatiently ridden ahead of his troops when he reached the field, and he and Bonaparte were soon agreed that as matters stood, the battle was lost. 'Let us get down from our horses,' Desaix said to him, 'and it will look as if we were more confident.' They did so, and together watched the battle they were conducting, and that meant so much for their country. The two men were still almost at the age when we are usually taken up with examinations, and shivering before dry and dusty professors.

It is said that Desaix remarked: 'The balls don't know me since I have been in Egypt.' French officers had a peculiar way of speaking when they were confronted with death, or their own presentiments of it. Desaix's words were regarded by everybody as a proof that he himself felt his impending fate. At length the first troops of Desaix's division swept on to the plain. The two generals shook hands and mounted their horses. Half an hour afterwards a cannon ball shattered Desaix's breast and killed him on the spot.

The first troops of Desaix's corps to reach Marengo and avenge his death belonged to General Boudet's division. In all the great battles, and whenever an important move is on, we find mention of this division. General Boudet was born in 1769, and had taken Guadeloupe in 1794. In 1807 he defeated the Swedes at Stralsund, and was made a count. He received large donations of land in Swedish Pomerania, and was besides Knight of the Danebrog, and received the Cross of the Legion of Honour. His men, especially his artillery, were models for the whole army.

These chosen troops came up at the last moment and put spirit into the half-demolished army. All weariness was forgotten, and confidence was restored in the little man on the white horse whom they had seen in a kind of flight all day long. He cried out to the ranks as they closed once more and pressed forward: 'Remember, soldiers, that I am accustomed to sleep on the field of battle!'

General Zach had opposed Boudet with 5,000 good grenadiers. But, just at the right moment, General Kellermann flung his cavalry on the Austrian grenadiers, who were thrown into confusion and generally taken prisoners. From that point the French on the left wing advanced, and the plain was retaken before evening. The general was able to sleep in the village of Marengo, from which he had been driven in the early hours of the morning. In the course of the night Berthier concluded an arrangement with Melas, by which all that the French had lost in Italy was restored.

During the last hundred years it has often been said and written that it was Desaix and Kellermann who won the Battle of Marengo. In my opinion the general in command can only gain a victory when his officers obey his orders, keep their places, and do their duty at the proper time. One man can do no more once the battle has begun. Bonaparte won at Marengo because Desaix and Kellermann did their duty according to his calculations; he lost the battle of Waterloo because Grouchy did not do his duty, and was not where he ought to have been according to the calculation of the chief commander.

There were two General Kellermanns—father and son—with Napoleon. The elder was born in 1733 at Baden, and lived until 1820. While he was a republican general he won the artillery Battle at Valmy. Napoleon made him marshal and Duke of Valmy, and often employed him as commander in the fortresses where the young troops were trained. His son, Count of Valmy, was made a general after Marengo. In later years he generally fought against the English in Spain and Portugal.

It is difficult to realise the immense effect of the battle of Marengo. The success was so unexpected and so great that all ranks of society and all parties joined in the common rejoicings, Paris was at once illuminated when the news arrived, and from that day practically the whole of the government, indeed the whole of France and its destiny, was given into the hand of Napoleon. The banished king wrote the following letter to him:

> You will have known for a long time, general, in what esteem I hold you. Should you doubt my gratitude, I beg you to let me know what position you desire to have, and where you desire your friends to be placed in the State. As to my principles, I am a Frenchman. I am by nature indulgent, and will be more so where prudence dictates that quality. The victor of Lodi, Castiglione, and Arcole, and the restorer of Italy, cannot possibly prefer empty fame to true honour. Meantime, you are wasting valuable time. We two could secure the prosperity of France. I say, we two, because I need Bonaparte, and because he cannot do this without me. General, the eyes of Europe are upon you. Honour is waiting, and I am impatient to restore peace to my country.
>
> Louis.

Bonaparte's reply was dry and direct.

> Sir—I have received your letter and thank you for the gracious words you write of me. But you must not think of returning to France. You would have to walk over hundreds of thousands of corpses. If you will make the sacrifice of your own interests for the peace and prosperity of France, history will thank you. I am not insensitive to the misfortunes of your family, and I will gladly contribute to your tranquillity and security in the refuge that you have chosen.
>
> Bonaparte.

The almost naive assumption of superiority must have made a great impression on the Bourbons, who had stooped so low in a moment of weakness. Bonaparte himself, indeed, was hardly conscious what an impression of audacity his letter would give to people whose real attitude toward himself he never completely understood. But in the shadow of the shattered kingdom, and of the republic that had collapsed so quickly, there were figures that united in a common hatred of the man—a determination to rid the world of tyrants.

A number of conspiracies were discovered from time to time, in which older men of the revolutionary days, and others that belonged to the king's party, were involved. Some tried to penetrate into Malmaison in assumed uniforms; others attempted to kill him as he went to the opera. A few dangerous workers had begun to prepare a bomb, but when they came to test the explosive, the effect was so powerful that they became half afraid, and the noise attracted the attention of the police.

However, before the close of the year 1800, one of these murderous plans was put into execution and made a great impression on Paris. It was due to a conspiracy of some of the royalists, who had, with extreme calculation and cold-bloodedness, formed a plan that was only thwarted by an accident.

On Christmas night Bonaparte and Josephine were to hear Haydn's *Creation* at the Opera. It was a special performance and the whole of Paris was expected to be there. Shortly before seven a couple of the conspirators, dressed as working men, came along with a hand-cart, on which there was a vessel filled with powder and balls. They left the cart casually, as it were, in a street that the carriage of the First Consul had to pass. The time was accurately calculated, and the fuse lit. Everybody knew that Napoleon was punctual. But it happened that his coachman was rather drunk that evening. He raced furiously down the street, and was past the infernal machine two or three seconds before it exploded.

Fifty-six men were wounded and twenty-two killed, and several houses were demolished. In the opera-house people had just begun to whisper of an attempt on the First Consul's life, when he stepped coolly into his box, and there was an indescribable outburst. His wonderful luck made him seem miraculous. He was the chosen one of Providence in the eyes of many, and the attempt on his life lifted him to a higher pinnacle.

But, though he had shown his customary coolness during the catastrophe, he afterwards had a very close inquiry made into the source of the outrage, which clearly was no isolated crime. Fouché, either to conceal his ignorance of the plot, or out of a grudge against his old enemies, gave him the same night a list of 130 revolutionaries.

Napoleon's feeling was directed rather against the royalists, but he had these 130 individuals sent to Cayenne, after forcing through a law that empowered the Consuls to banish undesirable persons.

On February 12th, 1801, Paris heard of the Peace of Lunéville, which was the fruit of Marengo and of Moreau's equally brilliant victory at Hohenlinden. The frontiers of France were extended, and all its enemies humiliated. Thousands of people passed by the Tuileries, crying: 'Long live Bonaparte,' They danced in the streets, and the First Consul's orchestra played dance-music to the accompaniment of musketry and rockets. Once more the most splendid *fête* was that given by Talleyrand, Minister of Foreign Affairs. At his house the First Consul received all the distinguished people—French or foreign—who were then at Paris. The older royalty and the Revolution, nobles and republicans, new men of fortune, soldiers, scholars, poets, artists, and officials—all came together and paid homage for the first time to Napoleon Bonaparte as France's first citizen and the head of the State.

All who have read the memoirs of the period are familiar with the odour of summer-roses that clings to Malmaison. In later years, when the great French *châteaux* were reopened, there was more pomp and brilliance, but they never eclipsed the fairy days at Malmaison, with the court that was merely a troop of fine young ladies and gentlemen on a picnic. The First Consul, who was the centre of it all, was no longer the spare, dark general with the yellow Italian tint. His whole appearance was changed. When he was a young officer he suffered severely from a disease of the skin, a sort of vicious scab. He contracted it first on his hands in the trenches before Toulon, where he took part himself in loading and serving the guns.

It spread over his whole body and became a great plague to him. He was not then in a position to command the best attendance or to give sufficient time for a radical treatment of the ailment. When he had eventually got rid of it, his skin assumed the marble whiteness that characterised his family, and he paid great attention to the care of it. He often spoke about the treatment of it. First he would lie for hours in water heated to such a degree that others could hardly put a foot in it. He also had himself washed with *eau de Cologne*, of which he used enormous quantities. His whole body was then well rubbed, and his servants put on his under-clothing, and the narrow white trousers, all of the finest material and spotlessly clean. His uniform was always the blue or green coat of the bodyguard with red facings, and afterwards court dress and the fantastic imperial clothes.

He was now a handsome well-built man, with strong legs, small, firm feet, clear and clean-cut features, and the fine mouth of the Bonapartes, with faultless white teeth. That was his appearance when he took part in their games and ran races with Josephine and the other young women in the garden at Malmaison. But he did not like anyone to beat him in the race, and he was angry when he fell down and got grass-spots on his white hose. One had to be very serious then. The young men choked down their laughter, and did not know which way to turn, for he was a dangerous man.

No one, not even Josephine, knew how far he would take a joke. He was always irritable from youth upward. I have never read anywhere of Napoleon laughing. It seems that he could not. It is said that a good- natured smile of his could heal wounds, and make the man it was bestowed on follow him through fire and water. But there was never a laugh, or an outburst of hilarity; he had always the same marble coldness, with his lips firmly compressed, ready to issue the word of command or to frighten men to death with a voice that had no equal. His temper was always uncertain.

The painter Isabey was light and agile, and full of jokes, like all the others. One morning he came through the empty rooms—the company had gone to breakfast—and saw in the conservatory a young man whom he took to be Lucien Bonaparte. Isabey quietly approached on tiptoe, then made a spring, and jumped full on him. When he turned round in triumph to face him he met the dreaded look of the First Consul. The little artist ran as fast as he could into the garden and then the forest, and it was a long time before he would venture out, and still longer before he dare tell anyone of his adventure. The First Consul went on as if nothing had happened.

For my part I have never been in company with any great man, with the exception of Björnstjerne Björnson. He too has a look that can frighten people to death. When he opens his mouth, it is generally for the purpose of serious talk. But how he can laugh! His laughter has a full resounding ring, as if it came from the depths of his heart. There are few things so pleasant as to hear Björnson laugh.

Napoleon certainly never indulged in laughter or in jovial intercourse over a glass or a good story. He ate so quickly that no one had enough, and the young officers were dismayed as he rose from table before the soup was finished at the lower end of it. He drank a couple of glasses of his red wine and a little brandy when on the field; but I have never heard of him raising his glass to propose a health, and certainly the wine never reached his head in the smallest degree. Yet all are agreed that he had a most wonderful smile.

One night they were sitting together at St. Helena, and talking of old days, as usual. In the course of the conversation. Las Cases remarked: 'I do not understand why Your Majesty did not take the sword of Frederic the Great, when you had it in your hand.'

'Because I had my own,' said the Emperor quietly, with his characteristic smile; 'and he pinched my ear, without hurting me,' says Las Cases.

That was one of Napoleon's habits. When he was speaking to one of his generals or anybody that he liked, he would take hold of the lap of his ear, and pinch it more and more severely while he spoke. One needed to be very stolid to keep still during the ordeal. His fingers were not too gentle.

He was destructive by character and custom. He stuck his paper-knife into the costly chairs that were provided for him everywhere. He wasted huge quantities of paper. Whenever he took up anything that was frail or finely worked, he was quite certain to demolish it or damage it before putting it down. He pulled up the choicest plants in the hot-houses, and, when he could do it without being seen, he used to shoot Josephine's rare birds. As a matter of fact, however, he was not a good shot, and he did very little when he was out shooting. But it was a kingly pastime, and the whole apparatus was at hand, and so he took his marshals for great hunts in the forests of Fontainebleau. They were soldiers and accustomed to hear the balls whizzing past their ears, and they shot right and left on chance, to the consternation of the real sportsmen and servants that were there. One day the Emperor shot out one of the eyes of Masséna, the Duke of Rivoli, but nothing was said of it. Berthier took the blame for it, probably because he was master of the hunt.

As long as they were at Malmaison the lively and amiable Josephine succeeded in dispelling the chill that always surrounded the Emperor in later years. There they lived like good and loving *bourgeois*, sleeping in the same room. They were together all the time that he was not engaged with business, though these intervals were brief enough. It is incredible what an amount of work he got through in those days. His lively sisters, the young wives of his generals, and the handsomest officers in the army, played comedies and other performances, danced and made love to each other, without any serious consequences. Bonaparte himself had returned from Egypt with an unpleasant story

34

about Josephine. The stupid Junot had told it to him in the trenches before Acre. But she brought him round; he returned to the army, and all was forgiven and forgotten.

The only one that was missed from the gay company was the charming Pauline, the youngest sister of the First Consul. She had accompanied her husband, General Leclerc, in the expedition to San Domingo in 1801. During the Revolution the blacks in the French colony of Hayti had, freed themselves, and a negro called Toussaint l'Ouverture, had been put at the head of a sort of republic that the blacks had formed after the model at Paris. Bonaparte gave his brother-in-law a well-equipped expedition and fleet, and told him to restore order in the colony as peacefully as possible.

The expedition entirely failed. Unfortunately, Toussaint l'Ouverture had sailed for France the day that the fleet reached the island. He was a man of some ability. Leclerc, who could not even keep order amongst his own generals, met the wild negro-general Christopher, and the latter at once began an insurrection. The plague broke out. Leclerc himself died, and his successor, General Rochambeau, who afterwards fell at Leipsic, was a hard man, and allowed himself to be led by the French planters into, waging a fearful war of extermination against the blacks. They were driven into the sea and drowned; they were hunted with blood-hounds from Cuba. The expedition was a complete failure, and the colony was lost to France.

Pauline, untouched by plague and other horrors, returned as a widow to Paris. She was more charming than ever, and ready to begin again where she had left off.

During these years of comparative peace the First Consul was constantly occupied with plans against England, with which he was always at war. He collected enormous provisions of war by land and sea in the north of France, on the Channel, and especially at Boulogne. The Bourbons and emigrants at London were also working in their own way. They set afoot a fresh conspiracy which was to fall on the First Consul during one of his journeys to St. Cloud or Malmaison, overcome the body-guard riding by the carriage, and kill Bonaparte in the struggle. This seemed to them to be more like a fight than an assassination. They had put at the head of the conspiracy the old Vendean leader, Georges Cadoudal, the people of la Vendée being still distinguished by a fanatical loyalty to the royal house.

Cadoudal had always wished to see one or two French princes at his side, and his idea was to recall the Bourbons when Bonaparte should be got rid of. The army would be conciliated, and led to fresh achievements by General Moreau, who—though he was far from royalist in disposition—was understood to be willing to take part in the conspiracy, because he had been at variance with Napoleon for some time.

General Moreau, who was born in 1761, had covered himself with glory under the Republic. His retreat from Holland, when Jourdan had been beaten as usual, was and still is regarded as a masterpiece of military art. In the eyes of all his contemporaries, especially since the death of Desaix, he was next to Napoleon. With a very short interval they won the two most brilliant victories: Bonaparte at Marengo in Italy, and Moreau at Hohenlinden in Germany, For a time it was reported that he was going to marry Pauline Leclerc, but he chose a certain Mlle. Hulot, and from that day his and Napoleon's ways parted. The lady and her mother succeeded in inflaming him against Napoleon to such an extent that he made it his life-aim and his misfortune to destroy him and take his place.

In order to win General Moreau, the conspirators had chosen his old comrade. General Pichegru. The latter, though an old republican, had accepted the Bourbon plan at London, and then went to Paris to kill the common enemy. The next step was to bring Moreau and Pichegru together, and induce Moreau, who shared Pichegru's hatred of Napoleon, to join the plot. In August, 1803, Cadoudal left London with a million francs in Bank of England notes, which he had sewn into his belt. He landed on the sand-hills of Biville from a smuggler, and was led from man to man, using certain signs agreed upon, as far as Paris, where he began to collect suitable men for the attack, and get them uniforms, horses, arms, and all that was necessary.

Meantime others were endeavouring to bring Moreau and Pichegru together. Moreau spoke with great warmth of his old comrade, and offered to do all in his power to procure the reversal of the sentence that had banished Pichegru to Cayenne in 1797. It is possible that he also expressed himself somewhat sharply about Napoleon.

This was taken by the intermediary, a General Lajolais, as a safe indication that Moreau was ready to join the conspiracy. He hastened to London, via Hamburg, and gave such an account of Moreau's bitterness against Napoleon that the emigrants were beside themselves with joy, and even the Count Artois, who was afterwards King Charles X, compromised himself for life by taking part in meetings where the murder of the head of a State was decided. Toward the close of 1804,

Pichegru, with several of the highest French nobles, including the brothers Polignac, crossed the Channel in Captain Wright's yacht, and reached Paris.

A little later Lajolais brought about a meeting between Moreau and Pichegru. It took place during the night in the deserted Boulevard Madeleine. The two old friends were deeply moved at seeing each other in such circumstances, when Georges Cadoudal suddenly stepped out and joined in the conversation. Moreau at once became as cold as ice. At subsequent meetings it became clearer and clearer that Moreau was quite willing to work for himself, but by no means for the Bourbons. It was a serious disillusion, and was so discouraging to the rest of those who were in the plot, that many of them thought of giving up the whole enterprise and leaving Paris.

Just at that moment the arrests began. Fouché was not Minister of Police at that time, but he was prying round everywhere on his own account. Réal, an officer that Napoleon often used, was at the head of the Paris police, but he knew nothing of the conspiracy. It was really the First Consul himself who picked up the first threads. Even while he was Consul, and still more when he became Emperor, Napoleon's time was largely occupied in reading all kinds of police reports and making himself familiar with the statements of spies that were put before him every day.

At the very time when the royalist murder was being plotted, he was making a fool of the English envoy at Munich. He knew that the man had offered £50,000 for the black *portefeuille* in Bonaparte's private room, and so he read more carefully than ever the mass of reports on suspicious persons, and the lists of foreign and native individuals who had disappeared or turned up. From the large number of these he chose the names of five men who were to be submitted to judicial inquiry.

It was evident that he had a keen eye for this kind of work. Only two out of the five turned out innocent, and were set at liberty. Two of them were convicted of high treason and shot, without any information being got out of them. The fifth confessed that he was one of Georges Cadoudal's men, and had come with him from England over the sand-hills of Biville. At the same time, after a nocturnal struggle between custom-officers and smugglers at the coast, a piece of cartridge-paper was picked up with the name Troche written on it. It was found that this was the name of the young man who was leader of the conspirators that had come with the smugglers from London and secretly made their way to Paris. These were the first threads of the plot.

The next thing to be discovered was that General Moreau was involved in the affair. He was at once arrested, and gradually forty-five of the conspirators were landed in the various jails, but the leaders were still at liberty. When Moreau was arrested, the cry was raised immediately that Napoleon was trying to get rid of his one rival in this pitiable fashion. Moreau stood so high in the esteem of the army and the nation that he could not be conceived as helping the royalists and those who were considered guilty. Bonaparte's temper broke loose, and was turned furiously on the royalists, from whom he thought he had deserved better treatment.

From that time he spared no means of discovering the leaders, so that the whole world should know the plot to be a dangerous royalist conspiracy against the first man in France. The prisoners insisted that they had been acting with some of the most distinguished names in France, and that a prince of the blood—they thought it was the Duc de Berry—was to come to Paris, if he was not already there.

'I will forgive Moreau,' said Bonaparte, 'but I will shoot the first Bourbon that falls into my hands.'

He sent the judge Reynier to Moreau in prison, to extract a confession, and, so it was proposed, bring the general to the Tuileries. But the official conducted the business with so little tact that Moreau did not realise the good intention. Not knowing that the greater part had already been betrayed by the others, he denied everything, and made use of all kinds of foolish subterfuges.

'Very well,' said Bonaparte, 'he shall be put on trial.'

They still failed to discover Pichegru and Cadoudal and the other leaders in Paris, and an extraordinary law was passed that threatened with death all who were concerned in hiding them; those who knew it and did not give information would have six years in the galleys. Pichegru moved, as he did not like the company he had fallen into. He spent one night at the house of the minister Marbois, with whom he had been banished before. Napoleon appreciated the friendly act so far as to spare the minister, when he heard of it afterwards. At last someone was found who would betray Pichegru for 100,000 *francs*. He gave them the key of the rooms where he had himself conducted the general. The police entered the rooms at night, and seized the pistols that lay by the bed; though the powerful general fought them in his shirt before they could bind him and take him to prison.

They afterwards took the brothers Polignac, Rivière, and finally Cadoudal. He was caught in a small carriage on one of the outer boulevards by two policemen. He shot one dead and wounded the other, but the people prevented him from escaping. Cadoudal made no secret of his object in Paris, and was shot without asking any consideration. As Cadoudal and the Polignacs were now arrested, the matter got abroad, and people learned with astonishment that the royal family itself was privy to the plot to murder the deliverer of France. Unhappily, Napoleon was so much embittered that he would not rest until he had found traces of the Bourbons. He was ready even to pardon Pichegru, and send him as governor to Cayenne, to organise the colony there; but for the royal party there was to be no mercy.

One day he went through the Bourbon family with Talleyrand and Fouché, and when he heard of the Duc d'Enghien, whose name was scarcely known to him, he set his spies to work at once. He was soon informed that the young prince lived close to the French frontier—nearer than any of the other emigrants—at Ettenheim, in Baden, that he was often absent for days together, and that he received suspicious visitors.

One of these was falsely said to be Dumouriez, one of the republican generals who had fled to England to escape a charge of high treason. It agreed only too well with all that the prisoners had stated—that in their gatherings a distinguished young person appeared at times, and was treated with exceptional respect by the others. The First Consul firmly believed that he had now found the last link in the plot. He sent General Ordener across the frontier to arrest the duke at Ettenheim, and at the same time sent his best envoy, Count Caulaincourt, to the Baden court to excuse the infringement of territorial limits. He was occupied for a whole week with the affair, and he worked himself to such a pitch of excitement that no power in the world could restrain him. The unfortunate young duke, who was certainly innocent, was arrested in bed, brought to Paris, and was, after a very slight legal procedure, shot at Vincennes in the early morning.

The incident caused a stir in contemporary life that we can hardly appreciate. The unjust and hasty deed is one of the worst that Napoleon Bonaparte ever committed. It forms the refrain to all the vituperative songs of his enemies. We have to remember what a prince of the blood meant at that time; this one was the last of the house of Condé, which was closely related to the Bourbons. He belonged to the highest rank of European nobility. Moreover, Europe had already begun to speak of the Corsican monster, the bloody tyrant, etc., and was anxious to find some ground for this hatred.

Paris seemed to be shaken by a thunder-bolt. Nothing like it had been known since the Revolution, if even then. It had all taken place so quickly that at first people only knew that an emigrant prince had been violently seized on foreign territory, and passed before a court-martial with hardly any investigation. Although more than a third of the Parisians were ignorant who the Due d'Enghien was, all were horrified at this nocturnal trial—without a jury—coming, as it did, after the questionable treatment of the conspirators. Malmaison was intensely excited. Mme. Rémusat and the other ladies were paralysed with horror. Josephine threw herself sobbing on her husband's neck, crying:

Listen to me, Bonaparte! If you have your prisoner shot, you will be guillotined yourself—like my first husband; and this time you will take me with you.

Fouché was pleased in his sombre way. 'That was fortunate,' he said. 'I began to fear that this little Bonaparte would be content to play the part of General Monk.'

Bernadotte was of much the same opinion. He rubbed his hands, and said: 'We have him now!' He meant that the First Consul had played his stakes too high, and it might be his ruin.

Talleyrand expended his wit over it: 'It's worse than a crime; it's a blunder.'

The affected Lucien Bonaparte rushed into his wife's bedroom with the cry: 'Alexandrine, let us fly! He has tasted blood.' He posed as a noble republican, and so his brother was a blood-thirsty tyrant.

It would be impossible to form a more unjust estimate of Napoleon than that of his brother Lucien. He was neither cruel nor blood-thirsty. He did the sanguinary work of a soldier, in which he was a master, but he was devoid of the cruelty that characterised nearly all the other great soldiers with whose glory our children's lessons are poisoned. If in this case he made a violent end of an enemy, it was a sort of family revenge. The other Bourbons had sent men to murder him, and surrounded him with bravoes in his own country, though their machinations had happened to fail through a series of accidents.

As to the young man who became the victim, he belonged to a race whose degeneration is obvious to us today. The great military genius that had once been found in the family—in the great Condé—

had assumed a different shape. Insanity and suicide entered into the blood. One of the duke's ancestors at the siege of Belgrade shot sentinels and others who appeared on the walls from safe cover; and when he settled down at Paris, Louis XIV had to pardon him three times for shooting from his palace windows at slaters and other workmen on neighbouring roofs, merely for the entertainment of seeing them fall into the street below. Certainly, there is nothing of that kind against the Duc d'Enghien. But he was still young when he was killed.

Napoleon defended the deed to the last moment on the ground that it was necessary for the security of the State. He took the whole responsibility on himself, and he says in his will that he would act in the same way again in the same circumstances. However, that may be, it gave a wholesome fright to the royalists and the royal house. The conspiracy and all that went with it soon engendered in the people a feeling that demanded the empire and an hereditary dynasty as the sole means of assuring the future of the country.

CHAPTER 2

Emperor

In May, 1804, Napoleon Bonaparte was chosen Emperor of the French by the representatives of the people, and his family were declared to have an hereditary right to the throne.

The first thing to which he devoted his attention as Emperor was the army. He gave grateful distinction both to the older generals whom he had found in office at the time of his own rise, and to the younger men who had grown to be a power in France and a terror to Europe under his own supervision. With great pomp he elevated eighteen generals to the rank of marshals of the empire, and made them generous awards of land and money. There were a few amongst the older generals whose merits were slight in comparison with those of the younger men. But it was his intention, and a fine stroke of policy, to bring together the old and the new, so that the adventurous character of his own rise might not be too apparent. The six older men were:

Perrignon, Serrurier, Brune, Jourdan, Kellermann, and Lefebvre, as well as Augereau, Soult, and Masséna. The new men were: Bessières, Davoust, Moncey, Mortier, Ney, Lannes, Bernadotte, Berthier, and Murat. Most of these afterwards became dukes and princes, with titles taken from the battles they won. Kléber and Desaix, who were more worthy of the marshal's staff than any of the others, had fallen.

He then pardoned most of those who had been implicated in the conspiracy. Only Cadoudal and twelve others were shot. General Pichegru strangled himself in prison with his own neckerchief. Moreau was condemned to two years' imprisonment, but the sentence was commuted at the instance of his wife into a journey to North America. He bought some property at Delaware, and lived quietly there until the news of Napoleon's campaign in Russia gave him fresh hope of realising his ambitious dreams. He returned in 1813, and met his death in the midst of the enemies of France. Napoleon bought his French estate, Grosbois, and gave it to Berthier. His hotel at Paris he gave to Bernadotte. It was the same house in the *rue* Anjou from the garden of which Napoleon III sent pears to the widowed queen Desideria at Stockholm.

King Louis XVIII was now far from being in the mood in which he had written to General Bonaparte. He protested in the most lofty terms against 'the usurper,' etc. Napoleon's only reply was to publish the royal proclamation in the *Moniteur*.

Meantime, the Emperor's mind was no less taken up with great plans than that of the First Consul had been. He had to consolidate the new order of things that had arisen amidst the hatred of the whole of Europe, Throughout his whole life he had no peace with England, by day or night. There came a time when he felt the whole of the continent to be in his hands, but never England. It seemed in the end to be Russia that undid him, but that was not so in reality. He fell before Old England, 'tasteless Albion,' the cradle of freedom.

On the 8th of July, the Emperor left St. Cloud for the purpose of inspecting the vast forces with which he threatened England. It was in the midst of this army and fleet that he arranged the great festival at which he founded the order of the Legion of Honour. On the broad plain were 100,000 fine soldiers under the command of Marshal Soult, while the fleet, not quite so brilliant, lay in the neighbouring harbour. Surrounded by his brothers and the new marshals, Napoleon took the oath of the new order, and all repeated the words after him in a scene of enthusiasm that could never be forgotten.

He travelled about from place to place in the north of France for three months, and returned through Aix and Mayence on October 12th, in order to prepare for the coronation of himself and Josephine. It was a pompous and tedious ceremony, but perhaps more brilliant than it had been under the former kings. It was a point of honour with him to eclipse all other princes. The pope himself came from Rome, and blessed the imperial couple at Notre Dame. But when the pious pontiff had uttered the blessing on the two crowns that lay before him, Napoleon took up one of them and put it on his own head and the other on Josephine's, who was on her knees in front of the altar. Nothing so stupendous had ever been witnessed before. The festivals were brilliant beyond conception, but many of the older generals and some of the younger ones made fun of all his clerical performances and incense.

The execution of the Duc d'Enghien and the invasion of Baden had broken off all communication between the European courts and Paris, and had provoked a new coalition against Napoleon. The Emperor wrote another homely letter to his 'brother,' the King of England, but the only result was a cold and formal reply from the ministry, as before. On April 2nd, 1805, Napoleon travelled with the Empress to Milan, where he crowned himself with the ancient iron crown of Lombardy as King of Italy. There was enthusiastic rejoicing wherever they appeared in France and Italy. In the month of July they were back in his favourite *château* at Fontainebleau.

Meantime there was great activity in all the Cabinets of Europe, and in September, when Napoleon was again at Boulogne, where he conducted a general experiment in embarking his army, the Austrians under General Mack marched into Bavaria. Marshal Soult's whole corps was already aboard the fleet. But just at the moment of the Austrian outbreak, Napoleon learned that Admiral Villeneuve, whom he had selected for conveying the troops to England, and whose appearance in the Channel was daily expected, had been shut up in a Spanish harbour and blockaded by the English.

It was Napoleon's original intention to entrust the command to Admiral Latouche-Tréville, the only French admiral of any competence. But he unfortunately died just at the time. Count Daru, the *general-intendant* of the army, a man who approached Napoleon very closely in daily life, came into the Emperor's tent at Boulogne on the very morning that the news arrived. The Emperor was walking backwards and forwards in the greatest excitement.

'Sit down, Daru, and write,' he said.

In the course of one morning he altered his long and laborious plans. He wheeled round his army, which was facing London, and marched it without a break toward Vienna. At one sitting he dictated the plans of the campaign that ended at Austerlitz. Each army corps received its route, from Hanover and Holland, from Italy and the south of France. The march for each day was prescribed, and all the points were indicated at which the columns were to meet. The plan was so accurate that the troops marched 200 miles eastwards without having to make the slightest deviation from the prescribed route. They reached their destinations, and the whole plan was carried out with complete success.

We hardly know what to think when we find Fouché, the Minister of Police, declaring:

All the Austrian spies were bought much more easily than one would think. Most of them had already been secured by us in Italy, and this had had a good deal to do with the defeat of Wurmser and Alvinczy. Before the campaign of 1805, the operation was conducted on a larger scale, and nearly all the generals on the Austrian staff were accessible. I had given all my secret information on Germany to General Savary, the head of the intelligence department at the Emperor's headquarters, and he used it with success. As all the breaches were thus open, it was mere sham fighting for our brave soldiers and superior manoeuvres at Ulm, on the bridge at Vienna, and at Austerlitz.

It was also 'sham fighting' when Napoleon pretended one day at the Tuileries, after the Peace of Pressburg, to be angry with the Minister of Finance, because the treasury was in difficulties at the beginning of the war. These difficulties, Fouché says, had been created by the Emperor himself by abstracting fifty million *francs* from the cellars of the bank for the purpose of bribery. They had contributed in a high degree to the remarkable success of the improvised campaign. It is quite certain that, though Fouché chatters and exaggerates, he had good reason to regard many things with distrust that seem wonderful to us. It is not easy to determine how much was due to the superiority and bravery of the leaders, and how much was a shameless comedy, facilitated by previous payments of money.

Spies are now an essential part of international intercourse. Every country has them and every country hangs them. There was certainly nothing in Napoleon's character inconsistent with the use of spies and bribes. These indelicate weapons were as convenient to his hand as to anybody else's. Although the landing in England was his favourite plan, he may very well have had also a completely elaborated plan of the Austrian campaign, including all the corruption and treachery on which he could safely rely. His head had room for everything at that time. If one thing failed, he always had another plan.

The *grande armée* of the year 1805 was the first to be composed entirely on the lines of Napoleon's system. In the republican armies each corps was a sort of separate army, with its own arms of all kinds, commissariat, hospital, train, etc. In the course of time Napoleon organised the forces so as to have them better in hand himself. Each corps was complete with infantry and all that belonged to it, including field artillery. But of the cavalry only a few squadrons of hussars and mounted riflemen, for reconaissances and covering, were under the command of the head of the corps. A corps was usually commanded by a marshal. The whole of the heavy cavalry was under a particular general, who was usually Murat; and of these troops and the artillery Napoleon took what each corps needed, either in the course of the battle or to execute a manoeuvre.

The corps of the bodyguard had developed into the Imperial Guard. It consisted of horse and foot grenadiers, *mamelukes* from Egypt, a brilliant Italian battalion, and two squadrons of picked *gendarmes*, who kept order at headquarters. To these Napoleon added a chosen artillery-park of twenty-four guns, so that the Guard was really a small army of 7,000 men, with officers selected from the finest in the army. With the Guard, Lannes and Oudinot's grenadiers generally marched near the Emperor.

The army that began to march across Europe in September was divided into seven corps. The first was under Marshal Bernadotte in Hanover, with Generals Drouot, Rivaud, and the younger Kellermann. The second corps was that of General Marmont in Holland. With him were Boudet and Grouchy and a large number of Dutch auxiliaries. The third corps was under Davoust, with Generals Friant and Gudin; the fourth under Soult, with Saint Hilaire, Vandamme, and Legrand; the fifth under Lannes, with Suchet and Gazan, and Marshal Oudinot and his grenadiers; the sixth under Ney, with Dupont and Loison, and the cavalry-general Colbert; the seventh was led by Marshal Augereau. The cavalry, with its brilliant group of generals—Nansouty, Milhaud, l'Espagne, Lasalle, and the famous d'Hautpoul—was commanded by Murat. The mounted Imperial Guard was led by Marshal Bessières, and the foot-guards by Marshal Mortier. Marshal Brune remained in the abandoned camp at Boulogne.

All these army corps, with their vast appurtenances began to march on their various routes on the same day. They went straight across Germany in order to meet the Austrians, who had raised a large army under the Archduke Charles, and had Russian troops in their rear, led by the Emperor Alexander himself and General Kutusow. Marching was heavy work in those days. The roads were few and bad, and there were not many proper bridges; and they had a very heavy train and heavy artillery.

Bavaria, Baden, and Würtemberg received Napoleon as a friend and ally, and he adopted the dangerous practice of taking large masses of foreign troops into his service and expecting the same bravery and fidelity from them as from the French, when they were under his own officers. He had no pronounced national feeling. He himself travelled from Paris to Strassburg, and crossed the Rhine on the first of October. All the information he received assured him that everything was in order. The great plan matured quickly and accurately.

On October 15th, General Mack was surrounded in the neighbourhood of the fortress of Ulm, and completely cut off from the Russians, who tried to come to his support from the east. In the conflicts that followed Ney won special distinction. He was ordered to take a particularly strong position, the monastery of Elchingen, which was defended by General Laudon with 16,000 men and 40 guns. After heavy losses Ney succeeded in entering the abbey with a desperate charge. Two days afterwards Mack was forced to surrender the town and fortress of Ulm. Before Napoleon and his staff defiled 30,000 men, with 16 generals, 60 guns, 40 flags, and 3,000 horses.

Berthier received the sword of the unfortunate General Mack. It was not the first time that General Mack had had to surrender his sword. He had done so to General Championnet, in the republican days, at the taking of Naples. But Championnet was a good-natured man. 'Keep your sword, General,' he said. 'My government has forbidden me to receive presents of English manufacture.' Marshal Ney was made Duke of Elchingen and General Exelmans received the grand cross of the Legion of Honour for his behaviour at Wertingen.

After the capitulation of Ulm the troops, with Napoleon in the midst of them, marched from victory to victory. Marshal Mortier immortalised himself by a heroic struggle against a superior force at Dürnstein. Murat was to be found everywhere with his cavalry. The whole army, which had now been in Napoleon's hands for ten years, was perfect in every respect, and its generals were at their best. No one was ever tired. Rivalry had not yet become bitter. The generous gifts and distinctions were still at their beginning.

Oudinot marched straight with his grenadiers from the Boulogne camp to Vienna in 45 days. There he went himself with some of his officers on the undermined bridge over the Danube, and snatched the burning fuse out of the hands of the Austrian officers who stood ready to blow up the bridge. Murat, Lannes, and Sébastiani were with him.

On November 15th, 1805, Napoleon rode into Vienna for the first time. The Emperor Francis had retreated to Olmütz. The French army marched after him. Marshal Soult, afterwards Duke of Dalmatia, one of the solid generals who always led large divisions of the army with distinction, crossed the Danube, and defeated the enemy at Hollabrunn. An envoy came from the Emperor Francis with a proposal to conclude an armistice; but Napoleon knew very well that this was merely in order to give the Russians time to come up. Field-marshal Kutusow and the Emperor Alexander were already at Wischau.

Napoleon seized the opportunity to approach the man whom he regarded as his greatest rival in the world, and who was afterwards the last to be conquered—or won—by him. He proposed a personal interview with the Tsar, but Alexander merely sent Prince Dolgorucki. When the prince came. Napoleon had caused his army to retreat a couple of miles, and was busy strengthening his new position. Dolgorucki concluded from this that the French had lost courage, and would rather retreat than face the Russians. His impression was received with delight by the Russians, and they at once advanced. Napoleon took up his headquarters at Brünn, and was determined to choose his own field of battle.

On November 28th, the combined armies were far beyond Wischau and near to Pratzen. Napoleon acquainted his generals with the ground he had chosen, and said:

'If I merely wanted to keep the enemy off, I should remain here on the heights of Pratzen. But in that case I should only win an ordinary battle. I will, therefore, let my right wing take up a position in the direction of Brünn, and if the Russians are enticed by that to descend from these hills, they are hopelessly lost.'

On December 1st Napoleon was delighted to see that the Russians and Austrians were executing the very manoeuvre that he was luring them to do. They left the heights of Pratzen and marched on Brünn, in order to attack or surround the French right wing. Those with Napoleon heard him say repeatedly to himself 'Before tomorrow night the army is in my power.'

On the evening of December 1st he went round the camp. Some of the soldiers made torches out of the straw they slept on, in order to light the way for the Emperor in the dark winter night. The whole army noticed it, and as he went from corps to corps the straw-torches flamed out, until the whole camp was filled with fire and smoke, and the cry rang out from thousands of throats: 'Long live the Emperor !'

On the morning of December 2nd, 1805, the entire French army was drawn up in order of battle, as he had directed. Marshal Lannes formed the left wing with the divisions of Suchet and Cafarelli. Marshal Bernadotte was in the centre with Rivaud and Drouot. The right wing was led by Marshal Soult, and really decided the battle. The whole of the cavalry under Murat sat on horseback in two lines. Napoleon himself had under him ten battalions of the Guard, and ten battalions of grenadiers under Oudinot. The sun burst out of the wintry fog that lay on the plain and the ice-covered waters, and was mirrored on the panoply of war. At that moment the Russians were seen to leave Pratzen.

'How long will you need, Marshal,' Napoleon asked Soult, 'to occupy the hills that the enemy is leaving?'

'One hour, your Majesty!'

'Good! Then we'll wait another quarter of an hour,' said Napoleon.

Soon afterwards the guns opened fire and the battle began. Kutusow had divided his fighting forces into six corps. As reserves he had the famous Russian Guard, which was commanded by the Grand Duke Constantine. Although Field-marshal Kutusow had the chief command, the plan came from the Austrian General Weiroth. Kutusow had fruitlessly resisted it. When he now saw the turn that the battle was taking, as Marshal Soult's troops began to occupy the hills at Pratzen, he tried with all his forces to overpower them, and he fought with heavy losses to regain the position which he now clearly saw to be of decisive importance. For two hours there was a fierce conflict.

At length Kutusow had to give way, and from that moment the battle took such a turn that nothing could stand against the French. Lannes and Murat forced back the right wing under Prince Bagration; General Rapp made his famous attack with the *curassiers*, in which he took Prince Repnin prisoner; and when Napoleon came up to support Soult with his Guard and Oudinot's grenadiers, everything fell at once into the hands of the French—guns, artillery waggons, flags, etc. Those who tried to flee across the river were drowned, as the ice broke under the weight of the guns and owing to the holes made in it by the French balls. Whole divisions were demolished or gave up their arms.

The result was extraordinary. There were 26,000 killed and wounded and 25,000 taken prisoners, together with a number of flags, including the standard of the Imperial Russian Guard.

Only two French officers of high rank fell at Austerlitz. General Valhuet, whose leg was shot from under him, died at once, and Colonel Morland fell at the head of the riflemen of the Imperial Guard. His body was taken to Paris in a cask of rum, but was forgotten and left in it until 1814. The brave and active General Rapp was badly wounded. He was one of the unlucky officers. He got four wounds in the republican wars and three in Egypt. His arm especially was unlucky, and was always being hit. General Thiebault also was wounded.

After Austerlitz Napoleon's habit of rewarding his men assumed the most princely proportions, and he retained this generosity as long as he had anything to give away. He adopted the children of the soldiers who had fallen in the battle. They were to be reared at the expense of the State, and he gave them permission to add 'Napoleon 'to their names. He awarded pensions to all the widows, from the widows of generals to those of privates, and expressed his thanks to the army in fine language. 'My people will receive you with pride,' he said, 'and whenever one of you says "I was at Austerlitz," all will respond with one voice: "This is a brave man."'

In recognition of their aid Bavaria and Würtemberg were made kingdoms, and Baden a Grand Duchy. Murat was made Grand Duke of Berg, Berthier Prince of Neuchatel. Eugene Beauharnais, Josephine's son, was appointed Viceroy of Italy and married to a daughter of the King of Bavaria. Shortly afterwards Joseph became King of Naples, and Lucien King of Holland. A large number of officers received titles, decorations, money, and property. The Peace of Pressburg was soon concluded. Austria lost Venice, which went to Italy, and Tyrol, which was given to Bavaria. The Emperor Alexander, who might have been taken prisoner with his whole army, was allowed to escape. This was always Napoleon's way with the *Tsar*.

It rarely happens in descriptions of battles that one can get more than a series of pictures of the collision of various arms, the heroic attack or the stubborn resistance of the infantry that decides the important position. To see a battle as a connected whole, with plan opposed to plan, and with the various scenes subordinated to the general idea and the better calculation that eventually leads to victory, is not easy for any but a military expert. Nevertheless, I have succeeded in making a sort of survey of some of Napoleon's battles. It is not the case in all battles that one side steadily wins; that all the forces are tried, yet, taking all things together, the superiority is on the one side throughout.

In some battles the victory comes suddenly in the middle of the fight. In a moment one side utterly loses, and good solid troops are rendered quite useless at a stroke. Austerlitz was a battle of this kind. During the two hours when Kutusow attempted with his entire army to regain the heights of Pratzen, the struggle was equal in a sense, and on neither side was there any perceptible increase of success. It was as if a steel rod were strained more and more until it suddenly broke, and the destruction was complete. Troops like the invincible Russian Imperial Guard suddenly became of no more use than recruits.

I see the same thing in a different way at Marengo. Throughout the whole day the Austrians drove back Napoleon's right wing and centre further and further. In the afternoon he was in such a position that everybody thought it had been a steady defeat from morning to evening. But Bonaparte saw the strain on the steel bar. Firmly and judiciously he prevented the break until Desaix was at hand. Then the bent steel flew suddenly back upon the Austrians, and they were defeated. It was not merely that he had got reinforcements; the inexplicable moment of collapse had arrived. There was no retreat and no loss, but flight and capture.

It was the same at Waterloo. It is always said that Wellington was beaten strategically. Napoleon had strained the steel bar with his forces more than ever. The issue of the fight vacillated, and it was impossible to tell on which side the bar would spring. Napoleon alone knew that it was an hour too late. And when, not only Marshal Grouchy did not appear, but Blücher came instead, the bar sprang back at once and broke, but in the reverse direction, and Wellington won his great victory.

The Prussian campaign began immediately after the Austrian. Metternich was at Berlin in 1805, and made the greatest efforts to bring Prussia into the alliance, but Frederic William remained firm. Now, however, a year later and after the battle of Austerlitz, he opened the unfortunate war that brought Prussia to the verge of destruction. Without making any declaration of war, the Prussians moved into Saxony, just as the Austrians had invaded Bavaria in the previous year. It is a fact that on the 26th of September, 1806, Napoleon, with his finger on the map at Paris, foretold the destruction of the Prussian army about October 15th. It took place on October 14th. He then settled that Clarke should be Governor at Berlin at the end of October. When Daru asked permission to take the treasury with them, the Emperor replied: 'It will do if the treasurer comes.' He took only 24,000 *francs* with him on the campaign in Saxony. The vanquished must pay the bill.

The Imperial Guard at once left Paris, and went eastwards in post-chaises. Napoleon crossed the Rhine on October 1st, 1806, and set up his headquarters at Bamberg. Here he collected his troops under the seven marshals, Bernadotte, Lannes, Davoust, Ney, Soult, Augereau, and Lefebvre. Murat led the cavalry. It was an unfortunate beginning for the Prussians when the young and promising prince of the royal house, Louis, was cut down by a French hussar in a skirmish at Saalfeld, a few days before the decisive battles of Jena and Auerstädt. However, the King of Prussia and his generals were so sure of victory that they had taken up their position between Gotha, Erfurt, and Weimar, while Napoleon came from Gera, or eastwards.

Thus the armies were not face to face. The Germans had the Rhine in their rear and the French the Elbe, with an open field to Berlin and Dresden. The Prussians had themselves chosen Saxony for the fight. But it was the army of Frederic the Great, invincible in the opinion of contemporaries, and led by the generals and pupils of the famous king. We have only to think of such names as Kalkreuth, the Duke of Brunswick, Möllendorf, Schmettau, Hohenlohe, Rüchel, and Blücher, with 230,000 stout bronze-soldiers from Potsdam, well armed and well drilled.

Napoleon again sent one of his letters from monarch to monarch—this time to the King of Prussia:

If I were a novice in the art of war and had to fear the changes of fortune on the field, this letter to your Majesty would be senseless. But your Majesty will be beaten, and without a shadow of doubt you will put an end to your own peaceful existence and the lives of your subjects.

Napoleon's royal brother, Frederic William, sent no reply to the letter. He and Queen Louisa were with the army. The army was in two divisions, one of which, consisting of 70,000 men, led by the King and the Duke of Brunswick, marched toward Auerstädt; the rest, under Prince Hohenlohe, went toward Jena. The two places are about five miles from each other. Napoleon had made such good use of the night on October 14th, that his troops were ready for the attack in the early morning, and just at the points where the Prussians least expected them. The first to move was General Suchet. He opened the battle in the early hours, while the mist still lay thick on the fields. With him were Generals Wedel and Claparède, whose division had distinguished itself at Austerlitz in the preceding year.

They met with a long and stubborn and desperate resistance. Marshals Soult and Lannes attacked with all their forces. Ney came up during the fight with two divisions. Napoleon sent forward the reserve, and Murat threw himself on the enemy, as usual, with the whole of his cavalry. The Prussians gave way slowly at first, with the utmost coolness and the regularity of the parade ground. The infantry formed one square after another. But when five squares were completely ridden down, one after another, by the French hussars and *curassiers*, the Prussians gradually broke into dangerous disorder. Their cavalry began to fail before Soult's solid columns, and retreated in the direction of Weimar.

At this moment the reinforcements that Prince Hohenlohe expected came up. General Rüchel's corps, consisting of 26 battalions and 20 squadrons, reached the fighting line. The struggle now became extremely fierce, but in less than an hour the whole corps melted away under the repeated attacks that Napoleon showered on it. In the end there was nothing left of 'the army of Frederic the Great.' The older art of war had measured itself against the new, and utterly lost. The revolution was so great from the military point of view that contemporaries were more amazed than they were at any other of Napoleon's victories. The defeat was not in itself greater than many others in respect of the direct losses of men and material; but the military and moral effect of it was crushing at the time for the losers, if instructive for the future.

While Napoleon was fighting at Jena—on the same day, October 14th—Marshal Davoust encountered the division of the Prussian army that was led by the Duke of Brunswick, to which the King himself was attached. With Davoust were Generals Gudin, Friant, and Morand, whose distinguished divisions nearly always formed the nucleus of the army corps that he commanded. He had, however, not much more than a third of the forces opposed to him, and he found himself in a very dangerous position. Marshal Bernadotte was quite near to him, but he acted as if he did not hear the guns. He even took with him some regiments of dragoons that did not properly belong to his corps; his real reason being that he did not want to share the honours with Davoust, and would have liked to see him beaten by the Prussians, which might very well have happened.

The danger to Davoust's corps was at its height about six in the evening. He himself sat on his horse, serious and grave, as he always was, in the midst of the frightful turmoil. Already a ball had carried off his hat. He once more sent a messenger—one of his adjutants, the brave Romeuf, who afterwards fell at Borodino—to Bernadotte, imploring him to come to his help. Davoust—who knew him—even offered him the supreme command. But Bernadotte marched on, though he had only one turn to make to reach the battlefield. Even in the end, when Davoust had won the battle with his unflinching coolness and superior art, and when his men were so tired that they could hardly stand on their legs, Bernadotte would not throw himself on the demoralised Prussians, although he was near enough for his and Davoust's soldiers to see each other.

It is true that there was a deep personal enmity between the two marshals, but the whole army and all the officers were enraged against Bernadotte. The Emperor used to say afterwards: 'If I had sent Bernadotte before a court-martial at that time, he would certainly have been shot for his conduct.' It is said that Napoleon had the decree in his hand, but tore it up at the last moment out of consideration for Désirée, Bernadotte's wife, who had had some leaning to Napoleon in her younger days.

Davoust's victory at Auerstädt on October 14th, 1806, is always regarded as one of the most brilliant in the annals of the French army. The Emperor made him Duke of Auerstädt, and gave him splendid gifts. Davoust was of the old nobility, and he had known the Bonapartes since the military school at Brienne. He served under the generals of the Republic, but was excluded from the service because he was a noble. He afterwards became one of Napoleon's most reliable leaders, training and keeping his men together with a firm and hard hand, so that the third army corps was a model body.

The losses of the Prussians in the two battles were enormous. Davoust alone took 114 guns, while he himself had only 44. About 50,000 men fell or were made prisoners, and he captured flags and supplies of all sorts. Amongst the prisoners there were 6,000 Saxons with their officers. Napoleon had the officers brought before him at Weimar. He told them that it was one object of the campaign to prevent the incorporation of Saxony into Prussia. He then sent them on parole to Dresden, and entrusted to them a proclamation in which he posed as Saxony's protector. This was a finely calculated introduction to the intimacy he gradually formed with the Saxon court and the later king of Saxony.

The veterans of Frederic the Great were beaten, but most of them fought to the death. The defeat was still further embittered for Prussia as it meant the extinction of so many great names. The famous Duke of Brunswick had both eyes shot out, and he died shortly afterwards. Field-marshal Möllendorf and General-lieutenant Schmettau were fatally wounded. Prince Henry of Prussia and the Prince of Orange, afterwards King of Holland, were wounded, and so were General Rüchel and others. Frederic William, always moderate, was content with a fall from his horse, but he very nearly fell into the hands of the French horsemen.

An armistice was asked, but Napoleon at once replied that he would only treat with them at Berlin. He assumed a hard and unpleasant attitude toward Frederic William, whom he despised, and later toward Queen Louisa, whom he could not endure. It was quite a different matter when he was dealing with Alexander the First. A few days after Jena, General Kalkreuth, another of Frederic the Great's first generals, was annihilated by Marshal Soult. Bernadotte won a victory at Halle; and they went on from battle to battle, the unfortunate queen having to fly from town to town as far as Küstrin.

Prince Hohenlohe had to surrender to Murat with his whole army at Prentzlau. As prisoners of war, 16,000 foot and six regiments of cavalry of the best soldiers in Prussia, with 60 guns, and 40 flags, had to pass before the French lines. Stettin, which was then a strong fortress, surrendered to the brave cavalry-general Lasalle, who attacked it at the head of a few squadrons. Davoust took Küstrin. In the end Blücher alone remained, and he retreated before the advancing French with the remnants of the fine army, and established himself at Lübeck.

Three marshals—Soult, Bernadotte, and Murat—went after him. Blücher contested every foot of the ground in Lübeck. They fought in the fortifications, at the gates, and afterwards in the houses. Every street had to be stormed and taken, but after two days fighting Blücher had to surrender, with eleven generals, 500 officers, 60 flags, artillery, and supplies—all that was left after the catastrophes at Jena and Auerstädt.

On the following day Magdeburg fell, and then there was nothing left in Prussia to fight with. Meantime the French had set up their head-quarters at Potsdam. Marshals Lannes, Bessières, and Lefebvre, were there with the Guard, and General Bourcier erected a large cavalry depot there. The town was long held by the French.

On October 27th Napoleon rode with the Guard through the triumphal arch that had been raised to the memory of Frederic the Great at Berlin. The campaign with Prussia proper was now at an end, but as Russia came forth as the ally and deliverer of Prussia, the war had to continue, and the French armies gaily made their way eastwards towards Warsaw. During the following campaign the Emperor remained with the army, and spent the winter in the eastern provinces of Prussia. From his headquarters he ruled his entire empire, and kept his eye on everything, particularly Paris. Amongst other things during the winter, he worked out the plan of a monumental structure at Paris, which was to have the inscription: 'To the soldiers of Napoleon's grand army.' In it the heroes of all his campaigns were to be named on tablets of white marble, and those who fell on the field were to be inscribed in gold. The Madeleine church in its present form was the ultimate outcome of his plan.

Another task that engaged him was his great plan of blockading the continent against England. It was, perhaps, a larger plan than he suspected, and at all events it proved too big for him in the end. He also made the Elector of Saxony king; he was the only one among the legitimate princes who was a friend of Napoleon.

In the early days of February, 1807, there was a series of conflicts with the Russians, who were commanded by General Bennigsen, together with the remaining fighting forces of Prussia. The French broke out of their winter quarters, where they had spent a hard winter in the midst of snow and morasses and mud; though it was nothing to compare, as some may imagine, with the cold of Russia or the fearful snow-storms of the eastern plains. On February 8th the two armies faced each other at Eylau, at a distance of half a cannon shot.

The Russians had the better position, and were numerically superior. It was very bad weather. The snow was falling heavily and the French had the wind in their faces. Bennigsen opened the battle with a terrific gun- fire. The Russians, taught by Napoleon, had now a large and excellent artillery. Napoleon felt that it was a critical day. He spared nothing, even sending forward the valuable guns of the Guard.

Marshal Augereau had to lead forward his corps at the beginning of the battle in face of the heavy Russian fire. But just as the great masses were set in motion they were lashed by a particularly heavy and violent snowstorm, coming right in the faces of the advancing French. Augereau's columns lost their bearings, and found themselves in the middle of the Russian right wing, which was commanded by Generals Tutschukoff and Doctorow. The marshal himself was seriously wounded and had to be carried from the field, and his fine corps was routed and almost annihilated.

As soon as they could see their way again, it was clear to Napoleon that the whole army was put in a critical condition through Augereau's mishap. He ordered Murat and Bessières to collect 70 squadrons and throw them against the enemy's centre. The immense body of horse rushed forward and disappeared in the half-lost battle. Their attack at Eylau has become famous for all time. The Russian cavalry was routed, and the solid regiments of infantry were trodden down. At the head was a man who had the highest repute in the cavalry after Murat—General d'Hautpoul. When the battle began he was some distance from Eylau. But he at once obeyed Napoleon's old general order, always to march toward the guns. As soon as he heard them, he turned his *cuirassiers* and raced to Eylau.

Bernadotte, who was also not far off, behaved again as he had done at Auerstädt. D'Hautpoul begged and implored him to return and join in the battle, but he would neither hear nor see. He continued the march that had been directed to him—not because he was afraid: it was not possible for any one about Napoleon to be afraid—but the Prince of Ponte Corvo was so ambitious that he would not have minded seeing one of the others defeated, even if it was Napoleon—perhaps, especially Napoleon.

The brave d'Hautpoul rushed with his *cuirassiers* into the half-lost battle, and made a great breach through nearly the whole Russian army. He was brought back wounded and torn, and died a few days afterwards. Napoleon had given him the grand cross of the Legion of Honour and ample endowments after Austerlitz, and it was the common opinion that General d'Hautpoul was well on the way to become a marshal. Napoleon had a statue of him made from 24 of the guns taken at Eylau. It is still standing somewhere at Paris—I do not remember where.[1] But I recollect well a large equestrian statue of Bernadotte that is still seen in Christiania.

After the fierce attack of the cavalry had broken twice through the Russian lines, they concentrated for the third time. They now stood firm, and could not be shaken again. The fight continued all day with extraordinary spirit, but General Bennigsen established his position in the town of Eylau. The Prussian General L'Estocq came up with some reinforcements in the afternoon and the battle was left undecided when darkness set in. Marshal Soult urged Napoleon to remain on the battlefield.

About eight o'clock the camp fires were lit along the whole line in order to mark the fact that the French occupied the field. Bennigsen,

1. It was actually in Gaillac in Tarn. It was destroyed by the Vichy Government in 1942 and melted down to support the Nazi war effort.—Leonaur Editors

however, retreated during the night. He may have suffered more than Napoleon, who had a good many reserve troops to rely on. But the battle had run in such a way that both sides could claim the victory, as they really did. At all events neither side was defeated.

A number of high officers had fallen. Sixteen generals were lost on the French side including Corbineau, who fell at the Emperor's side. Heudelet received a ball through the middle of the body, but he recovered. Defrance and Desjardins fell. So did General Dahlmann, who commanded the *Chasseurs à Cheval* and fell with d'Hautpoul in the great cavalry attack. The loss was also very great amongst the soldiers and inferior officers. The Battle of Eylau was always spoken of afterwards in grave tones. It was the most sanguinary that was ever seen in the Emperor's campaigns. Napoleon himself spent a good deal of the following night on the field, helping the wounded and directing the burial of the enormous number of corpses.

The Emperor's bulletin on the Battle of Eylau caused great excitement at Paris. He made no effort to conceal his great losses and the doubtful issue. After Eylau several of the white uniforms were abandoned. There were a number of white regiments in the army, dating from the time of the kings; but it was said it was too terrible at Eylau to see the red blood pouring over the fine white uniforms.

During the battle the Emperor himself was in serious danger, partly because he recklessly exposed himself to it, and partly because of the close proximity of the two armies. Berthier had the greatest difficulty in keeping him out of the most dangerous spots. The Emperor was as cool and collected as usual, though the generals could not conceal the fact that they felt the whole issue to be hanging by a single thread. General Dorsenne commanded the section of the Guard that was nearest to the Emperor, and tried to protect him as much as possible. He was, like most of the officers of the Guard, a fine tall man, with some care for personal appearance. His men also were picked and they were just as proud of their general as he was content with them himself.

In the middle of the battle, at the height of the turmoil, General Dorsenne suddenly caught sight of a division of Russian cavalry that seemed about to storm the little hill where the Emperor and his attendants were standing. He called his men, and quick as lightning formed a square round the Emperor with the Guard. The soldiers stood with arms presented, but heard no command to fire or lower the bayonet. General Dorsenne sat erect and proud in his saddle, looking

at the approaching horsemen. It was enough for him that his grenadiers stood like a wall round the Emperor. In fact, when the Prussians
drew near and saw the grim faces of the famous Imperial Guard with
the high bear-skin helmets, standing shoulder to shoulder like an iron
frame, the troop instinctively turned aside and rode away. The Emperor smiled at Dorsenne.

On February 16th General Savary had his great day as a soldier.
He was generally employed in a political capacity, as an envoy or in
the police. As a friend of Napoleon's youth, who could be implicitly
trusted, he had often to do things that brought him the contempt and
hatred of others. At this time, however, he had temporary command
of the fifth army corps, during the illness of Marshal Lannes, and on
the 16th he succeeded in defeating the Russian General Essen after
a stiff fight at Ostrolenka. He had with him the divisions of Suchet,
Gazan, and Reille. He was given the grand cordon of the Legion of
Honour and an award of 20,000 *francs* a year, which had been set free
by General d'Hautpoul's death at Eylau. He afterwards became the
Duke of Rovigo. General Ordener was made a Count after the battle
of Ostrolenka.

After a long and spirited siege the elderly Marshal Lefebvre took
the fortress of Dantzig. He had with him the first two engineer-
generals of the army, Lariboisière and Chasseloup, and it was really
these who conducted the siege. The marshal was always for storming,
and they had the greatest difficulty in restraining him until they were
ready. In the end General Kalkreuth had to surrender Dantzig with
large stores of arms, ammunition, and corn. Lefebvre was afterwards
Duke of Dantzig.

A number of smaller battles were won by the French, and at last
the great Battle of Friedland put an end to the war with Russia. The
Tsar, like the King of Prussia before, had no army to fight with. Napoleon fought the battle of Friedland on the anniversary of Marengo,
the 14th of June. It did not begin until five in the afternoon, and
was a complete victory—one of the most thorough infantry victories,
won by the bayonet, the cavalry afterwards swooping like hawks on
the fugitives. This time the Emperor himself was on the heels of the
monarchs. When they reached Tilsit, the bridge across the Niemen
was still burning by which they had saved themselves and the remnants of their armies. The booty was enormous. At Königsberg, for
instance, they found 160,000 new English weapons, that had not yet
been unloaded.

The Emperors Napoleon and Alexander met eventually at Tilsit. They were daily together for a whole fortnight, discussing political matters. Napoleon wanted to have a free hand in regard to Spain, and Alexander in regard to Finland. He treated the *Tsar* with great moderation, in fact with a consideration that was foreign to his nature, and at his request, restored to Prussia sufficient territory to keep it in existence.

On the other hand Alexander recognised the three kings Joseph, Lucien, and Jerome, and the King of Saxony as Grand-duke of Warsaw. Finally, he joined the continental blockade; but he never seriously meant a single word that fell from his lips. However, Napoleon, who could at the time have divided the world into two parts, was glad to secure the recognition and the friendship of the man; he considered that this was all that was wanting to his power.

The armies then returned in triumph to France, where all the towns, with Paris at their head, received with the utmost hospitality the brave soldiers who had been away for ten months. The Emperor made a generous distribution of crosses of the Legion of Honour and awards, but with strict regard to justice, which gave an increased value to every gift.

CHAPTER 3

Ascendent

The Emperor was now quite at home in every part of Europe. He was familiar with all the castles of Italy and the continent. Every day the officers and servants of his court were brought before him; and when his travelling carriage galloped over the drawbridge at night, the torch-bearer stood at the steps, his own officers flung open the door of the carriage and received him, and the little man in the grey coat walked quietly in the torch light up the broad steps; the aged and powdered servants of the castle standing by with candelabra in their trembling hands. He strode through the well-lit halls to his own rooms, was relieved of his clothes by his own valet, and flung himself into his boiling bath as if he were at home.

Everything that belonged to his person was of the finest quality, arranged most punctiliously, and in his own grand style. His carriage horses were picked animals, and arranged in relays of three pairs each with an outrider. When he had to travel 20 *kilometres* (12½ miles) six relays of horses were arranged on the route, so that he only went a short distance with the same horses. He generally went at a sort of gallop, though one must remember what kind of roads were in existence a hundred years ago and the heaviness of the carriages. There was no question of reading or studying maps in the carriage. Nevertheless, there were books, writing materials, maps, and field glasses with each relay. Every object was marked with the number of the relay, so that it was easy to arrange in the night before a journey, without anyone knowing of it.

He had, in fact, plenty to think about. When he travelled eastwards, he reflected on his campaigns. Along the route he received couriers, or there might be a marshal with his staff at a prearranged point to confer with him. Day and night he galloped on through villages and dark woods. His coach thundered along the narrow streets, and the light of his torches flashed like lightning across the narrow windows. 'There he is again,' the Germans said, as they shrank underneath the bed-clothes. He sat confidently in his stout carriage, his escort rattling along at the side with gleaming sabres and pistols.

When he went westwards, he considered above all things what else he could do for Paris, which was never out of his thoughts. He mentally decided on fresh distinctions, promotions, and gifts for his men. Wherever he went he kept his eye on the crown property and the public domains. He accumulated property that he could share as he pleased amongst his marshals and dukes. It is difficult to appreciate the munificence of the man in his awards. He never loaded favourites and courtiers with wealth, as foolish princes do; still less dare women interfere in such matters. His gifts were a manly recognition of manly strength and courage, which never escaped his attention—from the marshal to the little drummer who ran out in his shirt and beat the alarm.

At one time Marshal Davoust, Duke of Auerstädt and Prince of Eckmühl had an annual income of 1,800,000 *francs* (£72,000) from his offices and domains. However, this did not last many years. In 1814 all property was lost that lay outside the strict limits of France. But when we recollect what an income of £72,000 meant a hundred years ago, we can realise how money circulated about the person of Napoleon. And Davoust was anything but a favourite! There was nothing between the Emperor and him to compare with Napoleon's feeling for Duroc, Lannes, Junot, or Marmont. The awards to Davoust were merely a recognition of the qualities that made him an indispensable and invincible leader.

Napoleon's princely titles were not empty ones like those that victorious monarchs of our own time bestow with silken sashes. Most of his officers and chief servants received with their titles incomes that enabled them to keep good house at Paris. We still find amongst the highest French aristocracy many of the princely names that were originally given to Napoleon's soldiers. In point of fact, it is difficult to identify sometimes the titles that cover the names of distinguished soldiers and statesmen. Murat was first Grand-duke of Cleve and Berg, and afterwards King of Naples. Berthier was the reigning Prince of Neuchâtel. Ponte Corvo and Benevento also were real and independent principalities, and were given to Bernadotte and Talleyrand and their heirs.

In 1806 Napoleon created 22 principalities out of the annexed territories, such as Venice, the hereditary title bringing with it five-tenths of the revenue of the respective district. Many of the marshals received duchies of this character—Soult was Duke of Dalmatia, Bessières of Istria, Victor of Belluno, Moncey of Conegliano, Mortier of Treviso, Macdonald of Tarentum, Oudinot of Reggio. Besides the marshals General Duroc became Duke of Friaul, Maret of Bassano, Savary of Rovigo, Fouché of Otranto, and a Corsican relative of the Bonaparte family, Arrighi, a courageous cavalry general, was made Duke of Padua. The best titles were those that were taken from the battles, and designated the victors throughout life. The aged Kellermann was made Duke of Valmy; Lefebvre, Duke of Dantzig; Masséna, Duke of Rivoli and Prince of Esslingen; Lannes, Duke of Montebello; Ney, Duke of Elchingen and Prince of Moskwa and Beresina; Davoust, Duke of Auerstädt and Prince of Eckmühl.

For all these and many others the Emperor provided generous incomes, either in the form of productive property, or, if there was any difficulty in this, in the form of princely gifts. He kept them all in mind, and although he did not Like them or their wives to waste, he equally disliked parsimony. He wanted his men to fill the space vacated at the Revolution, and effect the transition from France's older nobility to the new society that he would create. He therefore surrounded himself with a brilliant circle at home and abroad. Wherever he went, a court was formed about him—it was done for the first time at the chateau of Montebello. In every town in Europe and in the deserted castles his daily life had the same invariable tenour as at St. Cloud or Fontainebleau.

There was the same regularity and continuity in his work from morning till night. Reviews of troops that were off to the war; reorganisation of the corps that returned suffering from the field; work in his own cabinet with his secretaries and general-staff officers or with foreign envoys. He ate when he pleased; and he always had something good. Even in the worst days in Russia, when all the others suffered great privations, the Emperor always had his chamber-tin; and there was always a little meat or fowl at his meals. He had only to nod and a small table was spread for him as rapidly as at the Tuileries. He used to say himself that it seemed to be done by magic.

When he was in the field they put a chicken to roast every half-hour, and it often happened that they roasted twelve before he would eat. During the fight his head cook would make his way through the confusion, and bring the Emperor something to eat and a glass of wine on horseback. Although Napoleon seemed to set little store on such things, he was waited upon on every side with a devotion that no other man ever experienced. Everything pertaining to his person and his daily life was of the best quality; and wherever he was—at home or abroad—he lived like the best-served prince in Europe.

His officers also were well treated in the first campaigns on the continent. The highest of them began to display a certain luxury, but there was no effeminacy or excess. It was said of Junot alone, the Duke of Abrantes, that his prodigality was ridiculous; that, for instance, his carriages and his fine stables were equal to the Emperor's. For the younger officers the first campaigns to Vienna and Berlin were mere picnics. They knew that they were going out for victory and promotion, and they reached courts and circles where there were no other young men besides themselves, but a large number of the finest ladies, who could not withstand the handsome cavaliers from Paris that swept in like a hurricane from the field, laughing and amorous, and were off in the morning—perhaps forever. The gay Lasalle, the handsome Colbert, Gardanne with the famous moustache, Turenne, Ségur—they were the greatest names the old ladies could imagine, as they blushingly asked: 'How is your father, the Duke?'

The officers who were not elegant enough for these circles found open houses and hunting properties, with as much shooting, gaiety, and dancing as they wished. In the kitchen and the cellar they found natives who could serve them in Parisian fashion, and the butlers were only too pleased to produce for them their master's old French wine. When they were garrisoned in large German towns, they turned everything upside down with their follies, infatuated the women and drove the men to despair.

One young general confided to his German tailor that the latest fashion at Paris was to wear close-fitting white silk hose with red tassels at the knees; but the tailor was not to tell anybody, because the general wanted to be the only one in fashion at the next ball. It turned out as he expected. The tailor had not kept silence, and the general and his friends had the satisfaction of seeing one local lion after another enter the ballroom in close-fitting white silk hose with red tassels at the knees.

The ordinary soldier and the lower officers filled themselves with wine and German beer, and pulled the maids about until they fled in their heavy skirts. No one could resist the gallants, speaking the fine language of the ruling power, with such busy hands and so sure a grip of the figure, dancing and leaping as if they had springs in their legs.

The fights were harder and the whole art of war more severe than in Italy. Nevertheless, one could long hear the melody of a polka amid the bustle of the war in the early German campaigns; but it gradually ceased as the settlement with the princes became a settlement with the people. Napoleon now knew that he could beat the Russians or the Germans, whatever they might call themselves. He made little distinction between the various Germanic peoples. Their racial differences were immaterial to him.

Hence, when he had taken the power away from the reigning prince, he chose auxiliary troops from the beaten army, gave them French officers, and let them march and fight with his own soldiers. It was fortunate that many of the inhabitants of the borderlands and almost all the German officers, at least those of higher rank, knew a little French. Napoleon saw no danger in it, and when, in 1813, these troops returned to their own powers—a matter which can hardly surprise us—Napoleon thought it the blackest treachery.

He had himself no strong feeling of nationality. He was no more French than the Norwegians were Danes when, as did Tordenskjold, Rye, Helgesen, and Schleppegrell, they went to the assistance of Denmark. Nevertheless, apart from the fact that Norway was always above everything else in their minds, the long period of union had engendered a more patriotic feeling toward Denmark in Norwegians than one could expect in an entirely Italian race, that had lived only a comparatively short time on the island of Corsica, which in turn was only for a short time, and against its will, brought under French rule. Napoleon's national feeling was really a natural consciousness that he was the greatest son of the greatest nation, and that what he did for other nations was the best they could receive, because it was French. He knew no love of country apart from and beyond his own person. He did not know that there is a patriotism beyond the range of reason, a peculiar love of one's own country that would rather fight and perish any day than receive even the best conditions from the hand of a foreigner.

When there was question of an invasion of England, which many think was never seriously intended. Napoleon faced all kinds of difficulties and made all kinds of preparations on land and sea. But he did not reckon with the English nation. He was hardly able to imagine what would happen if an enemy were to march upon London. Napoleon's experience had been built up on the level continent, where the frontiers of the countries had been shifted backwards and forwards in the extravagant wars of princes. Hence Spain, on which he now threw himself, was a fatal enigma to him, and he wore himself out in a fruitless endeavour to solve it. The Spaniards had been a hundred years before a nation that would rather die than surrender.

It is quite true that, under exceptionally bad rulers, Spain had made a most foolish declaration of war upon France before the battle of Jena. But it is just as certain that, when the Spanish pretence of war had been at once crushed out. Napoleon interfered most unjustly in Spanish affairs. His aim was clear enough. He wanted the crown of Spain for some member of his own family, and at the same time to reach through Spain his worst enemy, England, which had made a sort of market of Portugal.

General Junot was therefore ordered to march peacefully through Spain and besiege Lisbon. Junot was not a distinguished general and still less a diplomatist. The important commission was entrusted to him mainly because Napoleon knew that he would carry out any order, however, difficult, with the most uncalulating courage. He took Portugal in a month, and reached Lisbon, as he was directed to do, on November 30th, 1807, with the remains of his army, which he had worn out with marches and fights.

As he approached, the royal house of Portugal, the Braganza family, went on board the fleet with the court and immense wealth and sailed to the empire of Brazil, Napoleon made Junot Duke of Abrantes, after a battle he had fought in Portugal. He had marched peacefully through Spain, as if the war with it was over. It was the same with the 70,000 men that the Emperor sent after Junot to Portugal in 1806. However, these troops, commanded by Marshal Moncey, Duke of Conegliano, and General Dupont, were suddenly directed to fall on the Spanish towns and fortresses.

On June 6th, 1808, Joseph Bonaparte was proclaimed King of Spain. He had hitherto amused himself so well as king of the gay Neapolitans, at a safe distance from his restless brother, that he was not particularly pleased with a promotion that put him on the ancient and unfamiliar throne of Spain, and events justified his concern. The shrewd General Exelmans knew the Spanish nation better than Napoleon did, and he had endeavoured to make him understand that this was the worst conceivable way of treating the Spaniards; but no one would listen to him. The result was that the whole of Spain offered a resistance that had the character of a revolution from the first. It was a revolt against a king imposed on them by a foreign power. From this moment began the bitter struggle between French and Spaniards, that went on without interruption until the fall of Napoleon.

The radical differences between the Spanish wars and the open campaigns in Italy and Germany where the French generals had hitherto conquered, was due firstly to the natural character of the country, which offered better opportunities for small fights, surprises, and descents. Then there was the circumstance that the war was a general rising of the people. The haughty nation took part in it to a man—indeed, to a woman. They fought in bands, and by ambush and assassination. More French soldiers were killed in this way than in the pitched battles. Another feature that gave the Spanish wars a unique complexion was the levity with which the French troops were wont to regard the women in conquered territory as so much booty. The Spanish women declined to see this, and what the French had begun almost in jest, soon assumed the most alarming pro- portions on account of the unexpected resistance, and at last it degenerated into violence and shameful abuse on the part of the conquerors.

The rage of the Spaniards was unbounded. They continued the scattered fight with cold-blooded ferocity, and punished, maltreated, and mutilated their prisoners. No isolated Frenchman was safe in Spain. When the troops marched onward, they found the corpses of their comrades hanging along the streets, naked and mutilated; and the nature of the mutilation clearly indicated that this was vengeance for the treatment of their women.

The worst of all was that the French arms met with a serious reverse from the outset. A French corps under General Dupont advanced along the Andujar. Dupont belonged to an old family of officers, and had narrowly escaped the guillotine. Carnot had had him installed in the topographical department of the Ministry of War together with Clarke, but he had a command as early as Marengo, and was the officer who conducted the negotiations with General Melas after the battle. He had served under Marshal Mortier at Dürnstein, and after Friedland he received on the field the broad ribbon of the Legion of Honour. He was, therefore, one of the chief generals, and the Emperor had confidence in him.

One day in June, 1808, he was opposed with a small part of his corps to the Spanish General Reding, a Swiss by birth, at Baylen. One of Dupont's generals, Gobert, fell in a skirmish, and his successor,

Dufour, a good general, who afterwards fell at Beresina, was not prepared and not at his post. Other accidents happened. Orderlies went astray; commands were intercepted by the enemy, and this gave rise to misunderstandings and a number of bad manoeuvres. In addition, the heat was extraordinary, and General Dupont was ill.

General Reding profited so well by all this that he compelled Dupont to seek an armistice after an unequal fight on June 20th. But Reding was attacked from another side at the same time by General Wedel. He was between Dupont and Wedel, and would have been crushed if he had not succeeded in inducing Dupont to inform Wedel by an orderly of the armistice. Thus Wedel was forced to desist from attacking, and let slip a Spanish regiment that he might have captured. But while Wedel was still fighting, one of Dupont's adjutants, Villoutrai, who had completely misunderstood his commands, had brought news of the armistice, out of consideration for General Castanos, who was still a long way off.

Castanos advanced by forced marches to Baylen, and the situation became so desperate with his arrival that the armistice was converted into a capitulation. Nor was this all. Generals Wedel and Dufour, hearing that Dupont had capitulated and marching on to reach Madrid, heard from Dupont by an adjutant after a day's march that their divisions were included in the capitulation. In a moment of incredible stupidity the generals obeyed, surrendered, and had their brave soldiers disarmed, and thrown into Spanish prisons.

The whole army—21,000 men, with 40 guns and 2,400 cavalry—became prisoners of war. Very few of these fine soldiers ever reached France again. Most of them met their death by hunger and filth and ill treatment in the horrible prisons of Spain. As was usually done—perhaps especially in Spain—the higher officers had collected an immense amount of booty, which was amongst the baggage of the army. It has been hinted that the generals thought more of their valuable spoil than they ought to have done. But when the soldiers saw that their poor knapsacks were to be searched they handed over to the officers the driving of the waggons, in which there were great quantities of pictures and other valuables taken from churches and castles.

It was the greatest blow that the French army ever experienced under Napoleon. He heard the news at Bordeaux on August 1st, and his pain and anger were unbounded. 'Would that I could wipe out the disgrace with my blood,' he exclaimed. The celebrated engineer-general Marescot and General Privé had protested against the capitulation, and could not be included in the infamy of it. General Privé was detained in England until 1814, and Dupont was imprisoned. His case was never concluded, as far as I can learn; but after 1814 he received fresh honours and dignity under the Bourbons.

When the Baylen capitulation was known throughout Spain, it made a deep impression. The bubble of French invincibility was pricked, as it were, and the revolution could not be suppressed. Joseph had to fly from Madrid after being King of Spain for eight days. The misfortunes of France in Spain were completed in 1808 when Wellesley landed to the north of Lisbon with an English army. Joined the Portuguese, and marched on Vimeiro with a force of 26,000 men. The intrepid Junot did not budge a step, but opposed the advance of the enemy with his 10,000 men. He fought for five hours and lost the battle, but his position remained so strong that the English general offered him honourable terms, and the capitulation was concluded in the famous monastery at Cintra near Lisbon. Junot's army with all arms and stores was sent in English ships to France, so that he and his men left the Peninsula without disgrace.

However, coming after the Baylen scandal, the Cintra capitulation put the French in a desperate position, and the English, who remained in Portugal, were greeted as friends and allies by the Spaniards. After a short time the Spanish nation, which might have entered into an alliance with the French by a rational and considerate treatment, to drive the English invaders out of the Peninsula, joined with the English in antagonism to Napoleon.

When Napoleon and Alexander met at Tilsit in July, 1807, they had both expressed a wish to meet again before the end of the year. Affairs in Spain, and the presence of the English army in Portugal made a meeting more than advisable for Napoleon. Prussia's fate was to be decided. Austria was making strenuous preparations, and had reorganised its reserve. When Napoleon went to Erfurt for the promised interview in July, 1808, his forces were as follows, according to a letter to his brother Joseph:

> I have one army at Passau, one at Warschau, one in Schleswig, one at Hamburg, one at Berlin, one at Boulogne, and one marching against Portugal. I am collecting a reserve army at Boulogne, I have another in Italy, another in Dalmatia, and another at Naples. And there are garrisons all along the coast.

All the German princes, except the King of Prussia and the Emperor of Austria were at Erfurt. Baron Vincent came, as representative, with an excuse for the latter. The truth was that the Emperor was concerned to see Napoleon caring about nobody but the *Tsar*, and the two arranging the affairs of Europe without inviting him. Moreover, Austria was fully occupied just then with its own organisation.

During the fortnight they were together at Erfurt, the two Emperors had most intimate conversations, and it seemed to everybody that the Russian autocrat was proud of the consideration and friendship with which Napoleon treated him. 'The friendship of a great man is a gift of the gods,' was said one night from the stage, where Talma and the other actors from the *Théâtre Français* were playing tragedies. Alexander grasped Napoleon's hand and said with some warmth: 'I feel that every day.' Napoleon was as generous as ever. He presented the Grand Duke Constantine with a very valuable sword, and gave his own to Emperor Alexander, As he took the weapon, the Tsar said: 'I accept this token of friendship, and your Majesty may be quite sure that I will never draw it against you.' They parted on October 14th, the one going to his kingdom in the east, the other to the west, and they never saw such other again.

It has been stated that Napoleon's ultimate aim in all his wars was universal peace. That may be true in the sense that he certainly aimed at bringing about a state of things in which all the others would be on the floor, and he would be recognised as the greatest of all. The princes he met were personally inferior to him, and their enforced recognition had little value in his eyes. He cared little about England. It was not a kingdom in his opinion. But to win Russia's mighty *Tsar* was an object worth seeking. He was prepared to divide the world with him. He therefore gave greater attention to winning him than he had ever done in regard to anyone else. With his great superior mind, his knowledge, and the amiability that he really had, he overshadowed the younger man. The *Tsar* would have had to be of marble for all this to make no impression on him. Whereas Alexander I was in some respects very sensitive and easy to move.

Yet it was Napoleon who was duped. Not that the other man could have hoodwinked him. Napoleon was cunning enough to scent duplicity at any distance. But there is a great difference between what we may call Napoleon's occasional deceptiveness and the Asiatic form of absolute and unvarying duplicity that had been impressed in the training of the young prince and was the chief prerogative of the mature ruler. Alexander might be caught and enchanted, and he might mean every word that he said. But it was not associated in him with the least particle of what we call duty, to say nothing of his altering his opinion of Napoleon, or forgetting for a second that this enchanting individual was merely a Corsican adventurer of the name of Bonaparte, on whose neck he would one day set his stout Russian boot.

The more the King of Saxony approached him, and the smaller German princes humbled themselves before him, the more Napoleon attracted the young *Tsar*. He made no vain comparison of his power with that of the other monarch. It was enough for him as the elder to eclipse the younger man with his personal superiority. With Alexander, and recognised by him, he would renounce further plans, and, once England was shattered, each would possess his half of the world in peace. Meantime, Russia was to take Finland, and France the Spanish Peninsula.

On October 19th, Napoleon was back at St. Cloud. A few days afterwards he made a speech at the opening of the Legislative Assembly, in which he said:

> I set out for Spain in a few days to put myself at the head of my army, crown my brother King of Spain at Madrid, and plant our nobility in the fortresses of Portugal. The Emperor of Russia and I have been together at Erfurt. We are at one and indissolubly joined in war and peace.

He entered Spain on November 4th, 1808, and victory at once followed in his steps. Joseph met his brother, and joined the march on Madrid. Many of Napoleon's best generals were then in Spain, and in time they nearly all came. Davoust was spared, but Suchet, Soult, Ney, Masséna, Victor, and Marmont, were all called into the war, and few came out of it without hurt.

At Somo-Sierra the army corps to which the Emperor was attached had a fierce and famous fight. General Victor, who had been made marshal and Duke of Belluno after the Battle of Friedland, was at the foot of the pass of Somo-Sierra. It was protected by redoubts, in which there were 16 guns, while 10,000 infantry were distributed over the rising ground on each side of the narrow pass. They were commanded by General San-Benito. The position seemed impregnable for any troops but a numerous infantry with great staying power. But after a few attacks had failed, Napoleon became impatient. He ordered General Montbrun to take the position with the Polish lancers that he commanded, and that belonged to the Emperor's own guard.

It was an unheard-of thing to send cavalry against such a position, but the Emperor was impatient, and he knew that there were no better troops than the Poles to do it, if it were to be done. They did not fail him, but rushed forward. They ran their horses up the mountain, and leaped over the redoubts. The Spanish artillerymen were cut down at the guns, and, though with heavy losses, Montbrun succeeded in driving the enemy from the pass, and the army could advance. A large number of prisoners and stores were taken.

When the Polish lancers advanced to the attack, they were followed by the young Ségur. His place was in the immediate vicinity of the Emperor, acting as adjutant on tour and as an officer of the palace at home. The Emperor ordered him to take the place of an officer who had fallen, and thus he came to take part in the battle, which is regarded as a very remarkable piece of cavalry work. He was so severely wounded that he very narrowly escaped death. Afterwards he was liberally rewarded. He followed the Emperor as a general to the end, and died at the age of 91, in 1871. It is he who has written the excellent memoirs which have made famous the Russian campaign. His father had been in the service of Catherine II of Russia, and afterwards entered that of Napoleon, acting as head marshal of the court and master of ceremonies at the Tuileries. Napoleon was very proud of him.

The Emperor was not generous to the Poles. Not that he used them hardly in his service, or slighted them. On the contrary, the attack on Somo-Sierra was, and would certainly continue to be, regarded on both sides as a compliment. Many of the Polish officers rose to high positions. There were several generals amongst them, such as Prince Poniatowski, who was marshal only for a few days before he fell at Leipsic. General Dombrowski led the Poles into Russia, and in his early years one of Napoleon's favourite adjutants was the Pole Sulkowski, who fell in Egypt. But on the political side Napoleon gravely deceived the Poles. He understood well that they were not a people out of which he could make a kingdom for a Bonaparte, that would obey all orders emanating from Paris; and that was what he wanted. Moreover, he did not want to act contrary to the wishes of his friend the *Tsar*. The intense love of the Poles for liberty and their burning hatred of tyrants were by no means to his taste. Hence it was that he never realised their constant dream of a Polish kingdom. He accepted their services, and held them with hints and half-promises, but never went any further.

After the Battle of Somo-Sierra Napoleon was free to march on Madrid, which he could easily have taken by force. But he saw that it would be a bad beginning to set up Joseph by force in a kingdom with a pillaged capital. He took his time, therefore, and surrounded the city, which surrendered of itself. With a good deal of trouble the Spanish officials succeeded in keeping the people sufficiently in hand to permit the reinstatement of King Joseph in apparent tranquillity. Napoleon issued high-toned proclamations to the Spanish nation, but they did not make the least impression.

On the other hand he was himself greatly impressed with the fact that, in spite of their hostility to the French, the Spaniards were so honourable and loyal that King Joseph found his palace at Madrid intact, just as he had left it. Even the family portraits of the Bonaparte's, including David's famous picture of General Bonaparte on the Alps, were hanging in their places. Napoleon could not understand the national trait that made a compulsory king an object of hatred, yet left him safe in his chateau. If from the first Joseph had taken the place of the old and hated and disreputable royal house, without any use of force, all might have been well. Now it was too late.

On December 22nd, Napoleon left Madrid for the purpose of personally conducting the war. It was mainly a war with the English, who had crossed the Duero, and were drawing near Valladolid. The Emperor left Marshals Victor and Lefebvre, and the cavalry-generals Lasalle, Milhaud, and Latour-Maubourg to protect Joseph at Madrid. He immediately met with several mishaps. General Lefebvre-Desnouettes incautiously went with 400 dragoons across a ford with the object of occupying the village of Bonavente, which he thought to be deserted.

Unfortunately, there were still 2,000 English cavalry there, and they threw themselves on the small detachment. Lefebvre-Desnouettes was wounded, and his horse shot under him. He fell into the water, and was captured. General August Colbert—there were three brothers—received the command of Lefebvre's troops, which formed part of Marshal Bessières' cavalry of the advance guard. The young man fell two days afterwards. Before he died he said: 'I die like a brave soldier of the grand army, because I see before me the worst enemy of my country in flight.' He was one of the lions of the court; one of the finest men in the army.

Under the Emperor's lead Marshals Ney and Soult beat the English in a number of battles. General Moore fell, and General Baird was dangerously wounded on the *del* Curgo bridge before Corunna. It was to be expected that the war would soon end, under Napoleon's lead, with the reoccupation of the Peninsula and the destruction of the English. He was the only man who could handle several armies simultaneously and keep his eye on the generals.

However, in the middle of January, 1809, he received such news from Paris at Valladolid, especially in regard to the hostile attitude of Austria, that he at once mounted his horse and left Spain to Joseph with Marshal Jourdan in supreme command. Napoleon's suddenly leaving his army in a hostile country recalled his abrupt departure from Egypt. When the same thing happened later in life, it made a great deal of bad blood amongst the officers. The soldiers never resented anything he did.

There was one point that all aristocratic travellers hastened to write home to their circles—namely, that Napoleon could not ride, did not sit well on horseback, cut a poor figure, and so on. There was a certain consolation in thinking that the man who towered above them in everything else could not compare with them in personal bearing, at least in the fine art of riding. The truth was that Napoleon was a careless rider, a man whose chief concern was through thick and thin to get to his destination as quickly as possible. He had never had time or inclination to study that demeanour on which the sons of princes set such store. It is a great strain for man and beast to sit faultlessly, without moving, on a horse for hours together, reviewing large masses of troops.

The Emperor of Russia had a number of horses that were trained to stand as rigidly as if they were made of bronze. But Napoleon was always moving. Even during a review he was here and there and everywhere, because he had to see everything, and his thoughts were on what he saw, and he did not care a jot how he himself looked. Hence strangers who saw the little man in the grey coat on his noble horse, without giving a moment's thought to the animal or to the art of riding, found that he was a poor horseman. But when there was question of crossing a dangerous country, or of endurance, there were few in Europe who could ride like him.

On January 16th he rode at a sharp gallop from Valladolid to Burgos, which he had quitted the same morning—23 miles in five hours—from there, without leaving the carriage, he drove to Bayonne, and then on to Paris, where he arrived quite alone; no one had been able to keep up with him. On the evening of January 23rd his carriage entered the Tuileries, and the following morning Paris was astounded to learn from the *Moniteur* that Napoleon had returned from Spain.

Austria had been quiet for four years. But it could never lose its hatred of the arrogant son of the Revolution, who had annihilated its armies, and taken his place amongst the sovereigns of Europe. Moreover, money and entreaties came from England, and these were redoubled when the Emperor promised to succeed in driving the English out of the Peninsula. Thus, when Austria caused Napoleon to leave Spain on account of its menacing attitude, it did a great service to England, while the Emperor Francis Joseph was left to pay dearly for his imprudent declaration of war.

The Austrians had gathered a large and superior army of nearly 300,000 men, and they had at least one of the chief commanders of the time, the Archduke Charles. The troops were in Poland, Saxony, Tyrol, and Italy, under the Archdukes Charles, Ferdinand, and John, and Generals Kolowrat, Bellegarde, and Hiller. The French fighting forces were distributed under Poniatowski in Poland, Bernadotte in Saxony, General Gratien in Holland, and King Jerome in Westphalia. These were really reserve troops. The chief army, which was under the immediate command of the Emperor, consisted of the corps of Lannes and Oudinot, the third corps under Davoust at Regensburg, and the fourth under Masséna at Ulm. The seventh corps, consisting of 30,000 Bavarians under the Duke of Dantzig, was at Munich. The eighth, under Vandamme, was made up of 12,000 Würtembergers and 12,000 other German soldiers. Macdonald and Marmont advanced northwards from Italy. Altogether there were 267,000 men.

At last, after many bitter words and tedious intrigues. Napoleon learned on the evening of April 12th that the Archduke Charles had crossed the Inn. On the 17th Napoleon fixed his headquarters at Donauwörth. From the very beginning of this campaign there was scarcely a day on which one or other of the French generals did not distinguish himself, and the tide of war rolled steadily eastwards toward Vienna, some of the battles being great and sanguinary.

At Abensberg Napoleon left it chiefly to the Bavarians and Würtembergers to defeat the Austrians under General Hiller; and under the command of Davoust, Lannes, and Vandamme, they won a decisive victory. Marshal Davoust, who was already Duke of Auerstädt, was made Prince of Eckmühl, a small village near Regensburg, where he annihilated the army-corps of the Archduke Charles in a fierce three hours' battle, and opened the way to Vienna. General Cervoni, who came of an Italian family, was killed while he was spreading out a map before the Emperor. General Clement lost an arm at Eckmühl.

Napoleon was wounded at Regensburg for the only time in his life. He received a slight laceration of the heel. The King of Bavaria, whom the Austrians had driven from Munich, returned to his capital in triumph. The French armies then converged on Vienna, driving the enemy before them. Napoleon was marching for the first time without his Guard. He had been pleased to keep the Bavarians and Würtembergers near him, to reward them for Abensberg and attach them more closely to his person.

At nine o'clock on May 10th he reached the gates of Vienna. As the city was not surrendered for some time, he on the evening of the 11th caused a battery of fifteen guns to throw 1,800 bombs into it, and they at once set fire to it in different places. It capitulated on the morning of May 12th, and General Andreossy was appointed Governor.

After the taking of Vienna, it was necessary to cross the Danube, where the enemy were still drawn up for battle under the Archduke and General Hiller. Four bridges were used for crossing the river, as there were several islands to be passed, the last being separated from the left bank by an arm of the river some three or four hundred feet wide. The work began under the direction of engineer-generals Pernetti and Bernard. The latter was not yet so famous as he afterwards became, and was not considered so distinguished an engineer as Lariboisière, Chasseloup, Marescot, and Haxo, or as the great Eblé, who made the bridges over the Beresina.

On May 19th Napoleon ordered the pontoons to be put together and the bridges made. Masséna crossed it on the 20th with Molitor's division. He drove the Austrians out of the island after two hours' fighting, and by twelve o'clock he had the whole of the fourth corps on it. It is fairly large, and was at that time overgrown with bushes and intersected with ditches.

On the evening of May 20th Napoleon matured his plan of crossing the last arm of the river early the following morning and attacking the villages of Aspern and Esslingen. Neither he nor anyone else suspected that the Archduke Charles and General Hiller had entrenched themselves so strongly in these positions that the French had to fight two very critical battles before they could get a safe footing on the left bank; and even then they only half succeeded.

On the evening of the 20th the officers and soldiers sat round the camp fires and were chatting gaily as was usual on the night before a battle. A young officer named Albuquerque—of a Spanish family—had come with Lannes' troops from Spain. He had been fortunate enough to receive the sword of the brave General Palafox, when he surrendered Saragossa. He now sat and sang gay and sentimental Spanish songs to his comrades, who knew his fine voice and gathered round his fire. He fell at Aspern the following afternoon.

On the following morning, while Napoleon's troops were in the act of crossing the bridge, the enemy deployed all his forces, and attacked with a superior force the divisions that had crossed over. The battle centred about the two villages, which passed alternately to one or other party five or six times in the course of the day. Masséna was engaged at Aspern and Lannes at Esslingen. The French were outnumbered, but they were the best soldiers in Europe, and they kept off the enemy until dark came on. Marshal Bessières had exposed his cavalry to fire, and they had done wonders of bravery, but had also suffered a great loss in the death of General d'Espagne, one of the finest cavalry leaders, and three colonels. In the awful night between the 21st and 22nd of May, Masséna camped in the ruins of the burning village of Aspern, the Austrians under Bellegarde holding the church and churchyard in the same village. But both armies were overcome with fatigue, and they allowed each other a few hours' rest.

In the midst of the battle there was a heated private quarrel between Marshals Bessières and Lannes. By the Emperor's orders, Bessières's cavalry was at the disposal of Lannes, so that the former was, to some extent, under the supreme command of Lannes, and he found this intolerable. A violent quarrel broke out between them, and they very nearly came to fight a duel that evening. The armies had not a long sleep. At two in the morning the Austrians began to stir. Napoleon sent adjutants incessantly to the other army-corps which were still on the island and on the right bank, directing them to cross over as quickly as possible.

Meantime, the bridges themselves were in the greatest danger. The Austrians filled boats with heavy stones, and flung mills and mill-wheels and anything that could float into the river above the bridge. The mass was carried down by the current, and borne against the French bridges, bringing great pressure to bear on the piles and pontoons. In the early morning Marshal Davoust rode alone across the bridge to tell the Emperor that his men would soon be there. Some of them had already arrived, and were fighting with the heroes of the preceding day. Napoleon therefore began the day with full confidence, though the Archduke was again pressing forward his superior forces with great energy. The French stood as firm as they had done the day before.

Napoleon then, relying confidently on the closeness of reinforcements, commanded an advance, and directed his marshals to break through the Austrian centre and hurl them back on to the plains. This manoeuvre, which they knew well from many of his earlier battles, was at once and so brilliantly carried out that a broad and dangerous gap appeared in the enemy's fighting-line. Archduke Charles seized the flag of General Zach's regiment to lead his troops forward once more. He exposed himself as boldly as the bravest soldier amongst them, but he was borne back in the retreating masses of the army. Napoleon also was so imprudent on that day that General Walther, who had to guard him with the grenadiers, went up to him and said: 'If your Majesty does not withdraw I shall order my grenadiers to remove you by force.'

It was still no later than eight o'clock in the morning, and Napoleon was quite sure of seeing Davoust's columns come over the bridge any moment. Then came the news that the largest bridge had broken down. Quietly, without a word of impatience, he saw the certain victory slip from his hands. He directed Lannes to suspend the attack, whilst he got more detailed information. The news he heard soon convinced him that for that day he could not possibly expect any help from the other side of the Danube, and he had no more ammunition on his own side. The Austrians had succeeded in floating so much stuff against the longest bridge that the current at length broke it in the middle.

The Archduke was not long in learning that Napoleon was more or less isolated. He gathered his men, who were subjected to no further attacks, and there ensued one of the fiercest struggles that was ever witnessed. It lasted twelve hours, and was confined to one comparatively small field. The French defended themselves all day long with incredible bravery, and an unusually large number of officers fell. Amongst them was General Saint-Hilaire, one of the most important. He had received the grand eagle of the Legion of Honour and the cross of a Commander of the Iron Crown at Austerlitz. A worse loss was that of Marshal Lannes himself, the Duke of Montebello. His adjutants had succeeded in inducing him to dismount for a moment and stretch his legs, when a cannon ball broke both his knees. He lived for a few days in great pain, and died on May 30th.

Lannes was one of the best friends of Napoleon's youth and the most important of all. The writers who have sought to make everything about Napoleon as bad as possible, have tried to represent the relations between Lannes and Napoleon as anything but friendly. It is quite possible that he said some very straight things to Napoleon at times, and did not mince matters with him. Napoleon was not the kind of man that one could feel very tender towards; even in his relations with his intimate friends he preserved the coldness that he always deliberately cultivated. But when he heaped gratitude, praise, and rewards on them, they knew it, and they saw from a single look or a smile that he was a true friend of theirs. The Emperor never mentioned Lannes without warmly praising his fine qualities, and he missed the man all his life.

After the frightful Battle of Aspern and Esslingen, which is generally regarded as the Archduke Charles's greatest victory. General Mouton received the title of Count of Lobau, with rich awards, for his coolness and unflinching bravery. The Emperor was quiet and cool, as usual, when he summoned his marshals to a council in the evening. They all advised that the army be brought into safety on the right bank of the Danube. But it was impossible for him to retreat so far. He could not be induced to go farther than the island of Lobau. Orders were issued to begin the crossing as soon as the short bridge to Lobau was ready. But the villages were to be held as long as possible in order to deceive the enemy. During the night Napoleon rowed across the Danube with Berthier, to console Davoust and the other generals, who had been condemned to inaction during the great battle.

At two in the morning the Guard began to pass quietly ever the short bridge to Lobau. After them came the cavalry and Oudinot's grenadiers, and before it was quite daylight everything had been got across the single bridge to Lobau. They had then to make a better bridge over the river, and the best engineers in the army worked for forty-three days to prepare the piles, etc., for the crossing of 160,000 men with all their appurtenances. In the meantime the camp on Lobau was converted into one of the strongest positions in Europe, and French armies were converging upon it from all sides. A number of honourable fights were engaged in at the same time by Napoleon's generals, while he himself kept court at Schönbrunn.

The engineers had their work, which was regarded as a masterpiece in those days, ready in the early days of July. Three bridges, as broad as columns of troops, so that three waggons could pass each other on them, led from the right bank over the small island to Lobau. The bridges that were to lead from this point to the left bank were ready to be thrown over the left arm of the river at a given moment. The whole was protected by a palisade-work that ran out to a point up the stream from one of the small islands. Eight across the island of Lobau there was a forty-foot wide road made, running out on a mole; and on this road and on the bridges lanterns were set up every 60 feet. At each crossing there were sign-posts with orders for each army-corps.

Men now poured in from all quarters, and soldiers of every corps in the grand army, who had fought all over Europe, met on Lobau. At nightfall on July 3rd they sat round the bivouac fires; comrades, friends, and relatives, who had not seen each other for six years, found each other again in the crowd. Besides Masséna, Davoust, and Oudinot, the Viceroy Eugene came from the Tyrol, Marmont from Italy, Bernadotte, Vandamme, and Lefebvre, King Jerome from Dresden, and Junot from Bayreuth.

On July 4th, the order to cross was given. A number of small bridges that stood ready were thrown over the remaining narrow arm of the river to the left bank. One of them was an especial object of admiration. It consisted of a single piece and was placed in from eight to ten minutes. In the evening occurred one of the most frightful storms ever experienced. Wind and rain lashed the whole island with great violence and in the midst of it broke out the roar of the guns that were to protect the crossing. But nothing could hold them or damp their ardour. One corps after another began its march over the bridges and islands into the darkness and storm. The Emperor was on horseback all night. It was calculated that he spent 60 hours in the saddle between the 4th and 6th of July.

On the following morning the vast army was across, and when the sun rose it shone on the spreading masses of the French drawn up in line of battle in all their splendour. That day the Archduke Charles retreated. In the afternoon there was a fight at Wagram, in which General Macdonald distinguished himself with the army from Italy. Bernadotte, who commanded the Saxon auxiliaries, made a feeble and fruitless attack on the town of Wagram. His troops were beaten, and retreated in great disorder. The Archduke held the heights of Wagram and spent the night there.

Early the next morning, July 7th, the day of the real Battle of Wagram, the Austrians attacked the village of Aderklaa that Bernadotte was supposed to hold. Once more his Saxons fled in wild confusion, and the Archduke drove Napoleon's left wing so far back that the batteries on Lobau had to open fire to protect the bridges. Masséna commanded the left wing, and had with him Generals Molitor, Legrand, and Boudet, with his fine artillery. General Carra Saint-Cyr was also with them. He was sent first to recover Aderklaa, but owing to an unskilful manoeuvre his troops fell into such a bad position that they were deprived of cover, and driven back, taking the whole of the left wing with them.

Both Legrand and Boudet, who lost his beloved guns, were swept away. At this critical moment General Reille went to inform the Emperor that the Austrians threatened to overpower Masséna, whose entire corps had been thrown into disorder. The Emperor sent Marshal Berthier with the Guard and 80 guns right across the field from right to left. He must have been reduced to extremities when he sent Berthier and the Guard.

General Lauriston led the artillery and General Reille the young guard in the attack on Aderklaa, the chief point on the left wing. Marshal Bessières received a similar order, but at that moment he was struck by a very curious ball on the leg. It tore his trousers as far as the knees, and left a zigzag mark on the leg. The Emperor heard that one of his friends had been hit, and had fallen from his horse.

'Who is it?' he asked, without turning.

'The Duke of Istria,' was the reply.

'Ride on,' said the Emperor; 'we have no more time for weeping.' He was thinking of Lannes.

It is this moment in the battle of Wagram that we so often find represented in the photographs of the great pictures at Versailles. Napoleon was that day riding one of his most famous horses. It was called 'Euphrates 'and was a present from the Shah of Persia. No one had ever seen so white a horse before in Europe. In the midst of the hottest fire he galloped on this horse right across the field, in front of the French lines, to the labouring left wing. Savary and the other generals, who followed him as well as they could, expected every moment to see him drop. The Emperor took up a position in Lamarque's division, and remained there a full hour while the left wing was being restored to order. He sat upright on his white horse amidst the shower of bullets, so that friend and foe could see him at the short distance that separated fighting armies in those days.

Davoust was on the left wing, where he was opposed to Prince John of Liechtenstein. He was ordered to make a grand attack on the village of Neusiedel. With Davoust were the cavalry-generals Nansouty and Arrighi, Duke of Padua, who had taken the place of the fallen d'Espagne. The enemy slowly retreated before the skilful manoeuvres of the Duke of Auerstädt. The Emperor told his servant Roustan, a *mameluke* whom he had brought from Egypt, to spread a bear-skin on the ground. He dismounted, stretched himself on it, and went to sleep, as he was accustomed to do. He had every right to be tired.

When he awoke, a quarter of an hour afterwards, he found a circle of adjutants with reports from all parts of the field. He arose quietly and turned his telescope on Neusiedel; when he saw that Davoust's troops were on the heights, where he wanted them to be, he pushed in his telescope again, and said to his adjutants: 'Ride to Masséna and tell him he may withdraw. The battle is won.' The fight raged until one in the afternoon on the great plains, where the horses nearly disappeared in the high corn. At the edge of the battlefield the ripe corn was set on fire. Whole acres of it were burning, and the fire reached the well-protected train, and exploded many of the powder waggons.

Macdonald was the real hero of the day. He at length succeeded in breaking the centre and making a gap in it that offered a fine opportunity for the cavalry to rush in and take prisoners and spoils. But Murat was in Spain, Bessières wounded, d'Espagne dead, and, to crown the misfortune. General Lasalle, the greatest cavalry-leader that Napoleon had left, also fell on this day. Lasalle was one of the most handsome men in the French army, and a trained horseman from his early years, but he had grown rather wild in the course of time. He swore and drank, sang and rioted, and wasted all his money.

When he was in Egypt he corresponded with a lady at Paris. The English intercepted his letters, and, with the incredible lack of taste that they showed in all that related to Napoleon, they published them in the European press. The lady was married to a brother of General Berthier, and the publication of the letters caused a fearful scandal, followed by divorce, etc., at Paris. However, Lasalle afterwards married Mme. Berthier, and gradually reached so high a rank that he became one of the men who were most trusted and most frequently employed by the Emperor. He was exceptionally liked by his comrades. When he swung into his saddle and drew his sabre, his men would follow him like the wind over stock and stone, through fire and blood. But there was a wild spirit in the light cavalry long after Lasalle's death.

The night before the battle of Wagram General Lasalle had written a letter to the Emperor asking him to take care of the family he would leave behind him. It often happened that even the bravest had these fits of despondency before a great battle, and wrote letters that had the nature of presentiments if the writer fell.

The loss of officers was great on both sides at Wagram. The French lost Generals Gauthier and Lacour, besides Lasalle, and seven colonels. Gauthier had distinguished himself under Davoust at Auerstädt. At Wagram he lost a leg, and died of the wound. General Gudin, who kept quite close to Davoust, and always fought under him, received four wounds in the course of the day. Twenty other generals, besides Bessières, were wounded, but recovered. General Lamarque had four horses shot under him, Masséna, on the other hand, who was perhaps most exposed of all to the enemy's fire in these days, did not receive the slightest scratch. It was said in the army that Masséna, and Murat, and Ney, were bulletproof. But it was considered dangerous to be near Masséna. The very spot that he had just left was shunned. If any one came up and occupied it, they would shout to him that the marshal had just been there.

A few days before the battle Masséna had the misfortune to collide with a waggon during a reconnaissance. He was so badly shaken that he could not keep his horse during the battle, and had to lead his corps in a carriage. But when the left wing was in a dangerous plight he took to horse in spite of the pain. He called one of his orderlies to lengthen the stirrup, and by this means lifted his injured leg, with a great effort, on to the horse's neck. At that very moment a cannonball came singing along and knocked down the soldier who was busy with his saddle.

Masséna had begun his career as a private soldier in the republican armies, like Bernadotte and many others. But he was one of the greatest leaders, and Napoleon always described him as the first, although their relations were not particularly good. Masséna was easily led into small intrigues with the other malcontents, and Napoleon was well acquainted with the fact, as well as with the circumstance that Masséna was an incurable pillager wherever he went. After Eylau he had been made Duke of Rivoli, and he now became Prince of Esslingen.

Napoleon embraced Macdonald, and made him Marshal and Duke of Tarentum, which was rather a tardy recognition of Macdonald's deeds and merits. But it was some time before the Emperor came to trust entirely this man of Scottish descent, with his rather stiff and self-conscious ways. Napoleon never really liked him. Macdonald was fairly tall, and had an open and energetic countenance, though his nose was too short.

At the Battle of Wagram he wore the antiquated uniform of a republican general, with huge feathers in his hat. He distinguished himself wherever he went. Amongst other things he succeeded in arresting the flight of Bernadotte's Saxons, and inducing them to advance once more. Oudinot and Marmont also received the marshal's staff. It was, perhaps, a little prematur for Marmont. But Napoleon appreciated the brave and brilliant Marmont in his cold and unemotional way.

Bernadotte's corps was dissolved, and he himself was sent in disgrace from the army. The army bulletin of July 30th contains the following passage: 'The ninth army-corps, which was commanded by Ponte-Corvo, is dissolved. The Saxons who belonged to it pass under the command of General Regnier. The Prince of Ponte-Corvo has gone to the baths.'

The fact was that Marshal Bernadotte had been exceptionally slipshod during the whole campaign of 1809. He is never mentioned amongst the generals whose bravery decided a great battle. But he continued just the same to swagger and to criticise the Emperor. The night before the battle he was sitting in a circle of officers, saying that Napoleon's crossing of the Danube and subsequent manoeuvres were quite wrong and unsuccessful. He himself would have forced the Archduke, by a few well-directed movements, to surrender almost without a fight.

When his Saxons fled on the following day, and Bernadotte galloped after them, the Emperor stopped him and asked if this was the well-directed movement with which he would crush the Archduke. His spies had reported to him the conversation of the night before. It is certain, at all events, that Bernadotte's corps took to flight on July 5th at Wagram, and July 6th at Aderklaa, and Napoleon spoke sharply about him in the order of the day to his marshals.

But that was not the worst. After he and his corps had done so badly in the battle, the Prince of Ponte Corvo had the impudence to issue an order of the day, a thing that was reserved for the commander-in-chief, and no marshal had a right to do. He sent out a proclamation in which he claimed, the honours of the Battle of Wagram for himself and his Saxons. The whole army, and especially the officers and the Emperor, were infuriated. He refused to see the marshal, and wrote to the Minister of War at Paris:

If you have occasion to see the Prince of Ponte Corvo, inform him of my displeasure at the ridiculous order of the day that he had inserted in all the journals; it is doubly incorrect, since he was complaining to me all day about his Saxons. I will not conceal from you the fact that the Prince of Ponte Corvo has deserved little praise during this campaign. To say the truth, this "granite column" has been always in flight.

The victory at Wagram was decisive enough, but it had been dearly bought, and there was not the usual corollary of prisoners, guns, flags, etc. The day of the good old bayonet-fights was over. The artillery had to work hard to support the new infantry columns, which were swollen with recruits and foreign auxiliaries. Hence it was that more officers fell than had been the case in earlier battles. Finally, it seemed to the Emperor for the first time that he perceived a certain amount of laxity in his highest generals. He was only moderately pleased with the battle. On the Austrian side three generals were killed and ten wounded, including the Archduke himself. He had not spared himself the whole day, and was hit twice. But he directed the fight to the end like the unflinching soldier and great leader that he was. The days of Aspern, Esslingen, and Wagram, showed what the brave Austrians could do when they were led by a great general.

Napoleon held his court at Schönbrunn while the diplomatists were discussing the terms of peace. One day he was nearly murdered by a German fanatic of the name of Stabbs. He had drawn quite close to the Emperor during a parade, when General Rapp suddenly seized him at the last moment as a suspicious-looking individual. After the enormous strain at Esslingen and Wagram Napoleon had an attack of illness during his stay at Schönbrunn, but we know nothing of its nature. The high officers about him have never betrayed the secret, but we can gather that it was serious from the anxious deliberations of Murat, Berthier, and Duroc, and the haste with which they sent for Corvisart, the Emperor's physician, and a famous professor at Vienna. It may possibly have been only an exceptionally bad attack of dysuria, from which he suffered as early as 1796, and at Borodino, where he was ill and kept out of sight of the army for several days.

On October 19th peace was concluded at Vienna, under sufficiently humiliating conditions for Austria. Although he waged war for six years afterwards, and won most brilliant victories, this peace was the last that Napoleon ever effected. Europe never made peace with him. On October 26th he returned to Fontainebleau, having won fresh victories for France and made his empire stronger than ever.

CHAPTER 4

Zenith

In the years 1810 and 1811 Napoleon was ruling at Paris. It was, apparently at least, his zenith. The frontiers of France had been pushed to the mouth of the Elbe, and Rome was the second capital of the empire. The whole of Europe recognised his predominance, with the exception of England, which, in spite of the injury done to its trade by its exclusion from the continent, always had money for those who dared to resist Napoleon, and slowly and surely undermined his vast empire from the Spanish Peninsula, and enfeebled his fighting forces.

The resistance of the Spaniards became more and more bitter and savage, while England poured fresh troops continually into Portugal. Marshal Soult, Duke of Dalmatia, imagined at one time that he would be King of Portugal. But Wellington drove him out of Oporto with such thoroughness that Soult lost the whole of his baggage. The news of this battle reached Napoleon the day after Aspern and Esslingen, through a courier that the Minister of War had hastily despatched from Paris.

In the year 1810 there were 400,000 of the best French troops in Spain under leaders Like Soult, Masséna, Ney, Victor, and Suchet. The latter was the only one who was able to keep regular government in his province. There was no cohesion, and there were many accidents. In the course of time it came to be looked upon as a sort of banishment and a sign of disgrace when an officer at Paris was ordered to go to Spain.

The handsome secretary and palace officer, Canouvuille, was one of Pauline's many lovers. Napoleon had sent her a Russian mantle of exceptionally fine fur and diamond clasps. One day, with the searching eyes that saw everything, he recognised his present in the secretary's ante-room. An hour later Canouville was on his way to Spain.

It was somewhat different with Septeuil, another lion of the court. He declined to see Pauline's attempts to approach him, and she was so enraged that the young officer was sent to Spain at her request. He had one of his legs shot off in his first battle, and while the surgeons were amputating it—sawing and hacking as they did a century ago—he said to his valet: 'Don't cry. You will now have only one boot to polish.'

The elaborate equipment of the French court, that the Revolution had scattered to the winds, had at last been restored under the Emperor. It took a very different form from that it had had under the old regime, but it was no less magnificent in regard to the correctness of etiquette and the lavish expenditure on festivities. Napoleon's new court was, of course, not filled with aged superfluities and useless folk, who did nothing beyond drawing their salaries, as the earlier one had been. However, he revived many of the old titles and bestowed them on his own men and women; or he attracted men and women with ancient names to his court, a thing that always gave him great satisfaction. He used to say that no one could render court-service like the old nobles. A Montmorency would not hesitate to stoop and tie Josephine's shoe-laces, but many of the new ladies had no mind for acting as chamber-maids in this way. He praised the men of the older nobility in the same way, and sent them on diplomatic missions. He used to say that he learned more through them than through his own people.

At the same time he did not like his own people to be cast in the shade by the older nobles. He had some of the feeling of the Revolution, and rewarded merit without regard to origin. He mingled the old and the new, in order to bring about a harmonious system, but he took good care that one should not quarrel with the other. He was proud to have Count Ségur, of the old nobility, as his master of ceremonies, yet he never liked even a hint to be given to Marshal Lefebvre about his unconventional wife, the Duchess of Dantzig, whose incorrect behaviour filled Paris with laughter and gave some consolation to the fine courts of Europe, This attitude of the Emperor kept the old nobles in check and protected the new ones. All felt that the sovereign knew well what was worthy of gratitude and honour.

Las Cases, who himself belonged to a noble Franco-Spanish family of distinction, and had taken service in the imperial court at an early date—and eventually followed the Emperor to St. Helena—tells us that he one day heard the following story about Mme. Lefebvre, the

Duchess of Dantzig. She gave help to poor emigrants, amongst others to a noble family that was so proud and sensitive that the duchess, knowing well what people thought and said of her, dare not offer it herself. She therefore went to the family in which she and her husband were at one time simple servants, and gave her help anonymously through them. They themselves belonged to the higher social circles. 'When I heard this,' says Las Cases, 'I ceased to make fun of the Duchess. I rather esteemed it a pleasure after that to offer her my arm at the Tuileries and lead her round the magnificent rooms, and took no notice of the sarcasm and the round eyes of my comrades.'

But though the mingling of the new and the old was carried out with the utmost discretion and without ostentation, it begot neither life nor gaiety. The tone of the Tuileries was stiff and cold, because Napoleon, not very pleasant as First Consul, became positively disagreeable as Emperor. The Duchess of Abrantes and the other ladies recalled with tears the happy days of Malmaison, when they had to do duty in their stiff court-dresses at the Tuileries, St. Cloud, or Fontainebleau. When they gave luxurious parties themselves, at his desire, they were no longer free to enjoy the dance or masquerade. They had to think of nothing but *him*. When the cry rang out, 'The Emperor,' the company, already nervous with waiting, became as quiet as mice. The eyes and thoughts of all were on him to discover what sort of humour he was in. He was as unreliable as a Sultan. At times he might be disposed to joke; otherwise he would at the most amuse himself at their balls with frightening the younger ladies to death when his spies had told him their little secrets.

The festivals that the Emperor gave, or caused to be given, were generally so tedious that they were a great trial to the younger folk. He held audiences in the morning before breakfast, as the French kings had used to do, when they left their beds and were clothed by their valets. At other times he gave large audiences before one or other festival at the Tuileries. The whole court was in attendance, the ambassadors of foreign powers being in the front rank. The Emperor would stride rapidly in, and go along the row of bowing and bending courtiers. Those were the most anxious moments for the whole of Europe. From the few words he spoke to the ambassadors, or even from the way in which he would pass one by in silence or offer another a pinch of snuff, there were conclusions drawn all over Paris and Europe. It was like prophesying from the grounds in a tea-cup. As a rule the brief conversations with the ambassadors ran in this wise:

Emperor: 'Why is your government gathering such large masses of troops in the Tyrol.'

Metternich: 'Indeed! your Majesty astonishes me . . . .'

Emperor: 'Bah! I know all about it, and I want a satisfactory explanation.'

Metternich: 'I will send a courier to Vienna at once. Perhaps I could send my court by the same messenger a satisfactory assurance from your Majesty about the advance of the Duke of Ragusa from Italy.'

Napoleon: 'How do you know that'

Metternich: 'Ah! It is true, then, Sire.'

Napoleon: 'Whether it is true or not, I have no explanation to give.'

That was pretty much the tenor of these conversations. They assumed enormous proportions in the eyes of diplomatists, and brought Metternich the reputation of being the most astute of all. As a rule, however, they were mere bluff. Each side was well acquainted with the other's intrigues and manoeuvres. They knew also that it was only a question of time when they should be at war again. But the art consisted in talking peace and meaning war, and they waltzed round, like cats round a basin of hot broth.

At this time Napoleon was still a handsome-looking man when he strode in on the waxed floors, with firm short steps that resounded in the respectful silence, to the accompaniment of a slight jingle of spurs when he had his high boots on, and the faint odour of *eau de cologne* that always clung to him. But he soon became rather too stout, and it increased every year, even when he was in the field. The Empress Josephine had easily adapted herself to her high position at court by her grace and amiability, as well as tact and judgement. The great men, the kings and princes, who more or less willingly visited Paris, looked in vain for something to tell against her. Even Louis XVIII, when he returned and saw the great changes in the Louvre and the Tuileries, had to admit that everything had been done in a style that neither he nor anyone else cared to alter.

But while Napoleon gave his court a pompous air through the rules he had drawn up, he worked day and night with a versatility and endurance that his contemporaries were never tired of admiring. Just as he injured his horses by riding in the field, so he nearly worked to death the secretaries and ministers who were in his service, without ever being overcome by fatigue himself. His first private secretary was Bourrienne, one of the friends of his youth. They agreed very well for a number of years, but there was one fault that Napoleon could not bear or forgive, and that was carelessness in money-matters. He could forgive his generals for stupid mistakes when they redeemed them.

He could overlook infidelity of all kinds, even Josephine's—he was, in fact, not very sound on that point himself; but in money-matters he tolerated no irregularities. He was a terror to bankers and army-contractors. The large houses of the time—Hope of Amsterdam, Lafitte, Séguin—lived in daily dread of fresh surprises from the Emperor. He twice ruined the great speculator Ouvrard. As soon as he suspected dishonesty, or merely heard of some illegitimate profit, or that one of his men had used his position to enrich himself, he came down on him at once.

Marshal Masséna once returned from a campaign in Italy with his pockets well filled. The Emperor at once ordered him to pay three million *francs* into the State-treasury, without giving any explanation. Masséna paid without a murmur; or, rather, he only complained in private. Another officer, Colonel Solignac, who had been with Masséna, and who was ordered to pay 800,000 *francs*, hesitated to obey, and was at once reduced to the ranks. However, Solignac coolly shouldered his gun, and fell into line; and the next time Napoleon's eye fell on him, he restored his rank and command. Solignac had been at Napoleon's side in the junior Council at St. Cloud on the 18th *Brumaire*. He liked best to be with General Masséna, and was, like him, an incurable pillager.

Bourrienne, Napoleon's private secretary, had the same weakness in regard to money, though it took a more pacific form. Nevertheless their friendship was at an end as soon as Napoleon found that his secretary was using his position to make money. Bourrienne was a brave man, with quick intelligence and a great capacity for work. He was also devoted to Napoleon. But he was tempted when he saw millions circulating about the great man, who was himself indifferent to them, and he began very soon to receive payments of a more or less questionable character.

He discovered, for instance, that the Minister of Police, Fouché, paid 100,000 *francs* a month to men who were in Napoleon's immediate vicinity, to tell him every day where the First Consul went, what he was doing, and who came to him. Bourrienne thought no one could do this better than himself. He went to Fouché and offered his services. Fouché accepted, and from that time Bourrienne received 25,000 *francs* a month for the work. But the Minister of Police and Spies had many others in the Tuileries to whom he paid large sums. Even Josephine received 1,000 *francs* a day for secret information about her husband.

Later Bourrienne had his finger in all sorts of affairs, and at length he indulged in large speculations, in which millions were at stake. He was secretly a partner in the firm of Coulon Frères, who contracted for the cavalry-supplies, and went bankrupt for a million. In the end he became impoverished and was prosecuted by his creditors.

After Bourrienne, Méneval became secretary, and he was Napoleon's favourite. He was an extraordinary man in regard to trustworthiness and capacity for work. But he was completely worn out; as a reward, and in order to rest himself, he was made private secretary to Marie Louise.

The chief of the Emperor's cabinet was Maret, Duke of Bassano. He was a man of mediocre talent and poor character, but he was faithful and devoted to Napoleon to the last. He was generally hated on account of his daily and intimate converse with the Emperor, and because he stood high in Napoleon's favour; but more evil was laid to his charge than he really deserved. Talleyrand once said of him: 'I only know one man who is more stupid than M. Maret, and that is the Duc de Bassano.' He was really not so stupid, but thoroughly conventional and petty. He was a subordinate flatterer and slave to his great master. Napoleon was one of the men who can make use of everything that has at least strength; and the Duke of Bassano had a capacity for work that even the Emperor could never exhaust. At the dangerous crisis of 1811, when Napoleon had most need of a cool and moderate counsellor, he dismissed the judicious Champagny, Duke of Cadore, and made Maret Minister for Foreign Affairs, as he never expressed the least resistance or hesitation when the Emperor wanted anything.

Still nearer to Napoleon in daily intercourse—nearer than any other of his generals—was his warm friend and counsellor, Duroc, Duke of Friaul and Master of the Court. Like most of the men about Napoleon he had originally been an officer, and had served under the French kings before the Revolution. Napoleon used him exclusively as an envoy and Master of the Court in everything that pertained to his private life—his *châteaux*, his court and domestic routine, his journeys and daily life at Paris, his family and all the storms that broke out in them. Duroc was quiet, precise, firm and modest. He was of an upright and well-minded character. Amidst the chaos of intrigues and jealousies that gathered about the great man—not the least amongst his own family—Duroc was like a tower rising above the waters. He was ambassador at Vienna, St. Petersburg, Berlin, Stockholm, and Copenhagen, and he was much esteemed everywhere. He was spared Spain.

A very different man from him was another of Napoleon's immediate servants, who did not properly belong to the rank of officers. This was the Minister of War, Clarke, Duke of Feltre. He was of Irish extraction, and began his career as private secretary in the Orleans family. After the Revolution he was sent by the Directors, according to their custom, to watch General Bonaparte during the first Italian campaign. In a few days the general saw through the spy, and Clarke candidly confessed it and offered his services. Napoleon accepted the offer, and gradually loaded him with gifts and distinctions. Clarke became ambassador, Governor at Vienna and Berlin, where he is still remembered, Minister of War, and Duke. When he married he received a *dot* from the Emperor's private purse. He was the worst flatterer in Napoleon's service, and was always ready to goad him on when the Emperor was going too far. He was rightly hated for his malice.

It is not easy to see how much or how little influence Napoleon's men had on his actions. On the whole it may be said that their influence was very slight at first, but it became stronger, and in the days of his downfall was greater than was desirable. Yet he was the man who ruled everything and everybody. This was not merely because he wished it; Napoleon's gifts and acquirements, not only in military matters, but in almost every branch of government, were so thorough and superior that everything came naturally to him. Hence every part of the State-machinery became purely ornamental and unimportant. Communal and governmental offices shrivelled up and were cast in the shade. The one thing that Napoleon cared for was the *Conseil d'Etat,* where he appeared fifty-seven times in the days when his famous legal code—the *Code Napoléon*—was being drawn up. He had spies in this assembly also, and distributed money amongst its members, without one knowing what the other received.

Napoleon was unique in financial matters. There never was any other man who treated money with such indifference, yet used it with such prodigality on the one hand and such cold accuracy on the other. But he had his own ideas, and was just as difficult with financiers and exchanges as with his own ministers. He had a faculty for detecting errors in calculation that astounded those about him. One day he said that there was an error of 2,000,000 *francs* in an account presented by the *Maison Séguin* for supplies to the army. The minister smiled and promised that the account would be examined. After a long search the error was detected, and the firm refunded the money. On another occasion he went through the accounts of an infantry-regiment—he went through all of them—and found an entry of 16,000 *francs* for a stay in Paris. He declared that neither the regiment nor any part of it had been at Paris. The minister smiled and said he would see to it; and it turned out that the Emperor was right.

It cannot possibly be all flattery when we find all the great men of the time, French and foreign, whatever branch they may be expert in, expressing their astonishment and admiration at the range of his knowledge and the lucidity with which he discussed all subjects. Learned and gifted men had not to confine themselves with him to a few phrases, as they generally did with princes—who know nothing beyond what they have been coached in for a particular audience. If Napoleon had made a poor impression, no one needed to conceal the fact, because there were plenty of people who would be glad to hear it. But the truth was that he compelled them all to marvel at the clear and vast mind that seemed to have room for everything.

The famous chemist, Chaptal, was his Minister of Foreign Affairs for four years, and they worked very well together until Napoleon at last carelessly wounded Chaptal's pride, and so kept him aloof for several years. One night they worked together until very late, when a servant entered and announced in a fairly loud tone of voice that Mlle. Bourgoing had arrived. She was the famous and inspired actress of the *Théatre Français*. The Emperor directed that she should be taken to his room and wait there. all this was done in a tone of voice that the minister could not help hearing. The offence was deliberate, for the whole of Paris knew that the Minister of Foreign Affairs had relations with the charming actress. Chaptal at once put his papers together, bowed, and departed. He sent in his resignation the same night. This was in 1804, and he did not return until 1815, when he was Napoleon's Minister of Trade during the 'Hundred Days.'

Another well-known form of unpleasantness in Napoleon's conversation was his habit of suddenly breaking into anger and coarseness. He would fall quite unexpectedly on someone present and call him to account for new or ancient faults in such bitter and exasperating language that many went away never to return. He used to have most violent encounters with the foreign ambassadors. Four of these are especially famous—with Lord Whitworth in 1803, with Metternich in 1809, with Prince Kourakin in 1811, and with General Balakoff at Wilna on July 12th, 1812.

It is said that in his altercation with Lord Whitworth Napoleon was so excited that he nearly struck the ambassador; some say, in fact, that he did. But Lord Whitworth's own account, which appeared in 1888, does not say a word of any such violent action on the part of the First Consul. There were some, even amongst those who knew Napoleon very well in daily life, who believed that these violent and passionate attacks were merely deliberate scenes, much like the one before signing the peace of Campo Formio, when he broke Count Cobentzl's tea-service.

In the service and in intercourse with his officers he was cold, almost repellent, severe, and inflexibly just. One day General Gouvion Saint-Cyr, afterwards marshal, appeared at the Emperor's morning audience at the Tuileries. Napoleon said quietly to him:

'You come from Naples, General?'

'Yes, Sire. I relinquished my command to Marshal Perignon, whom your Majesty sent to relieve me.'

'And no doubt you have leave of absence from the Minister of War?'

'No, your Majesty; but I had nothing else to do at Naples.'

'Unless you are on the way to Naples within two hours, you will be shot on the plain of Grenelle at twelve o'clock precisely,' said the Emperor, returning his watch to his pocket.

That was his method in the service. Exact in all military matters, he acted without respect of persons, and never allowed a favourite to offer him anything. Such a man was bound to appeal differently to different people; but it is clear that in the course of time he drew the best and most valuable to him like a magnet.

There was certainly not much gaiety about him in the imperial days, but that was what he wanted, and he was probably right. All those about him had risen with him, and it was necessary to keep a certain distance between them and himself. He had no sense of comradeship, no love of food or drink, and never gambled. It is true that in his early years, especially during the long voyage across the Mediterranean to Egypt and back, the commander-in-chief would join occasionally in a game with his officers. But he could never bear to lose, especially at cards, and so he cheated flagrantly, and no one dare say a word. However, when he had finished the game, he pushed the heap of money away from him, and told them with a smile to divide his unjust winnings between them.

What made service under Napoleon so attractive was not merely his luck in war and his generosity, but chiefly the fact that he knew his men far better that most generals do, and that he had the gift of making the whole army feel that each individual was known to him; that he knew where they were, what they had done, what were their wounds and their fights, and where they had distinguished themselves. Thousands fell and disappeared from the ranks, and the army was entirely renewed in the course of time; but from the moment when his eye first lit on them, the young recruits joined in an unwavering love of the man, and were ready to face death for him.

To be mentioned in an order of the day was enough for a regiment; a smile or a sign of recognition on his features when he reviewed them, a few quick words or a greeting, made them happy for a long time. And, if anything happened to them and they lay fatally wounded, the Emperor might ride by, with sabre and spurs jingling, dismount, and fix the cross on their breast.

The cross of the Legion of Honour, which he had founded in the camp at Boulogne in 1805, became identified with him, and as long as he gave it, was a link of mutual gratitude between him and the army— the most coveted honour, the recompense for wounds and prolonged sufferings, a pride and joy to thousands of brave men. Though military interests predominated in his mind, Napoleon had an idea that there ought to be a civil division of the Legion of Honour. It was with this object that he founded the Order of the Iron Crown. But the idea that there ought to be a decoration for civilians did not fall on fruitful soil. For a time it went well with scholars and writers, but when the Emperor decorated the famous soprano-tenor Crescentini with the Iron Crown, after a performance of his favourite opera, Romeo and Juliet, there was a good deal of annoyance felt in France and Italy.

It was in military circles, of course, that the most scorn was expressed about Crescentini's decoration. One night the officers present in a certain Parisian salon spoke in the bitterest terms of this wretched singer, this comedian, this buffoon and eunuch, and told of their own battles and scars. Suddenly the gay Mme. Grassini, the singer, broke in:

'But *messieurs! messieurs!* Have you completely forgotten poor Crescentini's wound?'

Napoleon still defended his idea in the conversations at St. Helena. Crescentini was a great artist and of good family, and Napoleon thought the decoration would give great pleasure to the Italians. But his calculation completely miscarried. It caused nothing but ridicule. If public opinion had been otherwise. Talma and other actors and musicians would have received the cross of the Legion of Honour. The prejudice of his contemporaries stayed his hand wrongly, he thought, because in his opinion every man was worthy of the Legion of Honour who was an honour to his country.

One of the things that gave the Emperor most trouble was his own family. As soon as he realised that he could make France the most powerful realm and Paris the centre of the world, he formed the plan of gathering the members of his family about him as a dynasty, a race of princes, like the old legitimate races, with his brothers on the thrones of neighbouring realms. But his family was made of very difficult material in some respects. They were all just as extravagant and vicious as any member of the old princely races, and were very fine-looking.

The men and women of his family were handsome individuals, some of them, in fact, of rare beauty. The men could wear the most splendid uniforms; indeed crowns and ermine sat better on them than on many a legitimate ruler. His sisters were so pretty and well-made (though rather short in the legs) that all the state and jewellery they won through their brother's rise only enhanced their fine appearance, and entirely harmonised with their natural grace. Pauline was one of the greatest beauties of the age. All of them had the same fine, clear-cut profile and engaging mouth. They all had, likewise, the same love of life, the same levity and unbounded faithlessness in love; and in this their great brother was worse than all the others.

Napoleon's parents were strong and healthy folk. The mother especially, Letitia Ramolino, was a fine healthy woman, and bore her husband eight well-formed children. She brought number two—the most remarkable of them all—into the world under very desperate conditions, as she accompanied her husband on horseback the whole of the day before, when they were flying to the Corsican hills in the struggle with the French. She held up bravely to the end, followed the rising splendour of her son, and never caused him a moment's embarrassment at the brilliant court, where she took her place as the stately and sagacious *Mme. Mère*.

His sisters brought him little profit or pleasure. They were not of the character that he needed for his purposes. He had disposed of his sisters so early that he had no occasion to seek husbands for them amongst princes. But his brothers were to be kings, whether they liked it or not. The eldest of them, Joseph, signed the treaties of peace at Lunéville in 1801 and Amiens in 1802; and in 1806, though he was a poor soldier, he drove out the King of Naples and occupied his throne.

So far all went well. But in 1808 he was to be King of Spain, and Murat received the gay kingdom of Naples. The intractable Spaniards gave Joseph much trouble, and his kingly dignity vanished after the Battle of Vittoria in the year 1813. He was married to Julie Clary of Marseilles, a sister of Mme. Bernadotte. She left him shortly after 1813.

Joseph was completely dominated by his passion for the fair sex and his love of pleasure and indolence. He was thrust against his character and inclination into a career of high politics and great distinctions. 'Joseph was never the slightest use to me,' said Napoleon; 'but he is a very good fellow and very fond of me—so was Julie.' The truth was that Joseph was made for private life, and it was not his fault that he became an absolute monarch. However, with the beauty and the charm that all the Bonaparte's possessed, he was able to make his way everywhere without compromising his great brother or his high positions.

Lucien gave some help to his brother on the 18th *Brumaire* as President of the Council of the Five Hundred at St. Cloud, and he had diplomatic missions under the Consulate. He was, perhaps, the most sober of the whole family, and had many natural endowments, a good deal of knowledge, and a firm character. But he was resolutely bent on being an irreconcilable Republican, and so after 1804 he affected hostility to his brother. Those writers who say Lucien kept aloof from public affairs because he had no ambition are on the wrong line. He was nearly bursting with envy of Napoleon, and devoted his whole life to an effort to attain power himself. Hence, when he came from Elba to Paris in 1815, it was because he thought he could quit Napoleon, put himself at the head of the government, and end as President of the French Republic.

For his eldest sister, Elisa, who had married an Italian noble named Bacciochi in 1797, he created the Grand Duchy of Tuscany. His youngest sister he married to Murat, who rose from the ranks to the position of marshal. Grand Admiral, Prince of France, and King of Naples. The beautiful Pauline was first married to General Leclerc, who died at Hayti; then to Camillo Borghese, who was a fool. She was, perhaps, the most frivolous of them, and had many lovers. Otherwise she was amiable, bright, and always willing; but she was so extravagant that her mother always predicted she would spend her last days in the poorhouse. It did not come to that pass.

The youngest brother, Jerome, lived until 1860. He was with General Leclerc at Hayti, and led a fleet to Martinique as rear-admiral. In 1807 he was made King of Westphalia. He was first married to an American, Miss Paterson, but Napoleon afterwards secured his marriage with a princess of Würtemberg. He was not without natural gifts, but when he was young it would have been hard to find a more arrogant, crude, and ignorant man. He was also extravagant beyond all measure. Napoleon was hard on him in 1812, at the beginning of the Russian campaign, but Jerome improved when calamity fell on the family. His rule as King of Westphalia was almost a farce. The whole thing would have been impossible if Napoleon had not assigned to him as French Ambassador Count Karl Friederich von Reinhardt, whom he often used for diplomatic work. It was he who really ruled the kingdom; Jerome only amused himself. It was due to the shrewd and judicious Reinhardt that the whole administration was no worse than it was.

The last of Napoleon's brothers, the unfortunate Louis, suffered at an early age from venereal disease. It destroyed his life, for he became morose and eccentric. He had good endowments, but his chronic ailment made him little fitted for a life of ambition and politics. He accepted with reluctance the positions of honour and the wealth that his brother offered him. He was, nevertheless, a wealthy man, and in the year 1802 he married the Empress's daughter Hortense. In 1806 his brother made him King of Holland; but as Louis was a man of some good feeling he could not endure to see how the Dutch suffered from Napoleon's continental system, and in 1810 he resigned the crown.

Fouché affirms as a well-known and easily intelligible fact, that when Josephine could no longer doubt her own sterility, she arranged herself a *liaison* between Napoleon and her own daughter Hortense, and at once married Hortense to Louis when she became *enceinte*. With such a beginning a marriage was bound to be unhappy. It is certain, at all events, that Louis acted sometimes as if he himself behoved that Napoleon was the father of Hortense's eldest son. It is also certain that there was exceptional mourning at the Tuileries when the little prince died of an infantile disease. There were many indications that Napoleon intended to adopt the child and educate him as his successor.

Queen Hortense never lived peacefully with her husband, and she was divorced in 1815. She was extremely frivolous, and in view of the malady of her husband it seems hardly probable that any of her sons were his. The first was the little Napoleon, who died, and was believed to be the son of the great Napoleon. The second became Grand Duke of Berg, and married his cousin, a daughter of King Jerome. The third was the Emperor Napoleon III, probably the son of the Dutch Admiral Verhuel. The latter two had taken part in some trouble in Italy, and on that account King Louis wrote the following letter to Pope Gregory XVI in 1830:

Holy Father! My heart is overcome with sorrow and indignation since I have heard that my sons have taken part in the criminal revolt against your Holiness's authority. My life, which was already full enough of care, has been still further embittered by the knowledge that one of my kindred could forget all your kindness to my unhappy family. The unfortunate young man is dead; God be merciful to him. As to the other who bears my name, he has, thank God, nothing to do with me, as your Highness is aware. I have had the misfortune to marry a Messalina, who bore children.

Hortense's fourth son, afterwards Duke of Morny, was the son of Count Flahault.

Among these terrible Bonapartes Josephine was a refined and radiant form; though she also had had her escapades in the salons of Barras and the other revolutionary chiefs, and at least once, while Napoleon was in Egypt, had had a brief *liaison* with an undistinguished officer. But she had a warm love of Napoleon, and he on his side accorded her the highest mark of confidence that he was capable of to a woman when he said that he was sure Josephine would leave a *rendezvous* if a message came to her from him. They slept in the same bedroom at first like good *bourgeois*. But in 1805 Napoleon, at the Boulogne camp, was detained far into the night with State matters. Josephine was so foolish as to make a scene when he came to bed. Napoleon was angry, and from that moment he could never be prevailed upon to return to the old arrangement, even with Marie Louise. He knew the species.

Josephine was not very judicious, yet she interfered little in things that she did not understand, and gave her busy husband as little trouble as possible. It was enough for her if she could retain his affec-

99

tion; and when other matters estranged him from her, she tried every means in her power to regain it. She attended to all his needs, and was generally such an Empress as he would desire; and she would not allow the clergy to come any nearer than he wanted, though she was religious in her way.

She once told the Archbishop of Nantes in the confessional that she ate meat on Fridays.

'Does the Emperor do the same?' asked the bishop.

'Yes.'

'Very well, then, do as he does. Your Majesty may be sure that he has a special dispensation for himself and his family.'

But when Josephine, to make quite sure, put the same question to Cardinal Fesch, he replied that when the Emperor wanted her to break the fast she was to throw the plate in his face. 'The doctors differ,' said Napoleon, laughing, as he told Chaptal the story, which he had heard from Josephine. 'The bishop is right; the other is a fool. He wants to give himself an air of austerity that does not go well with his own private life.'

In the course of time Josephine became more and more nervous and strained when it was seen that she would have no more children than the two she had borne to her first husband, General Beauharnais—Eugene and Hortense. She brooded constantly over it, and she could see that Napoleon also did so. She tried every possible means and advice, and even suggested to Napoleon a fictitious pregnancy and an adopted child. She had a presentiment long before it came that there would be a divorce.

Her extravagance was unbounded and almost amounted to a mania. It was impossible for her to resist the jewellers and dressmakers when they came to her rooms with the finest trinkets and richest toilets that the best artists of Paris had produced—all of fabulous prices. She had an incredible number of hats, the cost of which was enormous during a single season, and she lived in constant dread of her bills, though Napoleon paid freely and generously. His Empress could afford to be extravagant. She must put all the other princesses of Europe in the shade. There was no niggardliness about her husband. But he could not bear himself or her to be cheated, and he knew that Josephine was paying seven times the price of things, because she had no more idea of money than a bird.

Hence, when he was settling her bills, he never paid the full price, but offered the vendors a half or three-fourths of the sum. They generally took it, and did good business. But he never got to the bottom of her bills, as she always concealed the worst from him, although she must have known that they would all come to light one day. Josephine's first word was always 'No.' she denied things by instinct. Hence she lived in an ocean of debts, and the flood of bills even found its way to Elba.

Otherwise, and in so far as there can be any question of female influence on Napoleon, Josephine was certainly the most suitable wife for him. If she had only been able to bear him a child—even a girl—Napoleon would never have parted with her. He did not propose the new marriage because he was discontented with Josephine, still less because he loved anybody else, nor in any desire for a more distinguished partner. He was quite high enough to afford the luxury of retaining the woman to whom he had always returned, and he was very unwilling to inflict on Josephine the pain and humiliation of a separation. But fortune had favoured him, and he felt bound to put himself right for the future by ensuring descendants. Moreover, his followers were hinting every day—some quite openly, others by suggestion—that all the legitimate princely houses had their future assured; he alone was without past and without future. He must found a Bonaparte dynasty.

It has seemed to many that the man was insatiable, and was driven from one delusive plan to another by his unbounded ambition. But, apart from the great masters of politics who have never sought anything for themselves, but been raised higher and higher by the admiration and affection of their compatriots, it seems to me that we all, in our various ways, seek self-expression. When Napoleon saw that he had met all the claims that his wonderful fate had made on him, he had no reason to halt. He rightly felt that he was so far superior to other princes that the first place amongst them fell naturally to him, at the head of his great nation; and this expressly demanded of him some security for the future. He only hesitated so long to take the painful step out of tenderness for Josephine; there is no ground whatever for doubting that the step was very painful to him.

As in all other matters. Napoleon once more distinguished himself from other kings and princes who had a mind to repudiate their wives. No bull came from the pope; no black ring of priests terrified the poor queen; there was no incriminating law-suit with bought witnesses and charges of infidelity. Even in his separation from his wife he was a perfect gentleman, a *grand seigneur*, and the usual order and ceremony were observed as to form.

On her side Josephine deserves all praise for the way in which she met her hard fate, when all hope was lost. She remained a true friend of Napoleon, and never put herself in the way of the new wife and Empress. We rarely find so clear and clean a light on the relation between two eminent personages as in the case of these two at the time of their separation. When Napoleon's mind was made up, he directed Eugene Beauharnais to go and explain to his mother that the divorce was now unavoidable, for political reasons, as France demanded the continuation of the Bonaparte dynasty. The viceroy conducted the affair in the admirable spirit that he always showed. He had not only developed into a courageous and reliable officer, but was also a man of honour in every respect, and a good son to his mother and his step-father. Napoleon had a high opinion of him, though he never gave the least indication of looking on Eugene as a possible successor. Josephine had long hoped that he would do so, but she was too prudent and reserved ever to ask anything for her son. She wanted to leave it entirely to Napoleon to advance him.

As the widow of General Beauharnais, who had been guillotined, she had lived in such straitened circumstances that Hortense had been sent to learn dressmaking and Eugene to learn carpentering, when Napoleon appeared as a suitor. Now Hortense was Queen of Holland, and Eugene Duke of Leuchtenberg, Prince of Eichstädt, Prince of France, and Viceroy of Italy.

On the evening of December 15th, 1805, Prince Cambacérès, the chancellor of the empire, and Count Regnault assembled with the whole imperial family at the Tuileries. Josephine gave her consent to the dissolution of the marriage, after Napoleon had thanked her in sincere and moving words for the happiness they had had together for fifteen years. The divorce was communicated to the Senate the following day. Eugene again appeared and expressed the loyal attitude of his mother and the sacrifice she willingly made for her country. The marriage was then declared invalid on the ground that a priest and two witnesses were not present at its celebration.

General Bonaparte's civil marriage of 1796 was effected by no other formality than registering before the proper republican authorities. Bernadotte and the other officers were married in the same way. According to French law it could be dissolved by the consent of the contracting parties. It was, therefore, not this marriage that the Senate had to dissolve before Napoleon could marry a Catholic princess.

But when the coronation of the Emperor and Empress drew near in 1804, Cardinal Fesch feared that the republican marriage would put difficulties in the way of Josephine's coronation, and proposed that he should marry them in the Tuileries, a few days before the coronation, but with closed doors and no witnesses. When Josephine learned, at the time of the divorce, that her marriage had been declared invalid, she sent for Fesch to Malmaison, and he gave her a legal certificate of marriage. However, she made no use of this document, and was content to keep it in her possession.

In a sense both the cardinal and the Senate were right. In French law the marriage was invalid because there were no witnesses. But according to the Canon Law of the Church a marriage of this kind may be valid when it is conducted by a cardinal. However, Napoleon had to pay a fine of six *francs* to the poor, because he had omitted to have witnesses.

The divorce caused the greatest excitement in all the European courts. If he decided to contract a fresh marriage, it was clear that he would seek his wife in the most elevated circles. For some time there was question of a princess of Saxony, whom he could easily marry, but Napoleon himself desired a Russian princess, one of the Tsar's sisters. Alexander acted as though he was extremely flattered by Napoleon's choice, but begged a postponement on account of the youth of the Grand Princess. He knew as well as anybody that there was no question of delay.

On March 1st, 1810, Marshal Berthier, Prince of Neuchatel, went to Vienna to ask the hand of the Archduchess Marie Louise for the Emperor of France. The preliminaries had already taken place, and the Emperor Francis met the suit with the greatest complaisance. It must, however, have been hard for the old Hapsburger to give his own daughter to bear children to the man who had humiliated Austria, beaten her armies, and brought the house of Hapsburg to the dust time after time; and he a mere Corsican adventurer.

On March 11th, Marie Louise was entrusted to Berthier in the name of the Emperor, and two days afterwards they left Vienna. She was accompanied by a suite of 300 persons. Between Braunau and Altheim Napoleon had, in an incredibly short time, erected a very large and handsomely decorated wooden structure. At one end of the building was Austria, at the other France, with a neutral space between. Here the Queen of Naples, Caroline Murat, went down from Paris with a numerous escort, and received Marie Louise. The archduchess, who then received the title of Empress, was conducted from Austria into France with a splendid ceremony arranged by the Emperor himself. The bridal gifts he sent her included a *trousseau* of the finest Parisian work and taste, and put in the shade anything that Vienna could offer the ladies of the court.

After the ceremonies the Empress continued her journey westward in short daily stages, as was customary a century ago. Large carriages with four horses were ready at each stage, and no time was lost. She had now parted from her Viennese friends, and was only accompanied by the small temporary French court that the Emperor had sent. At each station where they were to spend a night she found a letter from her gallant bridegroom. March 29th was to be the last day of the journey. She was to reach the castle of Compiègne in the evening, where the Emperor and all his family awaited her, and Berthier was to present the kneeling Empress to Napoleon on the following day.

But the whole of these arrangements were upset. When all Napoleon's preparations were made, he took Murat and slipped out of the castle in the grey coat he had worn at Wagram. They drove to meet the Empress in a simple carriage, with one coachman without livery. When they reached Courcelles, in the pouring rain, they drove under the porch of an old church, and waited for the Empress and her suite. It was the last spot for changing horses, and the moment the Empress's carriage drove up Napoleon hastened to it. The next morning they had breakfast together in the Empress's bedroom. The frightful scandal flew through Europe, and shook the very pillars of Viennese society.

On March 30th the civil marriage was completed at St, Cloud, and on the following day the newly-wedded pair made a triumphant entry into Paris, followed by a festival at the Louvre which Napoleon had arranged, according to his own taste, on the most magnificent scale. Part of the Louvre was used for the festivity. There were tribunes for kings and princes, ambassadors, and marshals. The imperial family stood round Napoleon and Marie Louise in all their beauty and splendour, besides all the nobles and potentates in France and a number of foreigners. Altogether there were about 8,000 persons.

A shadow was cast on the festive period that followed the marriage. Some two months afterwards a terrible fire broke out at a ball given by the Austrian ambassador. Prince Schwartzenberg, in honour of his master's daughter. The accident not only cost the lives of several persons and interrupted the festive spirit, but it reminded contemporaries of a similar mishap that had occurred the last time an Austrian

Archduchess married a French ruler—in 1770, when Marie Antoinette married Louis XVI. Prince Schwartzenberg had committed one of those imprudent acts that we often read of in connection with the old Parisian palaces. To provide a room for the dancing the inner court of the hotel had been converted into a large hall. A wooden floor had been put in, with steps and approaches to the other rooms and the corridors, a roof of canvas was stretched over it, and the walls were hung with beautiful curtains and tapestry, and decorated with an infinite number of flowers and candles.

It is dangerous enough today, for all our electric-light and modern heating-apparatus. At that time, when illumination had to be got by thousands of wax candles, it was pure folly. It only needed one curtain to fall over a chandelier, as they danced or crowded on the steps, and the whole would be in flames in three minutes. That was what happened, at the very height of the festivities. The Emperor did not wait for assistance, but quietly took his wife in his arms like a good *bourgeois*, and carried her into the security of the palace.

Many were killed, especially ladies, whose light dresses caught fire at once, and who fell and were suffocated in the crowd, or ran in flames into the garden. There were plenty of men there who were accustomed to keep their heads in the greatest danger, but the whole thing passed with such frightful rapidity. The cavalry-general, Durosnel, found his wife, and carried her out of the crowd. As he pushed through he saw a hand stealing a valuable comb from her hair without being able to prevent it.

At the close of the year 1810, Napoleon received a request from Norway that led to the appointment of Marshal Bernadotte, Prince of Ponte Corvo, as Crown-prince and successor to the throne of Sweden. During and after the Consulate Bernadotte was a secret enemy of Bonaparte's. Napoleon treated him with the greatest generosity, but it was returned with ingratitude. On the 18th *Brumaire* he held back until he saw whether Napoleon's *coup* failed. When it succeeded Bernadotte at once joined him, and began fresh intrigues against him. Although Napoleon was fully informed of it all, he made Bernadotte marshal at the first selection, gave him the grand cross and the title of Prince of France and Duke of Ponte Corvo, with considerable revenues, and in the end appointed him King of Sweden with a gift of a million francs out of the Emperor's private purse. Bernadotte repaid it all with ingratitude and treachery.

In 1799, when Napoleon was in Egypt, Joseph Bonaparte married his wife's sister to General Bernadotte. The Mlles. Clary were the daughters of a merchant at Marseilles, and Désirée, who became Mme. Bernadotte, had been Bonaparte's first love. She was afterwards to marry a General Duphot, but he was murdered at Rome at the very time appointed for the wedding.

In the end she married Bernadotte, and his continuous rise, until he became king, was entirely due to his marriage with Napoleon's friend. Bernadotte had no great name in military circles. There were twenty generals in France, who had commanded independent army-corps, whose name and fame put his entirely in the shade. He was at the same time wholly uneducated and little liked in the army. But when Napoleon became Emperor, he was pleased to make his early love a princess and a queen.

Their son was Napoleon's god-child. They had deferred baptising him until Napoleon's return from Egypt, and the name Oscar had been chosen by Napoleon himself; it was taken from Ossian's poem, over which he and his contemporaries were very enthusiastic. That was how the kings of Sweden came to bear a name taken from the supposed poetry of the ancient Scottish bard. Neither Napoleon nor anyone else then suspected that the work was a forgery of Macpherson's.

It was really a small party of nobles and officers that pressed the aged and childless King of Sweden to ask Napoleon for a Prince of France as successor to the throne. They had at first thought of the Viceroy of Italy, but the need for changing his religion proved an insurmountable obstacle—especially for the viceroy. As there was no other prince of France except Ponte Corvo the choice fell on him, and Napoleon consented. As soon as it was all arranged Jean Baptiste Bernadotte promptly embraced the Lutheran creed! His wife's conversion was not quite so speedy. Indeed she seemed to be in no hurry to leave the court at Paris and go to Stockholm.

'I might be enthusiastic about Josephine,' said a contemporary, 'but I should be quite the opposite with the wife of Marshal Bernadotte. Her intolerable pride repelled everybody, and her way of conducting herself is very much out of place now that she is Queen of Sweden, and in striking contract to the amiability of Josephine, and even of Hortense.'

However, this was a small matter in comparison with other liberties she took, in spite of her pride and her regal position. The whole of Europe was scandalised by the way in which she ran after the Duc de

Richelieu, whom she loved. The duke himself writes in a letter that is dated from Zurich, July 19th, 1819:

This morning I found a bouquet on my table at the hotel. So my infatuated queen has come here.

On the 25th he again wrote to one of his friends:

'My infatuated queen is here in the profoundest *incognito*, and so heavily veiled that when I meet her I can never be quite sure it is she. This sort of things gets rather troublesome.'

At the time the women of Norway were meeting at church every Sunday and offering prayer for the mother of their country. It was not superfluous.

Bernadotte went at once to Sweden, where Charles III adopted him as his son. On November 1st he took the oath as Crown-prince, and on the 15th the Swedish government allied itself with Napoleon, and joined the continental system against Great Britain. Sweden had played a very poor part during the whole of the Napoleonic wars, but it was soon to astonish Europe with its infidelity. As the old king grew feebler, Sweden's policy reflected more and more the nature of the intriguing and untruthful Gascon. It was well known in what intrigues and conspiracies he had been involved since the beginning of 1804, before the great conspiracy of Georges Cadoudal and the royalists.

He had at that time a command in the north-west of France, and a revolt was planned amongst the soldiers of the Rennes garrison with the object of breaking into insurrection against the First Consul on an appointed day. Shortly before this date Bernadotte slunk to Paris on the pretext that he must be there when the rising took place, though his real object was, of course, to be out of the way in case of the affair failing at Rennes, as it actually did. The conspiracy was discovered on the very day the trouble was to begin, and the proclamations that were to be spread amongst the people, and that contained the names of Bernadotte and Moreau, were confiscated.

Bernadotte was saved by the fact that he had given nothing in writing, and his guilt could not be proved. But a young son of General Marbot, an adjutant of Bernadotte's had had his carriage filled with these dangerous proclamations, without his knowledge. He was at once arrested and his mother implored Bernadotte's aid. He had been a friend of General Marbot, and was guardian of his sons; and it was the conspirators who had put the proclamations in the young man's carriage. Bernadotte promised everything—and did nothing.

Mme. Marbot ran from one to another, and at last obtained a promise from Napoleon that her son would be released if General Bernadotte personally requested it.

The lady hastened with this information to Bernadotte. He delivered a short speech on friendship, etc., and promised to see Bonaparte the same evening. He did not; but departed the same night with his wife to the baths of Plombières. When Bonaparte heard it, he said: 'Yes, I know him.' The young Marbot was released, but Napoleon always distrusted him.

The struggle in the Spanish Peninsula went on vigorously in the years 1810 and 1811. Masséna was unlucky for the first time in his life. He fought Wellington in Portugal and lost the Battle of Busaco. Although he had Ney and Junot and General Reynier with him, he was powerless against Wellington's splendid entrenchments at Torres Vedras. In Spain things went a little better for the French. Marshals Soult and Suchet had the supreme command there, but the right force for controlling the whole had gone when the Emperor departed. Marshal Victor had the good fortune to free 600 of those who had been taken prisoners at Baylen. His corps was on board a section of the fleet that lay in the roads at Cadiz. When the unfortunate prisoners, who were at work dredging in the harbour, saw the French flag, they seized a wretched little ferry-boat, without any tackle, and rowed through the hot fire of the Spanish and English warships out into the roads, where they were picked up by their delighted countrymen.

But Napoleon had turned his eyes eastward, now that the divorce was effected and the new marriage answered his expectations so well. On March 20th, 1811, Paris was in a state of feverish excitement. They knew that the Empress was approaching confinement. But serious difficulties arose, and the life either of the mother or the child might be endangered. Dr. Dubois went to the Emperor, who was in one of the adjacent rooms. The physician wanted to know if he was to look mainly to saving the child or the mother. 'You will treat the Empress,' said Napoleon warmly, 'as if you were assisting an ordinary patient in one of the slums of Paris.'

Dr. Dubois returned to the Empress, threw off his coat, and set to work. The child was in a serious condition when it came into the world, but it recovered. As soon as it did so the Emperor took it from the nurse and carried it into the large hall, where the dignitaries of the realm were waiting in the greatest tension.

'Here is the King of Rome,' cried the Emperor, who was—for

once—beside himself with joy.

At the same moment the cannons of the Invalides opened fire, and announced to Paris that the Emperor had a child. At the first shot Paris stood still and held its breath. Everybody—men, women, and children who could do so—was counting. They knew that if the guns fired twenty-one shots it was only a princess; if twenty-two, then the roar would go on up to a hundred, for it meant the birth of a son, an heir to the throne. Napoleon the Second. It is said that the gunners at the Invalides played a joke by waiting for a few seconds before firing the twenty-second shot; but when they did so a thunder of rejoicing broke over the whole city, such as has never been heard before or since. So great was the enthusiasm they felt on hearing that the future of the country was assured that the imperial page who ran from the chateau to announce the birth to the councillors assembled in the Hotel de Ville was unanimously voted 10,000 *francs* a year. Three years afterwards, in 1814, the Emperor dissolved the Council. What became of the poor page's pension?

In the year 1811 there was broad sunshine in France; though a shadow fell on the land when 100,000 quite young men were drafted into the army towards the close of the year. The generous awards that the Emperor had made to his followers had given a brilliancy to social life at Paris almost equal to what it had been under the kings. The Emperor desired it, and most of his officers did not need telling twice. Most of them had also contrived to secure so many valuables and so much money that they returned with waggon-loads from every campaign. The salons of their wives and the splendid festivities they gave when they had any time at home in peace, were a welcome reward for the long days of war, when no one had spared himself and from which they brought wounds and injuries to Paris.

There was Napoleon's own family, with the Queen of Naples at its head, and even the Tuileries, which witnessed a continuous series of festive gatherings. Moreover, many members of the old nobility returned to their mysterious hotels on the Boulevard St. Germain. Some went on to the court and accepted service in it, and some of the best names are found in the army under Napoleon as well as under the Bourbons.

The higher circles at Paris were, therefore, as brilliant as ever. The lower strata of the population were content. The Emperor brought plenty of honour and fame, but he also brought work and business. He had an eye for everything, and, although he had a close knowledge only of the military section of his people, his practical judgment was of service to many branches of commerce. Paris was always his heaviest task. He once complained to Fouché:

> I shall be delighted if you can assure me that the *Faubourg* St. Germain is satisfied. I may tell you that in all my battles, in the greatest dangers, even in the middle of the desert, the question was always in my mind—what will Paris say, especially the *Faubourg* St. Germain?

There was a gulf between Napoleon Bonaparte and Paris that could never be filled. He was never a Parisian; he was not even sufficiently French.

It is not easy to say what subtle fluid it is that gives its character to a great city—a fluid of which everyone who feels himself a genuine Parisian, and insists on being regarded as such, must have a small drop. There is about Paris and everything Parisian a certain elegant perfume of depravity. Everything seems to be edged with a narrow red border. Napoleon was entirely devoid of it. He was, to his finger-tips, as hard and angular as crystal, without the stamp of any society, least of all that of Paris.

Now that he had founded a dynasty and put his troublesome metropolis in good humour, he felt himself superior to all the princes that he knew. The *Tsar* alone was an exception. As early as 1805 Napoleon had seen clearly that the Tsar would not allow Austria to fall too low. In 1810 Russia had abruptly withdrawn from the Tilsit arrangement, and left the continental system. Large musters of troops along the frontier of the Grand Duchy of Warschau seemed to forebode no good. But he had always evinced a curious attitude toward Russia, and he now hesitated to admit as a fact the patent defection of the *Tsar* to England and the other princes. He never understood the invincible comradeship that bound the other princes together, and alienated them from himself. He had learned from history, as we have seen a hundred years after his day, that the enmity of kings never lasts long.

After a certain time, after they have aired their armies and bled their peoples, they come together again and kiss each other on railway platforms, and the news flies over the telegraphic system of the world. He did not understand that if he had been a king's son—a bastard, at least—the others, impressed by his superiority, would have opened their circles to him and his son. But to him, as he was, the usurper, the child of the revolution—never! He might humble them and trade with their territory and capitals, but they would rather die than seriously recognise Napoleon as an equal. Bernadotte might do very well on the distant throne of Sweden. In the first place they needed him as a general, and further, they despised him, and let him feel that they did so. Napoleon was blind to all this.

Politically, he had the idea—an idea revived in our own time—that France in alliance with Russia had the fate of Europe in its hand; personally, he believed that the Tsar Alexander was his friend at the bottom. Sagacious as he was, suspicious even on the slightest indications, he clearly thought during the whole time, even when he was preparing to advance against Russia, that by a personal interview with Alexander—preferably after he had thoroughly beaten him—he could restore the friendly relations of Tilsit and Erfurt, commit him against England, and restore the equilibrium in Europe that he destined for his son.

When he saw clearly in February, 1812, that St. Petersburg had played him false, and had no intention of sending Count Nesselrode as extraordinary envoy to Paris, as he had long wished, he sent for Colonel Chernicheff, an adjutant of the Tsar who was at Paris, and gave him, in friendly mood, a number of explanations and a private letter to the *Tsar*. Colonel Chernicheff bowed and thanked him. But two days after his departure from Paris it was discovered that he had abused his position, and bribed a subordinate official in the ministry of war to give him a correct account of the strength of the French army. The official was arrested; but the perfidious Russian had got too good a start. They sent after him as quickly as possible, but he reached St. Petersburg with his prize.

The *Tsar's* reply to the letter that Napoleon sent by Colonel Chernicheff was brought by Baron Serobin in April. It contained an expression of Russia's desire that the French troops should evacuate Prussia and withdraw across the Rhine. Napoleon said that this was merely diplomatic effrontery, and would not take it literally. He sent Count Narbonne as extraordinary envoy to St. Petersburg, and told him to treat directly and personally with the Tsar, in accordance with the instructions of the Emperor Napoleon. A few days later the Russian ambassador, Prince Kourakin, broke off the negotiations that he had been conducting for some months with the Duc de Bassano, and the Emperor left Paris on May 9th, 1812. The Empress accompanied him to Dresden, it was the beginning of the great Russian campaign.

CHAPTER 5

Decline

In the year 1808, when the alliance still held good between Russia and France, Marshal Bernadotte occupied Jutland with Spanish troops, for the purpose of threatening Sweden on that side in order that Russia might annex Finland without opposition. As a fact, the marshal had explicit orders from the Emperor to do nothing against Sweden. But he concealed this part of his orders, and afterwards boasted of his inactivity, as if Sweden ought to be grateful to him for it. When however, it became clear, in the year 1811, that war was bound to break out between Napoleon and Alexander, Bernadotte pointed out to the French ambassador at Stockholm that it would be a great help to Napoleon if a Swedish army were to invade Finland.

For this service the Swedish Crown-prince demanded Norway. He had the effrontery even, Thiers says, to threaten to injure the French, if they did not support him in the taking of Norway; a remarkable procedure when we remember that he had himself worn the French uniform only a short time previously. He could never forget that Napoleon did not enter into his plans in regard to Norway. As he chiefly owed his elevation to the position of heir to the throne to the success of the French army, and as he by no means improved on closer acquaintance—for people soon found that he was vain, boastful, and prodigal of empty promises, while his military talent was very far below what he thought it to be—it was a fine dream that he would win favour in Sweden by this annexation.

In November, 1811, he had a conversation with M. Alquier, the French ambassador at Stockholm. After a few desultory observations on certain privileges that English merchants had enjoyed at Göteborg, Bernadotte audaciously asked 'why France rewarded his services so badly?' The ambassador hinted that the throne of Sweden was a very fair acknowledgment. If, says Thiers, one could have looked into the future at that moment, one would certainly have treated this foolish conceit with moderation. But we can understand the bitterness of the French ambassador. There are things that prove insupportable even under the menace of death.

The new-baked crown-prince was extremely arrogant throughout the conversation. He recalled all the battles in which he had taken part and declared—as he used to do amongst his confidants—that he had won the battle of Austerlitz (where he had not fired a shot); the battle of Friedland (where he was not even present); and the Battle of Wagram (where he had taken to flight both days with his 'granite column').

He then went on to say that he knew all about the bad feeling there was in regard to him at Paris; but he now ruled a race of giants, who adored him, and before whom no enemy could stand once he led them forward. 'That is too much,' cried the ambassador.

But Bernadotte, who was in a state of feverish excitement, called out to his boy Oscar: 'Isn't it true? You will follow the example of your father, and prefer death to disgrace.'

M. Alquier reported the whole conversation to Napoleon. The Emperor smiled, and broke all connection with Sweden. This caused some concern in Sweden, and both the old king and the crown-prince endeavoured to remedy the breach. But at the same time Bernadotte made secret overtures, on his own account, to Russia and England. He said, in explanation of his treachery to his benefactor, that Napoleon had unfortunately pursued him with jealousy throughout his whole life.

The truth was that jealousy was at the bottom of Bernadotte's hatred from the beginning. Jealous as he was by nature, he dared to be envious of the man who should have been far above the range of his jealousy; for there could be no comparison whatever between General Bernadotte and General Bonaparte. We can, more or less, understand his jealousy of Moreau, Masséna, Lannes, or Davoust, though they were all far superior to him. But for him to be jealous of Napoleon only shows his narrow-mindedness and slender intelligence.

After reading these things about Bernadotte, I was rather amazed to hear King Oscar II say in 1896: 'The one man who could have taken Napoleon's place was my grandfather.' He said it so quietly and unhesitatingly that one could see this was the way he had been taught history.

On May 20th, 1812, the French imperial couple were at Dresden. Napoleon feared that possibly, in view of the actual relations between the Russian and French courts, Count Narbonne would not succeed in reaching the Tsar personally. And, as he thought everything depended on that, he thought he would make one more effort to attain his end through his ambassador at St. Petersburg, Count Lauriston. He therefore said to Maret, the Duke of Bassano: 'Write to Lauriston, and tell him to go to Wilna (where the Emperor Alexander was with the army). Let him know that, as I wish to bring this war of words to an end, I command him to break through all formalities and see the *Tsar* in person, and learn from his own lips something that may lead to an understanding between us.'

When Lauriston received the order he at once asked for a passport to leave the capital and go to Wilna. He did not obtain one. In the meantime, a court such as Europe had never seen before and will never see again, had gathered about Napoleon and the Empress, who were staying with the aged King of Saxony at Dresden. The Emperor and Empress of Austria had come of their own initiative to greet their daughter and son-in-law and wish him success in his great campaign. The King of Prussia was there. He offered his son as an adjutant to Napoleon, though the Emperor declined the offer out of delicacy. All the kings and ruling princes from the rest of Germany came with their warmest wishes and an assurance of loyalty in the struggle against the *Tsar*, who now appeared to be the common enemy!

It was during the stay at Dresden that the elder Count Ségur made his famous *mot*. He happened to come late to a sitting, and the Emperor glanced sharply at him. The astute master of ceremonies answered: 'Your Majesty must forgive me for coming late. I was detained—there was such a crowd of kings in the ante-rooms.'

All these princes were to send troops to take part in the campaign. The Emperor had taken a liking to Prince Schwartzenberg at Paris, and wished him to lead the Austrian army, which was to advance across the Russian frontier in the south-west, and serve as cover and support to the grand army. There was not one of these foreigners who did not secretly wish that Napoleon would fare so badly that they might venture to abandon him. This feeling grew especially in Germany. The national upheaval had begun that sought to wipe out the unnatural frontiers between the smaller States of the ill-treated nation. It was not surprising that there were thoughts of vengeance everywhere, and that all were ready to cast off the frightful burden.

But it will be a matter of wonder for all time and an outrage on human honour to see the complicated intrigues of Bernadotte in the beginning of 1812. To the English party in Sweden he declared that he would not be Napoleon's slave, and that he thought most of the trade and advantages of his own kingdom. To his own party, which had chosen him as a general of Napoleon, he spoke in a lofty tone of the honour of the Swedish arms. To the Allies he said that he was prepared to cast off the yoke of France at the first signal. He would land with 30,000, if not 50,000, Swedes and annihilate the French in Poland, if they would only guarantee him Norway. Foreign powers could hardly credit his perfidy, and the King of Prussia especially felt himself injured. Bernadotte even went so far, in his desire to aid Russia, as to offer to bring about peace with the Turks. He was everywhere the most active enemy of France.

On April 5th, Sweden contracted an alliance with Russia, which promised to help it in the annexation of Norway. The condition was to remain secret. The Swedish cabinet was to deny officially that there was any alliance with Russia, and at a given moment its neutrality was to be converted into war with France. It was one of the most shameless instances of perfidy that history has ever known.

In the meantime the crown-princess Desideria, who was still at Paris occupied with other things, and could not be induced to go to Stockholm, began to regret the ill-feeling between Sweden and France, and tried to effect a reconciliation. Hence we find Bernadotte sending M. Signeul to Maret, who was with the Emperor at Dresden, with two documents. The first, the official note, declared candidly that for the moment Sweden was substantially on Russia's side, but Bernadotte again made a ridiculous proposal to mediate between Alexander and Napoleon.

The other, the secret note, said that Bernadotte had no interest in Finland; if he were guaranteed Norway he was ready to conclude an alliance with France at once. Napoleon who was perfectly aware of the secret treaty with Russia on April 5th, cried: 'The scoundrel! I want to hear no more of him.'

The *grande armée,* when it marched eastwards from its headquarters in all its splendour in the spring of 1812, was made up as follows.

The first corps, under Marshal Davoust, consisted of six divisions, the main strength of which were the divisions of Morand, Friant, and Gudin. The rest of the corps was mixed with Bavarian and Dutch regiments and Poles. Under Davoust there was also General Grawert with 17,000 Prussians. The corps consisted in all of 114,000 men of good troops. Besides the three generals, Gudin, Morand, and Friant, Davoust had also Compans and Pajol, the engineer Haxo, and the distinguished General Friedrich.

The second corps was led by Marshal Oudinot. He had with him Generals Merle and Maison, and the divisions of Legrand and Verdiers—the old soldiers of Lannes and Masséna. Altogether, with the cavalry under General Dumerc, there were 40,000 men.

The third corps was commanded by Marshal Ney with two divisions of veteran soldiers, who had been trained by the Duke of Montebello. There were also in it the Würtembergers, who had served before under Ney. That meant 39,000 men, with two corps of *curassiers* from the cavalry-reserve: 10,000 men.

The fourth corps was under Prince Eugene, with Junot second in command. It included Generals Grouchy and Broussier, the two brothers Delzon, and the best soldiers of the Italian army—45,000 men altogether.

The fifth corps numbered 26,000 men of all arms, mostly Poles, under the command of Prince Poniatowski.

The sixth corps consisted of 25,000 men, mostly foreigners who had served in the French army since 1809, under General St. Cyr.

The seventh corps was under General Reynier; 17,000 men, mostly Saxons, who were to act with the Poles.

The eighth corps consisted of King Jerome with 18,000 Westphalians and Hessians.

Besides these there were four corps of the reserve-infantry, divided amongst Davoust, Oudinot, and Ney. The rest, 15,000 fine horsemen marched with the Imperial Guard. The Guard was commanded by Marshals Mortier and Lefebvre, and distributed in two corps; the old guard, consisting of the green uniformed Chasseurs à Cheval and the blue uniformed foot-grenadiers; and the young Guard, *voltigeurs* and light cavalry. In all there were 47,000 men, including 6,000 picked cavalrymen and 200 guns with service. Then there was the corps of engineers, consisting of sappers, miners, bridge-constructers, and military artificers of all kinds; and the artillery and baggage with full equipment and horses—there were 18,000 horses in these two trains alone.

In the active army that marched against Russia there were 423,000 experienced soldiers, namely, 200,000 foot, 70,000 horse, and 30,000 artillery with 1,000 guns, besides six trains of bridges, ambulances, and supplies for one month. As a reserve there was the ninth corps under Marshal Victor, and the tenth corps under Augereau, in the neighbourhood of Magdeburg, which were to keep up the complement of the army. The total number of men to face the Russians was 620,000. Besides these there were 150,000 men in French depots and fortresses, 60,000 men in Italy, and 300,000 fighting in the Spanish Peninsula under the command of generals like Masséna, Soult, and Suchet. The entire French forces under the supreme command of one man amounted to more than a million armed soldiers.

If we consider the representation of the different nationalities in the great army against Russia, we have the following figures; 370,000 were French; 50,000 Poles; 20,000 Italians; and 10,000 Swiss. These could all be counted upon as reliable soldiers. But there were also 160,000 Prussians, Bavarians, Saxons, Würtembergers, Westphalians, Croatians, Spanish, and Portuguese, who were all more or less unreliable and dangerous.

As I said, Napoleon did not concern himself about this. To him soldiers were soldiers and nothing else. Moreover, there was such a feeling of hostility between the smaller States and between the north and the south that Germans often fought Germans with great zeal under Napoleon's banner; at least until the day when the French administration pressed so heavily on them that the princes were forced to seek the aid of their peoples.

On June 17th the Emperor reached Dantzig. From there he proceeded to Königsberg, and reviewed Davoust's six model divisions on the route. On the 18th he reached Insterburg, where he found the banks of the Pregel covered with supplies of all kinds. At the same time 220,000 soldiers, ready for the fight, converged on the place by different routes. On June 19th he at last received precise information that the Emperor Alexander could not be induced to see Lauriston. He had now to rely on force. The *Tsar* must be compelled. One way or the other he was determined to see the *Tsar* in person. And so Napoleon crossed the Niemen.

He proposed to advance into Russia through the district between the Dnieper, where it turns southwards near Orscha, and the Dwina, where it flows northwards near Ostrowno. The first movement of the Russians was to draw up their northern army, under General Barclay de Tolly, at the fortified camp of Drissa, where the *Tsar* himself was, and seemed to be preparing for a fight. The southern army, under Prince Bagration, was to be brought into touch with the northern by marching rapidly northwards and slipping past the advancing French. Napoleon's plan was to prevent the junction with the help of Davoust's corps, keep the two Russian armies apart, engage them separately, and drive Bagration into the morasses. Meantime, the Tsar had retreated so far without the great and decisive battle that Napoleon was eager to engage in, that the French reached Wilna, the old capital of Poland.

The Poles, so often deluded, thought that their day had come at last. The Polish nobility declared that the kingdom of Poland was re-established, and sent a deputation to Napoleon asking him to recognise it. That would be enough for them. But Napoleon, who never had much sympathy with the national aspirations of the Poles, gave an equivocal reply. His words deprived the Poles of all spirit and hope, and caused great disappointment even in France.

Meantime, if Napoleon's manoeuvre was to succeed, and the junction of De Tolly and Bagration to be prevented. King Jerome ought to be much further advanced than he was with his army-corps. As a matter of fact, even a strong general would not have been able to get so far by the end of June on account of the bad weather and the violent rains. But Napoleon, who was waiting at Wilna, was impatient; so was Davoust. At last King Jerome received an order, in a somewhat offensive form, to put himself under the command of Davoust. Jerome felt aggrieved, as was quite natural. He left the army and returned home. This quarrel between the two brothers lost Napoleon the favourable moment when Bagration might have been isolated and ruined. What was even worse, eleven valuable June days were spent idly at Wilna.

That was precisely what the Russians hoped, and what those Frenchmen dreaded who knew the Russian climate; it meant that the campaign would run into the winter. The story was going round the Russian quarters of the smith who laughed when someone showed him a French horse-shoe, that had been found on the road. 'Not one of those horses will ever leave Russia, if they are here when the frost comes,' said the smith. The French horse-shoes had neither spikes nor barbs, and it would be impossible for the horses to drag guns and heavy waggons up and down hills when the roads were hard and slippery.

When Bonaparte was a young general on his early campaigns, he would jump out of his carriage when there was some lengthy delay on the march and stand at the side of the road, and point to one of the heavier waggons, with the question: 'What is in this waggon?' The officer who was responsible had to ride up. The entire contents of the waggon had to be laid out on the field and checked—harness, horse-cloths, nails, tools, screws, metal-work, etc. The unfortunate young officer would have to give an account of the smallest details, and the general knew perfectly well what ought to be there. If the young man had to admit some blunder or other, he might pass into eternal oblivion; but if he was any good he might die a general. The Russian campaign was not equipped in this way.

When Napoleon at last marched on Drissa at the close of June, the *Tsar* quitted his strong position, though they had worked at it for a whole year to make it impregnable. He retreated as far as St. Peters-burg, and remained there. At Napoleon's command all the French troops reached the Dwina on the same day, but they found nothing but the empty camp. The campaign had to go on, without a decisive battle having been fought, with the same end in view— to keep the two Russian armies apart.

Barclay de Tolly retreated steadily before the advance of the main army. At the beginning of July he seemed to be going to take up a stand at Witebsk, in order to give Bagration time to come up and join him at Smolensk. But Bagration encountered Davoust at Mohilew, and the French marshal had one of his great days. He inflicted such a crushing defeat on Bagration that there could be no more question of a junction with Tolly at Smolensk.

In some mysterious way Prince Bagration succeeded in sending the news of his defeat through or round the French lines, and on the morning of July 27th, when Napoleon and the entire main army reached Witebsk, anxious for a decisive battle, they found Barclay de Tolly in full retreat once more. There was no pitched battle, such as the French had hoped for, though there was a sharp skirmish at Ostrowno, in which Murat and Eugene won. In the course of this fight a band of young Parisians, about 300 in number, who belonged to the ninth regiment of the line, cut their way through a mass of Russian *curassiers* before the eyes of the whole French army. The Emperor himself saw their bravery, and called out: 'Each of them has deserved the cross.'

It was a fresh disappointment for Napoleon that there was no ac-tion sufficiently decisive at Witebsk to bring on the question of ne-gotiations. At this time the French army was suffering terribly from the heat, and the desertions began—especially amongst the Germans. Napoleon remained quiet at Witebsk for a fortnight. He was not like his old self at all in this campaign. Astonishment has often been expressed that he did so little every day, since his power had been mainly in the swiftness with which he would astonish the enemy and push on a campaign. Even granting that he had less idea what a Russian winter was like than a general of his rank ought to have had, and much less than he would himself have been content with in earlier years, nevertheless, it was very unlike his real self to waste so much time at Wilna and then at Witebsk.

It seems to me that everything points to the conclusion that Napoleon had expected every day to receive the adjutant from the *Tsar*, who would turn the war into an agreement between them. He was convinced all along that the *Tsar* was deceived by his followers, and only needed correct information to accept the modern ideas that Napoleon wished to press on him. The same opinion of the *Tsar* of Russia's attitude toward modern ideas has been entertained by many shrewd observers a hundred years since those days.

The army took up quarters in the vicinity of Witebsk. Supplies were collected, and deserters and stragglers were brought up to the colours. Although not more than 7,000 men had fallen as yet, there were 150,000 men missing from the ranks. The destruction of the grand army during the Russian campaign must not be attributed wholly to the cold and the terrible retreat. In reality, the army was ruined before it reached Moscow; partly because there were far too many foreigners in it, and partly because there had been a foolish levy of boys. The latter could fight, it is true, but they were unable to endure the exceptional strain and privations of the campaign.

Moreover, a large number of the cavalry were already compelled to go on foot. When we examine the map showing the places of battle on the march in and out of Russia, we see that the French sword penetrated to no great depth in the bulky colossus. From the Niemen to Mohilew, Ostrowno, Polotsk, Krasnoi (the first time), Smolensk, Walutina, Borodino, and burning Moscow, and back through the fields of Winkowo, Malo, Jaroslawetz, Wiasma, Wop, Krasnoi (the second time), Beresina, Wilna, and Kowno, is not a long stretch of road. But it is a long stretch of history.

During his halt as Witebsk, the Emperor ruled with the same regularity as if he were at the Tuileries, except that he was thinking day and night of the movements of his troops and the care of his wounded. Nothing could daunt him; neither Bernadotte's desertion nor the rising in Russia, which the *Tsar* himself had instigated, and which caused the French to find only deserted country and abandoned or burning towns. He seemed to know nothing of the revulsion of feeling or the murmuring that began to be heard about him. Brooding alone over his plans and unshakeable in his resolution, he determined to pursue the retreating Russians with the main army, while keeping an eye on his flanks to the north and south.

Orders were given to Prince Schwartzenberg and Marshals Victor and Augereau to hasten to the relief of General Reynier, who was threatened by General Tormasoff from the south. In the north he had Macdonald in the vicinity of Dünaburg, and Marshal Oudinot was engaged in a fight with General Wittgenstein at Polotsk. General Gouvin St. Cyr was ordered to strengthen Oudinot's position with his Bavarian corps.

On August 17th Marshal Oudinot decided to withdraw a little, in order to take up a better position. Wittgenstein thought the manoeuvre was a retreat and advanced on him. In the battle that resulted the marshal was severely wounded, and had to be carried off. The command fell to General St. Cyr, who was also wounded, and he led the battle from a small Polish carriage.

This cool leader and great tactician executed a masterly manoeuvre at Polotsk on August 18th. He suddenly converted an ostensible retreat into a strenuous attack, and so won a victory which would have been even more brilliant if his carriage had not broken down at the decisive moment. He fell underneath the horses, and was only rescued with difficulty; and he at once resumed command. He took 1,500 prisoners and 14 guns, and gave Wittgenstein a severe lesson. After Polotsk the Emperor made him Marshal. Two Bavarian generals, Derois and Lieben, fell in this battle. Derois had led the Bavarians in 1805 at Ulm, and in 1809 at Wagram. He and his inseparable friend, Lieben, had spent their lives together from boyhood. They both became generals in Napoleon's service, and both fell on the same day at Polotsk.

On August 17th Napoleon reached Smolensk, the fortified outskirts of which he attacked at two in the afternoon with the famous divisions of Morand and Gudin. General Ledru, of Ney's army-corps, attacked the suburb of Krasnoi, the Russians making a determined resistance in all the fortresses round the town. On the right wing the Poles, under Poniatowski, fought like lions; they were taking the city of their fathers once more. By five o'clock the positions on the left bank of the river, under the Emperor's eye, were taken. But General de Tolly brought up strong reinforcements—General Baggowouth with his whole corps, the Prince of Würtemberg with a division of grenadiers and two battalions of the Russian Guard. It was six o'clock before they got far enough for the guns to reach the walls of the town. Eventually the French took it by storm, but it was so dark that Barclay de Tolly succeeded in withdrawing the remainder of his army from Smolensk.

The French regiments dashed in in triumph, proud of a victory that had caused Russia such severe losses, but it was quite deserted, and very shortly the whole of Smolensk was in flames. The bulletin that announced in France the taking of a town that was reduced to ashes excited little enthusiasm, if not the reverse; and even in the army some of the officers began to make disquieting remarks. But Napoleon pressed on from day to day in pursuit of the Russian armies in front of him. From Smolensk he sent the divisions of Compans and Gudin, General Bruyéres' cavalry and King Joachim Murat, to head off Barclay de Tolly. At the same time Junot was ordered to take up a position at Walutina and cut off the Russians from the narrow passes. But General de Tolly altered his original plan of retreating northwards towards St. Petersburg. He determined to make one more attempt to join Bagration on the road to Moscow.

Napoleon learned this and dispatched Ney in all haste to intercept him. The armies met at Walutina, and Ney won a brilliant victory, but here again, as in the whole of this campaign, something untoward happened. They had at last succeeded in attacking Barclay de Tolly's army apart from Bagration, and in such a position that not a single man could have escaped if General Junot had done his duty and taken up a position, as he was ordered, in the passes, which formed the only escape from the field at Walutina,

When General Grouchy brought the news of the battle to the Emperor, he rode over to Ney. All were agreed, when they saw the field of battle, that the carelessness and stupidity of the Duke of Abrantes alone were responsible for the failure to destroy or capture the whole Russian army. This brought his brilliant career to a close. Napoleon had loaded him with wealth, though he had dissipated this with the most tasteless prodigality and undermined his own strength with his excesses. He was one of the bravest and most daring, the first pistol-shot in the army, a good comrade and fine fellow; but a dangerous man, with unrestrained passions.

Whether his good luck was the cause, or his wild life, or a sabre-cut on the head (which the Duchess of Abrantes always alleged as his excuse), it is hard to say, but, after being unreliable and fantastic all his life, he became worse and worse, and ended in insanity.

At Smolensk, where Junot was to lead the attack, his orders were obscure and unsound. Murat galloped up to him.

'What are you doing?' he shouted. 'Why don't you advance?'

'My Westphalians won't move.'

'I will put some spirit into them,' cried King Joachim, and he flung himself on the Russians with a few squadrons and swept everything before him.

'See that?' he shouted again to Junot. 'There is half your marshal's staff won for you. Go in now and finish it yourself. The Russians are lost.'

Junot would not move however. His mind was really already going, though the others did not know it. When he failed in his duty again at Walutina and spoiled Ney's fine victory. Napoleon angrily determined to take his command away from him, but the other generals interceded for him, and he forgave him on account of their old friendship. But things went from bad to worse with him, and he had to be sent back to Illyria, where he was governor. Here he betrayed his condition in a very remarkable way. He gave a grand ball at his residence, and came to it with his shoes whitened instead of blackened, his sword and all his decorations round his neck, his hair curled, a three cornered hat under his arm, and white gloves—in other respects as naked as a savage.

He was sent at once to Milan. Here he had six horses harnessed to his finest carriage, sat on the coachman's box in full uniform, and as he drove through the streets of Milan filled his carriage with loose women. He was then sent to his native place, Montbard, in France, and put an end to his life in a fit of madness by leaping down from a garden wall and breaking his thigh. He was so violent that it was impossible to bind the leg, and he died in July, 1813. The Duchess of Abrantes bore with him in everything, and tried to keep him on his feet, and in good relations to the Emperor, as long as she could. In the end Junot had utterly forfeited the Emperor's friendship, though in earlier years he had been as good a friend of Napoleon as it was possible for anyone to be.

When the French army reached Wiasma on August 29th, they found the people in flight, as at Smolensk, and half the town in flames. They had to extinguish the fire themselves and save the great stores of provisions that were not yet destroyed. At this place the quarrel broke out between Davoust and Murat. The steady and methodical Duke of Auerstädt had for some time been annoyed with the volatile King of Naples, as he took off the cavalry every morning and exhausted them, so that they were being weakened every day. He was still less disposed to support these useless cavalry-demonstrations with his good infantry. He therefore forbade General Compans, in presence of the whole corps, to obey King Joachim. Napoleon himself came up, and, though he must have felt that Davoust was right, he was influenced by the relationship to Murat and his kingly dignity, and ordered Compans to put himself under Murat's command.

After Smolensk the army was weakened to a disquieting extent, and Berthier had the courage to point out to the Emperor that the outlook was bad. Napoleon called him an old woman, and asked him if he wanted to go to Paris. Prom the time when he had called them. out on this campaign, after they had had a short rest—some at Paris, others on their estates, or as governors and commanders in various parts of France, which was then a good deal of Europe—there had been a certain amount of bad feeling amongst the officers, especially the higher and older ones. The high positions and good incomes he had created for them had been used by them and their wives in a taste for luxury and splendour.

Most of them, moreover, like the Emperor himself, were between forty and fifty years of age. Their ambition was gradually fading. They had got enough; and their families, with which they only spent the brief interval between two campaigns, clung to them and wanted to detain them.

They all appeared at the Emperor's summons, nevertheless, and when they had shaken off their wives and children, and found themselves in the saddle once more, with the old soldiers and the eager young men crowding round them, they returned to their former spirit, and rushed on to fresh victories like the brave men that they were. Especially at the beginning of the campaign, when they marched eastwards with their fine regiments through the conquered territories, from town to town, and castle to castle, like the lords of the world; when they joined their comrades and friends at Dresden and saw all the crowned heads of Europe bowing before their Emperor they felt themselves in the *grande armée* once more, and every man from the highest officer to the common soldier was a hero.

No one could possibly have foreseen the horrors they were to encounter, but the march into Russia was from the first so utterly different from all they had been accustomed to, that the officers soon began to be uneasy. There had always been a certain number of malcontents, but they had never yet ventured to express their feelings, because Napoleon went on from one victory to another, and there was neither time nor mood for criticism. Now it was different. They began to find that he was a changed man. Possibly he was; but they themselves were not the men of a few years before.

CHAPTER 6

Reverse

As the French drew nearer to Moscow, the excitement increased in Russia and there was a growing dissatisfaction with Barclay de Tolly. A considerable party at the court and the great mass of the people showed an irresistible repugnance to the retreat-system, and at last everybody demanded that they should stand and make a fight. Public opinion singled out the elderly, one-eyed Field-marshal Kutusow as commander. It was not he that had lost the Battle of Austerlitz. They had followed General Weiroth's plan against his wish. On the other hand he had defeated the Turks several times, and was a great leader and a prudent and sagacious officer. Excess had reduced his strength so much that he could keep his horse only with difficulty. He was false and faithless and utterly bad; but he was patient and tough.

He received the supreme command, and had General Bennigsen, the victor of Eylau, as chief of the staff. It is said that Barclay de Tolly wanted to give battle before Kutusow reached the army, but it was the aged field-marshal who had indicated the heights of Borodino as the battlefield.

On September 5th the advancing French found the Russian army drawn up in line of battle on the heights in front of them. The important position Schwardina was fortified like a redoubt, and was defended by Prince Bagration in person. However, Compans' division took the redoubt early in the afternoon of the 5th with their usual brilliancy. It was the first triumph for the French. During the night and on the following day the French divisions pushed on and took up their positions. After a few hours' sleep in his tent, Napoleon mounted his horse in the early morning. In the midst of the confusion on the day before the battle M. Bausset, a stout and gouty officer of the palace, who was related to the imperial family, made his appearance. He had come straight from the Tuileries, and brought a letter from Marie Louise and a picture of the little King of Rome. The Emperor showed the picture to all the generals and officers, who had been brought together to receive their orders for the following day, and then had it placed on a chair in front of his tent, to the delight of the old grenadiers.

The same morning Colonel Fabvrier came from Spain, and brought the news of the unfortunate position of Marshal Marmont. Napoleon was not in the least disturbed. He was at work the whole day making preparations for the victory, of which neither he nor any man in the army doubted for a moment. On the following morning, September 7th, he strode cheerfully out of his tent and called out to his officers: 'See the glorious sun, gentlemen! That is the sun of Austerlitz.' His short and spirited proclamation to the soldiers was read to each company.

'At last,' it ran, 'you have come to face the great battle that you have sought so long. Now victory depends on you—the victory that is a necessity for us all. It means abundance for us, good quarters, and a speedy return to our country. Do as you did at Austerlitz, at Friedland, at Witebsk, at Smolensk, and the remote future will tell with pride of your deeds this day. Let it be said of every one of you: he was in the great battle on the plains of Moscow.'

Napoleon dismounted at the Schwardina redoubt, which Compans had taken and occupied, and the bloody Battle of Borodino opened. The French have named it after the stream Moskwa which flows by the spot, and one of Marshal Ney's descendants still bears the title of Prince of Moskwa. Under cover of two batteries of the Guard under General Sorbier, General Compans advanced with his own division and that of Desaix—a cousin of the great Desaix who fell at Marengo. They rushed the trenches that protected the Russian left wing under General Bagration, and all went well for a time. In a very short time, however, Compans got a bullet in the shoulder; Desaix, who replaced him in the chief command, was also severely wounded; and Rapp, who took Desaix's place, was hit four times in quick succession—first grazed twice with shots, then had a ball in his unlucky left arm, and lastly a shell caught him on the left hip and threw him to the ground.

At the same time Marshal Davoust had his horse shot under him, and one of his pistols went off and brought him also to the ground. General Sorbier sent word to the Emperor that the Prince of Eckmühl was killed. It was not so bad as that, however. Davoust raised himself and mounted a fresh horse. But these mishaps had the effect of spoiling the first attack.

Napoleon hastily sent Marshal Ney to replace him and make a fresh attack. Meantime the viceroy Eugene had taken the village of Borodino. Bagration's redoubts, which covered Kutusow's left wing, were then taken successively, after hard fighting, by Ney and Davoust. It was still only nine o'clock in the morning, and the Russian left wing was in a very dangerous and exposed position and almost unsupported. General Baggowouth was sent to help Prince Bagration on the left wing, though Kutusow had for some time had quite enough to do with his centre, where General Bonami had taken the trench known as the great redoubt.

The intrepid general made an obstinate resistance, until he fell covered with wounds, and the Russians, under General Paskiewitsch, reoccupied the redoubt, with heavy losses. Kutusow now sent considerable masses of troops to relieve the pressure on his left wing, but Napoleon sent into action a battery of the reserve with 24 guns. The Russians pressed forward once more, but General Lepoultre, St. Germain's curassiers, and Pajol's and Bruyéres' hussars opposed them, and forced them back after a bloody fight.

At last Napoleon gathered all his strength to break the enemy's lines, which had now been drawn up for the third time. In face of a furious cannonade at short range—there were 800 guns in action on either side—Poniatowski and his Poles advanced on the right wing. Prince Eugene attacked the large redoubt with three divisions. General Montbrun rode like the wind at the head of his *curassiers*. He fell, and August Caulaincourt took over the command. He rode with the *curassiers* right into the entrance to the redoubt and fell there. But at the same time Prince Eugene advanced from another side and the fight ended with appalling loss to the Russians. However, the rest of Kutusow's army remained under the French fire until dark, and retreated during the night.

Napoleon's victory was complete, but, like all the other victories in this campaign, it had no particular consequences. In order to thoroughly rout the Russian army it would have been necessary to use the Guard, which stood idle throughout the battle. It has often been questioned whether Napoleon was right in sparing his best troops.

General Ségur, who had certain relations with Russia, his father having served under Catherine II, and he himself having married into the family Rostoptschin, has said a good deal in his memoirs that is vigorously denied by General Gourgaud, who went with Napoleon to St. Helena. Ségur relates that in the battle of Borodino Murat had to seize a colonel by the throat to make him advance. Gourgaud, however, says this is impossible. The colonel in question was in General Friant's division, in which not a single man, much less a high officer, ever drew back; and the division did not belie its reputation at Borodino, but took and held the position at Semenowski with its usual bravery. Ségur describes Napoleon as ill and listless all day at Borodino, and says that all the generals were angry because he would not employ the Guard. Murat sent his adjutant Borelli to ask for help, but received none. General Mouton, Count of Lobau, let a part of the Guard advance on his own responsibility, and Lauriston at length received permission to go forward with the artillery.

Gourgaud describes all this as chatter on the part of the 'palace-official.' He declares that General Sorbier was under fire with part of the artillery of the Guard from the commencement of the battle; and that is true. When the Emperor saw the enemy advancing on Semenowski, he sent to the relief of Friant's division both Murat and the reserve artillery of the Guard. Besides that, Roquet's division was made to take up a position as reserve behind Friant, in front of the young Guard. During the battle the old Guard was drawn up in columns of battalions at intervals of 60 paces behind Napoleon, and this must have made the enemy think they were twice as strong as they really were. The young Guard was in front of them. The line of the enemy formed a triangle, with the apex towards the Schwardina position, where Napoleon was, and the wings drawn back somewhat.

Gourgand also contests everything that Ségur has said of the Emperor's listlessness and the general dissatisfaction with the inactivity of the Guard. He will only admit that the Emperor lost his voice for a time on September 7th and 8th, but says that he commanded with his usual vivacity, and tired out several horses. That Napoleon had a cold and was unwell all day is quite certain; but it is not at all probable that he had any other trouble, of a nature to interfere with his mental powers. If he would not use more of the Guard in compliance with Ney and Murat's repeated entreaties, we must remember that the issue was doubtful and they were far from Paris, and that the Guard was the only part of his army unaffected by the fighting. Finally, Napoleon could not see from the Schwardina trench the gap in the enemy's centre in front of Ney and Murat. However, these criticisms show that a change was beginning amongst Napoleon's followers.

'The bivouac at night after the Battle of Borodino was a sad one,' says one of the surviving officers. 'We put one corpse on another to make a seat by the fire.'

The imperfect victory had been won at an extraordinary loss in officers. Altogether there were 90,000 casualties on both sides. The Russians lost four generals, Kutaisoff, the two Toutchakoffs, and Prince Bagration himself. The French lost thirteen generals, and twenty others were more or less dangerously wounded. The most famous of all the dead officers was the cavalry-general Montbrun, the hero of Somo-Sierra, one of the best left after d'Hautpoul, d'Espagne, and Lasalle. August de Caulaincourt also was a brilliant and greatly liked officer, a brother of the Duke of Vicenza. Marshal Bessières lost his brother General Bessières.

The engineer-general Lariboisière and the brave General Friant each lost a son in the battle. General Bonami, who remained lying in the great redoubt with twenty wounds when the Russians reoccupied it, died of his wounds. Another victim was the handsome Canouville, who had become a general in the cavalry since the time when he received Pauline Borghese's fur with the diamond clasps.

We can form some idea of the intensity of the fight and the nearness of the opposing forces to each other, when we read on the list of wounded officers the names of Davoust, Morand, Friant, Compans, Rapp, Belliard, Nansouty, St. Germain, Teste, and Pajol—a marshal and a number of the leading generals of divisions. To these we must add hundreds of officers of all grades, men who had been in Italy and Egypt, and were all personally known to Napoleon. There had been such carnage immediately round him as had never been seen before, even at Eylau.

Of the highest generals, only three—and they were three of the most intrepid—were quite untouched: Barclay de Tolly on the Russian side, and Murat and Ney on the French. The latter two stood like statues in the rain of balls and were not touched. Ney made his men find cover by lying down, and he himself stood erect in the midst of them like a simple grenadier captain. Murat sprang from his horse and preceded Friant's division on foot at Semenowski.

After the Battle of Borodino Kutusow retreated in the direction of Moscow. For a moment it looked as if he were going to venture on a battle at Moshaisk. He had sworn by his grey hairs to defend the old capital of the Tsars with his last man. But on September 14th the field-marshal withdrew with his defeated army beyond Moscow, to the bitter sorrow of his officers and army.

He nevertheless sent a proclamation to Moscow that the French had lost at Borodino, and two bulletins were sent to St. Petersburg from his headquarters announcing that the French had been thoroughly beaten at Moshaisk, the Imperial Guard annihilated, 100 guns and 1,000 prisoners taken, including the Viceroy Eugene and the Duke of Auertstädt, and that the enemy was being pursued by General Platow's 30,000 *Cossacks*.

The *Tsar* distributed great distinctions and awards amongst the army on the strength of this. The truth was, however, that Kutusow was being pursued so hotly by Murat and Eugene that General Miloradowitsch, in order to save him on the streets of Moscow, threatened to set the town on fire if a brief armistice were not granted. Less out of fear of the threat than from the hope of the result of an interview with Alexander, Napoleon granted the armistice. It was given orally, without the usual formalities. The French army at last looked down from the summits of the hills on the great city, its white buildings and golden domes lying like a dream in the sunshine. Even Napoleon lost his balance for a moment. The others all broke out into jubilation.

Next day the Emperor entered the *Kremlin*, the ancient castle of the *Tsars*. It was the most remarkable of all the foreign castles he had visited, and his entry into it was the most romantic in his whole career. Moscow was not wholly abandoned. The French found many of the palaces of the Russian nobility open and provided with servants and all the rest. Wealthy merchants had put their property and stores under the protection of the French officers, with the intention of returning soon.

The *Kremlin* was full of powder and arms. The city, as it was then, offered convenient and comfortable winter-quarters for the army, and Napoleon at once began to issue orders and to organise; first of all in the army, where discipline had been relaxed, and many other things were not as they should be. He had troops enough to keep off Kutusow; and now that he was in one capital and the Emperor of Russia in the other, he was convinced that the noble ruler he had met at Erfurt would reach out the hand of reconciliation. Peace could be concluded between himself and his friend and admirer in the spring.

The soldiers, on their side, hailed Moscow as the end of all their trials. With boundless confidence in their great leader, whom fortune had never yet failed, they proudly turned to enjoy their rest in the beautiful capital of the *Tsars*. But Moscow broke into flames in the night between the 15th and 16th of September. The fires were of such a nature that the city had evidently been set in flames at several different points with a view to its total destruction.

The plot was furthered by the Governor of Moscow. He had stored up masses of inflammable materials in the garden of his palace, and this he distributed amongst criminals released from the jails. These had to spread them throughout the city, and set fire to it. He had had the hose-pipes removed, and all the efforts of the French to master the fearful conflagration proved ineffectual. They had to withdraw step by step from the city. Napoleon had to leave the *Kremlin*, in the vaults of which there were masses of explosive material. The fire already threatened the powder-waggons of the Guard, which had been brought into the courtyard.

From September 16th to 18th the city burned day and night, aided by a strong wind that veered round several times. In the end four-fifths of the city were destroyed—an immense stretch of desolation, as the oriental city extended far with its palaces and monasteries with large gardens and numerous outlying buildings. There were 15,000 wounded Russians in the hospitals. Prince Rostoptschin, the governor, lost all his wealth and the beautiful palace of his ancestors. 'I have brought nothing with me except the coat I have on,' he said. It has been stated that he had Moscow burned down in a fit of desperate patriotism, without telling his design to anyone.

That is altogether incredible. Such conduct on the part of a high-placed official is hardly possible in any country; it is quite inconceivable in a country where not the slightest thing is done without an order from above. Prince Rostoptschin sacrificed his palace and the holy city of Moscow because he was an obedient subject, and because, like every Russian, he had in his heart the law: 'Everything for the *Tsar!*' He either received an express command, or else he had powers entrusted to him that covered his desperate deed. The superstition that the white *Tsar* has never anything to do with the frightful things that happen in Russia is not confined to that country. The whole of Europe is stupid on Russian questions. Even today we are asked to play this childish game and regard the *Tsar* as the innocent dupe of his surroundings. In Russia nothing is done without the knowledge and wish of the *Tsar*.

After the fire Russian peasants and French soldiers poured into the cellars and stores in search of plunder. The Emperor fixed his headquarters in the *Kremlin* once more, as well as could be managed. He was determined to be there. On September 21st, however, General Sebastini sent word that he had lost sight of the enemy, and it was feared that they might be cut off and surrounded. In point of fact that was Kutusow's intention. He had marched toward the southwest. Murat and Bessières, who were sent in search of him, drove the Russians back in the direction of Kaluga.

Napoleon would not give up the hope of hearing from the *Tsar*. He had even tried a semi-official *rapprochement*. But he had to decide what to do with his army. It was now too weak to be able to attack Kutusow in the open field far in the interior of Russia. On the other hand the condition of Moscow made it impossible for them to spend the winter there. All the generals were for retreating to Poland. Napoleon was alone in his resistance to this proposal. It would have destroyed the idea of his invincibility and raised the whole of Europe against him.

There was now so great a change amongst Napoleon's followers that he had his plan written down and laid before the men who up to that time had been accustomed only to receive orders and obey them. His plan was to march north-west until they could unite with Marshals Victor, St. Cyr, and Macdonald, who were in the Baltic provinces. With these and all the other troops he could bring up he would advance on St. Petersburg in the spring. The plan was formed in the early days of October. All his generals were opposed to a fresh march to the north and fresh annexations, and Napoleon could no longer command as he had done in more fortunate days. He was forced to give way. He then wanted to send Caulaincourt to St. Petersburg, but that officer declared it to be of no use. He had heard the same from Count Narbonne.

These two nobles of the old court were the Emperor's most valued diplomatists and envoys in important matters, and they lived through all the hardships of the Russian campaign. Count Narbonne was the only man that preserved his good temper and his gaiety of manner; the gentlemanly air, that was more superficial in the others, was swept away in the evil days, and their disappointment and irritation were plainly manifested. It is said that right down to the awful days on the Beresina, Narbonne would sit on a stone or the root of a tree every morning and powder his wig. Although he was in his fiftieth year, he escaped with his life; but he died in 1813, as Governor of Torgau, after a fall from his horse.

General Lauriston was then sent to Kutusow for the purpose of securing a truce or at least an armistice. He was deceived and fooled at the Russian headquarters on all the rules of the art. In the meantime there was a kind of tacit armistice, though the Russians did not respect it. One of the *Tsar's* flying adjutants, who had been taken prisoner, was sent to St. Petersburg with fresh proposals for a rapprochement, and the Emperor decided to wait ten or twelve days for an answer. There was no idea of sending one at St. Petersburg.

Napoleon had been informed that the frost would set in about the middle of November. He collected provisions and ammunition, repaired and strengthened the *Kremlin*, opened the theatres, and led France and Europe from Moscow by means of couriers. There are regulations of the *Théâtre Français* that are dated from the *Kremlin* at this time. Meantime Russia had come into close touch with England. The Emperor Alexander also had an interview with Bernadotte at Aabo, where it was agreed to recognise the annexation of Norway, and send to Riga the Russian troops that were in Finland.

Peace was concluded with Turkey, and this enabled Admiral Tschitschagow to assume supreme command of the troops under General Tormasoff that threatened the French retreat from the south, and lead the whole force northward into the district of the Beresina. The plan for the demolition of the retreating army was as follows. Wittgenstein was to attack from the north, Kutusow from the rear, and Admiral Tschitschagow, who proved himself an able general on land, from the south.

When the French army had rested in Moscow and had once more been brought into order, there were still 100,000 splendid soldiers and 600 guns, but there was a lack of horses. The weather was fine, mild, and clear. Napoleon reflected all the time on his plan of advancing on St. Petersburg, but with the approach of winter his generals were less disposed every day to march northwards; they looked rather southwards, towards Kaluga and the fertile provinces. While they were still discussing it, the news came one day when Napoleon was reviewing Ney's corps, that was to march from Moscow, that Kutusow had broken the armistice on October 18th, and attacked King Jerome during the night with an overpowering force.

Murat was quite unprepared. As a man of honour he had relied on the negotiations that promised a few hours' rest before the cessation of the armistice. However, a series of brilliant actions and judicious manoeuvres enabled Murat and Poniatowski to escape with the loss of part of their baggage. This treacherous attack at Winkowo, where Kutusow sent Generals Baggowouth, Ostermann, Doctoroff, Orloff, Denisow, and Müller, against Murat, Poniatowski, and Sébastiani who were really only in charge of advanced posts, became a battle of which the French might well be proud. But the victory had no significance and the Emperor was displeased with Murat, because he had allowed himself to be surprised. Napoleon then ordered an advance against Kutusow. Moscow was abandoned on October 23rd.

On the same day Napoleon heard of Malet's conspiracy at Paris. The whole affair was really insignificant and more or less ridiculous, but it made a painful impression on the Emperor. General Malet was a fanatical republican, and had been imprisoned in 1807 for plotting against the constitution. In 1812 he was shut up in an asylum at Paris. One day he leaped out of the window, and ran into the city. He had a number of proclamations and nominations ready, and he began to distribute them. Some young men joined him, and hastily made themselves a sort of uniform with tricoloured scarves. At one o'clock in the morning Malet approached Colonel Soulier, a brave but stupid officer, and unacquainted with Malet. The latter represented himself as General Lamotte, and said he had come straight from Russia with the news that the Emperor had died on October 8th. He asked for a few troops to be put at his disposal.

Soulier was duped and gave him 1,200 men, but without cartridges or flints in their locks. With these General Malet went to the La Force prison, and set free Generals Guidal and Lahorie, who had been incarcerated for political intrigues. He then issued a number of orders, went to the commander at Paris, General Hullin, and shot him through the cheek with a pistol. However, other officers came up, and Malet was overpowered. In the meantime the released General Lahorie entered Savary's room—he was then Minister of Police and had him arrested and put in La Force. This curious state of things, however, only lasted half an hour. When Savary and the others came to their senses the whole thing fell to the ground. When the Minister of Police returned from the prison to his cabinet he found General Lahorie bound to a chair. But Savary never came to see the humorous side of the matter.

That was the whole episode. But from the fact that anything of the kind could happen at the mere rumour of his death the Emperor saw how frail the security really was of his vast power, and how little root he and his dynasty had taken in the people, apart from the army.

It had occurred to no one in Paris to hasten to the widowed Empress and the little heir to the throne. He therefore quitted Moscow, leaving Marshal Mortier behind to blow up the *Kremlin*. all now understood that the retreat had commenced, and all the French women, servants, and families, started with them on the long journey. The weather was still fine, and the soldiers were in good spirits.

It was Napoleon's first intention to march on the old route toward Kaluga against Kutusow, but he suddenly altered his plan, pressed on in a straight line, and struck the new road to Kaluga. By this change he expected to avoid an encounter with Kutusow, and pass through the town of Malo-Jaroslawetz. This difficult manoeuvre was moat ably and speedily executed. None but a French army could have deceived an enemy that was scattered all round it. The issue of it would have been assured if Eugene, or rather General Delzons, had occupied Malo-Jaroslawetz with an entire division, as the Emperor originally directed.

But Kutusow had discovered Napoleon's stratagem and sent General Doctoroff against Delzons' division, which was too weak to sustain the attack. Delzons redeemed his fault by retaking the position, but he himself was killed in the battle that ensued. There were two brothers of the name of Delzons, both generals. When the first one was killed, the other hastened to him, and soon fell dead beside him. Napoleon galloped up, and there was a hard fight round the little town of Malo-Jaroslawetz, which was lost and taken five or six times. At last Davoust came up with the divisions of Gerard and Compans, and drove the Russians back. But it was now growing dark, and the army had to remain in the position.

After the fight at Malo-Jaroslawetz, the French army no longer sought a regular battle; however successful, the result was always to weaken their forces. The weather began to be raw and rainy. The generals wanted to advance on Moshaisk in order to strike the road to Smolensk. On the 26th of October Napoleon had to give way and openly recognise that he was in retreat. It was the first time in his life that he yielded to the wishes of those about him. In the meantime Marshal Mortier rejoined the army. The retreating troops had heard the roar of the explosion as he blew up the *Kremlin*.

It was on the march back from Moscow that the terrors began. The generals gradually lost control of the desperate soldiers, the wounded remained lying along the route, the powder-waggons were exploded, and disorder spread over the whole army. Even Davoust could not arrest it. He marched in the rear with the relics of his splendid first corps, and had part of the responsibility for all that was done and in the daily fights with the enemy. Kutusow was content to march as closely as he could behind the army, and harass the French with his *Cossacks* and General Platow's light cavalry.

Although Davoust and his men performed their difficult task with incomparable bravery, the Emperor was so unjust as to remove the first corps—not to give it the rest that it so badly needed, but because, he said, the marshal was too slow and methodical in his march. Napoleon himself rode at the head of the Guard, who consumed all they found, and burned everything behind them. He saw nothing of the frightful misery or the endless trudging of unarmed men, who should have been protected every day from the *Cossacks* and provided with food. He did not want to see anything. He rode along in silence with Berthier, who had lost his head and was nearly beside himself. From time to time the Emperor rode on to a height, and complained bitterly of his generals.

One day there was an angry scene between the Emperor and Davoust, and they hardly spoke another word to each other until the end of the campaign. The rear-guard of the army now fell to Marshal Ney, the Prince of Moskwa. On November 9th, during the march from Dorogobusch, the snow-storms began. They caused 50,000 unarmed men and a number of women to fall out of the army. The whole of the cavalry, except the Guard, had lost their horses. The animals had already suffered heavily from the morasses and bad roads during the march, and now the frost set in and revealed the utter unfitness of the French horses for a campaign in Russia on slippery ice.

On the way from Dorogobusch to Smolensk, news came that the Russian armies were advancing from the north and the south, and were gathering on the Beresina and in the marshes along the river. This put an end to Napoleon's plan of making a halt at Smolensk to collect provisions and join with fresh troops. During the march the viceroy's corps had suffered heavily on crossing the river Wop. It had lost all its baggage and guns, and a large number of men.

Ney had been with Napoleon from his earliest years, in all the great battles and wherever desperate manoeuvres were to be carried out. But his name will always be most closely connected with the retreat from Russia. This remarkable man, with an unflinching courage supported by a frame of iron, knew neither fatigue nor illness; he slept on the ground, or watched day and night, ate or went hungry, and nothing seemed to affect him.

During the retreat he generally walked on foot amongst his men, and sometimes took 50 or 100 men, leading them like an ordinary captain of infantry against the bullets and shells. He was always cool and collected. He regarded himself as invulnerable, and really seemed to be so. In the middle of a fight he would take the rifle from the hands of a dying soldier, and shoot with it himself. It was he who awakened the sleepers and drove them into action; he was unmoved by the cries of the wounded for the ambulance. He would answer curtly that he had only two legs, and they were for moving forward, and that perhaps he himself would be on the ground tomorrow. Few men are made of iron, says Thiers, and one may be hard towards others when one does not spare oneself.

It was between Dorogobusch and Smolensk that Ney began his heroic daily fights to save the Emperor and the remains of the grand army. The snow now fell heavily, and an icy-cold wind swept the plains. There were hardly any horses left, and nearly everybody walked on foot. Some dropped out of sheer fatigue; others had their hands or feet frozen; all were tormented with hunger. The few who could hold their weapons had to defend the unarmed against the *Cossacks*, who followed the pitiful procession day and night, capturing, plundering, and maltreating stragglers, and then leaving them to die in the snow. In spite of all the laxity and misery, however, there was a nucleus of officers and men—the Emperor's old comrades—who maintained their coolness and fighting power, and forced Kutusow to respect them.

The Emperor himself met the reverse like a man. He rode along coolly, refusing to see anything, but taken up with fresh big plans. When he had abandoned his own plans and accepted those of the others, we no longer find in his orders the rigid accuracy of earlier days that rarely failed to reach the mark.

He had directed that the army should leave Dorogobusch in three divisions, with an interval of one day between each. The consequence of this was that he himself reached Smolensk first with the Guard, occupied all the available places, and appropriated all the provisions in the place. These, however, were by no means so abundant as Napoleon had been led to calculate. When the other divisions of the troops came up there was frightful confusion. The magazines were plundered, men fought for quarters, all discipline was lost, and the disorder was unbounded. Thus, there was little satisfaction in the halt at Smolensk, where Napoleon had hoped to be able to reorganise the best parts of the army, and at least to find them rest and provisions. They had to push on in the same state of confusion and misery in order to reach the bridge at Orscha.

At Smolensk Napoleon heard that General d'Hilliers had been completely beaten at Elna. The Emperor sent him in disgrace to Paris. Though it might seem an enviable lot to be sent home out of the horrors of Russia, the affliction was so overpowering for the proud officer that he did not get beyond Berlin. He died there of grief. He had been close to Napoleon ever since the first campaign in Italy. He was not in Egypt; he had permission to return home from Malta as he missed his wife at Paris so much.

Burdened with 60,000 unarmed and demoralised men, the remainder of the army left Smolensk in the same marching order. The Emperor started on the 14th, Eugene and Davoust on the 15th, and Ney on the 16th. Kutusow had caused his army to retreat after the hot fight at Malo-Jaroslawetz, so that for a time the armies had been back to back. Napoleon would have made a different use of this opportunity if he were still the commander of old. Now Kutusow was after him again in forced marches with his large army. He let the Emperor pass at Krasnoi, and then faced Eugene and Davoust with 80,000 men under Rajewsky and Miloradowitsch. Delzons' division which had now passed to General Gulleminot, a part of Broussière's cavalry, and General Ornano got safely past them. The viceroy also deceived the Russians by an astute manoeuvre and got past them. But Davoust was cut off, to say nothing of Ney, who was still a full day's march in the rear.

Napoleon could by this time have reached Orscha with the Guard and the other troops that followed him, and joined Marshal Victor and the other reserves, but he was very uneasy about the two marshals who were coming on. For a couple of days he seemed to be in a condition of dull indifference. Then he shook it off, and took the command in person. With a staff in his hand he preceded the Guard on foot and led them back from Krasnoi, to find Davoust in the midst of a fearful artillery-fire, rained on him from three sides. The small force he flung against the masses of Russians consisted of the remains of good corps: the young Guard under Marshal Mortier, a couple of hundred horse from Latour-Maubourg's famous dragoons, and a little artillery under the unflinching Drouot. General Claparède was in the meantime to defend Krasnoi against the Russians, who were everywhere.

During the battle General Laborde was ordered by Marshal Mortier to retreat slowly. He cried out to his men: 'The marshal has ordered us to retreat slowly, so march on, ordinary step, soldiers.'

They marched in perfect order, and were reduced to a few thousand. Kutusow was duped once more. He recalled Miloradowitsch's troops, and Davoust seized the opportunity to fight his way through, with heavy losses, and join the Emperor. But nothing could be seen or heard of Ney, who was a day's march in the rear. The great point now was to reach Orscha. As Napoleon marched away, he left an ambiguous order, because he did not want to have the responsibility of leaving Ney in the lurch. The order was that Davoust was to wait for Ney, but he was not to separate from Mortier. And as the latter had to start at the appointed time, Davoust was compelled to follow him.

The next rallying-point was Liady, where they were all full of concern about Ney, whose fate seemed certain. Ney had 7,000 men with him, to make his way through 60,000 Russians. His generals, Ricard, Dufour, and the brave Colonel Pelet, broke four times through Miloradowitsch's front ranks. But the 7,000 melted down to 3,000, and the marshal led these with bayonets levelled against the heights where there was a whole army with a vast artillery. Generals Marchand, Ledru, and Razoul followed him. They were flung back, and Ney collected them again as well as he could, with his usual coolness and firmness.

At this moment a colonel came from Miloradowitsch with a demand for Ney's surrender, but Ney would neither retreat nor surrender, though his men were falling all round him. Colonel Pelet sat on his horse, both legs and one arm torn with bullets. He had the idea of advising the marshal to retreat on the village of Dubrowna, where there was a bridge across the Dnieper. Davoust had marched past just before, and had blown up the bridge after him. There was no escape except to venture on the thin ice. Ney did this during the night. He got across and reached Orscha with 1,500 men.

There was, however, great rejoicing when the hero came in with his frozen and half-dead men, and they could rest for a time with their comrades. Napoleon, whose relations to Davoust were already strained, was so unjust as to support those who said it was Davoust who had abandoned Ney, whereas the Prince of Eckmühl had merely obeyed the Emperor's own orders.

At Orscha there were at the most 25,000 armed men, and about the same number of stragglers; altogether about one-eighth of the grand army that had crossed the Niemen in June. Here all the waggons were burned, all the Emperor's papers, and two complete trains of bridges. The news from Marshals Victor and Oudinot was disheartening. Wittgenstein from the north, and Tschitschagow from the south were bound to meet at the River Beresina, and bring the army to a last and decisive stand.

On November 22nd, Napoleon heard that his brave Polish General Dombrowski, one of his comrades in Egypt, had been beaten by the Russians under Ojarowski at Borissow, and the French had lost their own bridge over the Beresina.

The Emperor held a consultation with his best generals of the engineers. These were Lariboisière, Chasseloup, Eblé, Haxo, and the Swiss General Jomini, who was considered a great tactician. It was impossible to cross below Borissow. They would have to go further north, nearer to the source of the river, and try to cross there. It seemed impossible to all of them to throw a bridge across a river like the Beresina in face of the enemy. Then a fortunate accident occurred in the middle of their mishaps. General Corbineau, a brother of the one who fell by the side of the Emperor at Eylau, came from the west, from the right bank of the river. He had out through Wittgenstein's lines with 700 horse, and reached the bank of the river just at the moment when a Russian peasant, who knew the locality, was wading across it. This led to the discovery of the ford at Studjanka, and all agreed that this was the one way of escaping capture or destruction.

Tschitschakoff was deceived for a long time by their manoeuvres, and waited for the crossing below Borissow, and left the ford at Studjanka unguarded. It is quite inexplicable how the Russians, who knew the critical nature of the passage, and were so numerous in the district, did not manage better. Meantime, General Eblé and his men set to work to throw two bridges over the river. When Napoleon had the bridge trains burned, he had the foresight to save a few waggons, the tools, metal-work, and coal.

With the help of Chasseloup he and his clever bridge-builders saved the remains of the army and the Emperor. His work has rightly become as famous as any deed of war. The river was eight feet deep in places, and the strong current was filled with lumps of ice. He had to use balconies, wooden houses, and anything that could float, and throughout the whole of the work the officers and men were in the water.

While they were building it, the artillery bridge went to pieces three times, and the aged General Eblé had to go in the water himself. He was praised by all as a model officer, a man of fine appearance, as well as fine character. They said in the army that he and Larrey, the

Emperor's physician, could ask the impossible of the men, and it would be done. It was one of the most difficult tasks ever attempted to make bridges in such desperate circumstances, at such a speed, for a half-lost army such as the French then was. However, the troops passed over in good order, as soon as the bridges were ready. On the western bank they came up with Victor and Oudinot's advanced posts. The young soldiers shuddered as they gazed on the worn and dispirited relics of the grand army. If the stragglers had tried they also could have crossed during the night of the 26th and 27th. But the demoralisation was so great that they camped round the baggage on the eastern bank, and in a few houses they found there.

When the enemy saw the crossing, and gathered round from all sides, there was frightful confusion and pressure at the bridges, and a number of men came to a pitiful end. The bridges were to be burned on the morning of November 29th, to prevent the Russians from following. Eblé and Victor took the greatest possible pains to induce the half-mad stragglers to leave the eastern shore, but they would not. At half-past nine, the Russians coming on at a great pace, General Eblé himself fired his bridges. The poor wretches now saw for the first time that the position was serious, but it was too late. The *Cossacks* were upon them. They killed a good many, and drove the rest in scattered flocks into icy Russia, where they died a fearful death. The fight went on on both sides of the river daring the passage, and the remains of the French artillery gave their last reply to the overwhelming strength of the Russian guns. It was as in Tschaikowski's symphony, when the last notes of the *Marseillaise* die away, and there is only the pitiless thrust, thrust, thrust of the sabre, till at last the bells of Russia ring out clearly over the bloody plains.

In the fight on the eastern bank, which lasted throughout the crossing. Marshal Victor, the Duke of Belluno, performed a masterpiece of bravery and strategy, for which Napoleon requited him very badly, by blaming him for the destruction of the stragglers. Only one part of Victor's corps, which was under General Partouneaux's command, was lost during the fight and taken prisoner. It was the only body of French troops that was taken with arms in their hands throughout the whole campaign.

On the morning of the 28th, Marshal Oudinot, who was always unlucky in this respect, was severely wounded, and had to be carried from the field. Ney took over his command, and he was joined in the retreat by Lefebvre-Desnouettes—the aged Lefebvre, Duke of

Dantzig, went through the whole campaign—the generals of division, Maison and Legrand, and the cavalry-general Dumerc. Maison was a great help to Ney in the retreat. Legrand was one of the great infantry-generals of the good old times. He had been at Fleury and Hohenlinden and in all the later battles. He had been made a count after Tilsit. Napoleon married him to a young daughter of General Scherer; she appreciated her elderly hero, and fired him on to fresh deeds. On the Beresina it was Legrand that first reached the opposite bank. He was seriously wounded there, and his soldiers carried him for a long time on the retreat, but he died on the way. He was another of Napoleon's closest comrades.

There were many other good names on the list of dead and wounded officers on the Beresina—Dombrowski, Fournier, Gerard, Claparède, and the Pole Zayonchek, who lost a leg. After the battle the army made its way in the direction of Smorgoni. They knew that Maret, Duke of Bassano, had collected great stores at Wilna, and that the Bavarian General Wrede was not far off, and was ready to come to their assistance, as well as other generals with reserve troops.

On December 3rd no less than fourteen messengers came in from Paris. They had been riding hither and thither in search of the Emperor. For twenty-one days Europe had heard nothing of the grand army. The Emperor then drew up the 20th bulletin, dated December 3rd, 1812. He made no effort to conceal the whole miserable condition of the army and all the horrors of the retreat; and he concluded, curiously enough, with an assurance that 'the Emperor was never in better health.' Had he some consciousness himself that he had not been well on the campaign? Had he heard from Fouché that people hinted that in Paris? Did he think it would be more inspiring if people heard that he himself was unaffected, and was prepared to avenge his defeat? Whichever it was, his calculation was wrong. The 29th bulletin, and particularly its closing words, did him a great deal of harm in the eyes of the people.

General Heudelet came from the direction of the Niemen with 10,000 men, and General Loison brought the same amount from Wilna. But it seemed as if these apparently vigorous soldiers only came to perish in the frost and privations with the demoralised troops they met. At Smorgoni the Emperor secretly left the army on December 6th, and travelled westwards. He took with him Caulaincourt, Duroc, Mouton, and Lefebvre-Desnouettes. They drove the shortest possible way in simple peasant carts over the ice and snow.

On the way he met Maret, and with him inspected the large and ample stores at Wilna. There were provisions of all kinds there for 100,000 men for forty days. From that point the little troop passed through Warschau to Dresden, which they reached on the 16th, then through Leipsic and Mayence, and on December 19th, during the night, he was back in the Tuileries and held the little King of Rome in his arms. The secret journey right across Europe had been quite successful.

That the army, or what remained of it, was bitter about the Emperor for leaving them in their sufferings will be readily understood. It is always some consolation—the only one—when the man who is responsible for the mishap remains on the wreck to the end like a good comrade; one will forgive him much for the sake of his faithfulness. But Napoleon was not a good comrade. Neither in Egypt nor Russia did he think of anything but himself and his own power. He said himself, when he left Smorgoni: 'I am stronger when I speak from my throne in the Tuileries than at the head of an army that is perishing with the cold.'

This sort of reasoning was enough for him. He was by no means indifferent about his men. Few generals before him had done so much for their soldiers in the field and at home in the way of comfort and rewards. But to him an army was merely a power that he could use. When a thing was lost and destroyed he let it lie; it was of no further use. No one knows what that cost him, but he could not act otherwise.

When he left Smorgoni, he reckoned on the stores at Wilna, and they were certainly there. Marshal Macdonald was in the north with fresh troops, and in the south were his Austrian allies under Schwartzenberg. He wanted to concentrate these and other reinforcements that were on the way, at Wilna, and the Niemen was to be the line of defence against the enemy advancing from the east. Those were the ideas he imparted to Berthier. It is not impossible that this would have been enough for him, great leader as he was, to convert the defeat into a victory. He had been in difficulties before, and had never lost belief in himself.

But now the greatest danger of the whole campaign set in, the intense frost. The night after his departure from Smorgoni the temperature fell to sixty degrees below zero, and thousands of the men died every day. Even the fresh troops at Wilna suffered, because the Duke of Bassano caused them to march on Smorgoni, to meet the

Emperor and assist the army. The sudden and fearful cold wrought terrible havoc amongst the young men, many of whom were Italians. The generals who led them were Heudelet, and the one-armed Loison, Colonel Coutard, a relative of Davoust, and Franchesi, an Italian. In the course of five or six days 10,000 men of their brigades were frozen to death.

According to the Emperor's orders, Murat was to have the supreme command, because he was a king. But, brave as he was in battle, he had now lost all spirit. Berthier was sick and apathetic. Davoust was sombre and silent; he never spoke a word except when he was commanding. He was, perhaps, the one that suffered most at the sight of the general demoralisation, the lapse of discipline, the distrust of the Emperor, and the lack of co-operation amongst the generals, and when he looked at the scattered band that remained out of his model division. It was Ney, the incomparable Ney, that took everything on his shoulders.

It is not easy to understand how this general came so early to be known as the bravest of the brave. They were all brave. There could only be men who knew no fear about a leader like Napoleon. However, as some of them had a special reputation for bravery, like Ney and Murat, there must have been something in it. There must have been something more than ordinary coolness and contempt of death, something that fired the courage of others, and spurred them on to follow their brave leaders to death.

No man could have gone with a greater contempt of death, year in, year out, from battle to battle, than Joachim Murat, and no one possessed in a higher degree the gift of communicating his own courage to others. When he swung himself into the saddle—and he was a handsome man, in a fine suit of amaranth velvet, with enormously long white ostrich feathers, and arms and harness glittering with gold and precious stones—the devil was let loose in his squadrons; man and beast dashed after him, and there was nothing that could stop them. Yet it was found that there was a limit to this kind of courage. King Joachim collapsed when the supply of horses was exhausted, and there were no more cavalrymen to lead with jingling harness and flapping cloaks.

Certainly, he was just as fearless as ever; cowardice was impossible for him; but his courage had lost its glamour, when he could no longer command, but had to save an army that was shrunken out of all proportion. His sense of duty and manly courage sank behind other sensations. He must have thought of his beautiful Naples and his royal crown, which he must have been constantly feeling to see if it was quite secure. It seemed to him to be getting loose, and he lost his courage and his delight in chasing the *Cossacks* every morning.

Ney showed that he possessed the tenacious courage of the infantryman. Amongst the foot there are no fine horses or dashing attacks, but there is an unflinching courage in sustaining the daily struggle, a determination to keep on one's feet, and press onward to the appointed goal, or to retreat with order. Lannes had been of much the same character; but the Duke of Montebello was much more gifted in every respect than the poor Prince of Moskwa, who had nothing but his courage.

At Wilna things went much as they had done at Smolensk. The famished soldiers flung themselves on the stores, plundered and fought for food and drink in the most frightful disorder. There was now not a single corps with troops that had been under the colours. When Marshal Victor, whose corps was supposed to form the advanced guard, reached the gates of Wilna, he had not a single soldier with him. Of the newly-arrived division of Loison there were hardly 3,000 men left, and there were about the same number of the old Guard. On December 9th, Kutusow's first divisions came up with the French while they were plundering Wilna. Ney and the aged Duke of Dantzig ran through the town, and gathered men for the defence. Murat made no attempt to defend the town; he fled by night to Kowno.

The Bavarian General Wrede begged Marshal Ney to cut his way out of the town with the 60 horsemen that were still at his disposal. Ney pointed to the swarms of fugitives that filled the streets, and said they must be protected and got away during the night. He swore that all the *Cossacks* in the world would not drive him and his fifty grenadiers out, before eight o'clock the next morning, from the house which they had fortified, and from which they commanded the gate and kept off the Russians. Thousands of wounded men were left lying in the streets of Wilna, to be dispatched by the *Cossacks*. There were also crowds of stragglers who desperately preferred to remain in the houses rather than venture into a temperature of sixty degrees below freezing point.

A mile from Wilna the whole miserable procession was held up by an insignificant hill. The road was hard and slippery; men and horses slipped and fell, and guns and waggons rolled backward. At this point a number of Russian flags and trophies and a war-chest containing 10,000,000 *francs* in gold were lost. The marshal began to distribute the money amongst the Guard—and every soldier that reached Paris handed it back to the treasury—but as the *Cossacks* came on every vestige of order was lost and there was a general pillage, which was completed by the *Cossacks* when they had driven the French away.

On December 12th the fugitives poured into Kowno, where the same scenes were witnessed as at Smolensk and Wilna, only worse and wilder. The soldiers fell on the food Like wild animals, and men drank themselves to death with brandy. Murat held a council of war, and all but Ney and Davoust (who said nothing) vented their anger against the Emperor. Ney offered to defend Kowno until the fugitives had time to cross the Niemen and reach Königsberg or Macdonald's winter quarters, which were not far off. Positions were marked out for the various corps, and then all the generals made for Königsberg and left Ney behind.

There was now not even a shadow left of the grand army. Ney had only a couple of adjutants with him when he arrived at Kowno. He found 400 men under General Marchand and 300 Germans. The Russians were close behind him, and endeavoured to force an entrance by the gate on the Wilna road. Ney hurried up to it, but the three or four guns he found were spiked, and the artillerymen had fled. Even the Germans ran away, and the officer who led them shot himself in despair. But Ney would not yield. He was determined to defend Kowno until the following day. He took a rifle himself and shot away like a grenadier; a number of high officers did the same.

General Gerard, who bore himself with honour at Ney's side during these last spasms of the march, had gathered thirty men, and with these they defended the Wilna gate, and kept off the whole Russian army. The adjutant Rumigni had succeeded in collecting another small band of men of the 29th regiment, and when he came on with them the Marshal felt that Kowno was saved. He embraced the officer in his joy. Marchand was sent with all speed to the one bridge across the Niemen on which their hopes rested, and which had been attacked by the enemy; Ney fought the whole day and kept his position till nightfall. During the night they escaped from Kowno and reached the river, where Marchand had retaken the bridge. It was quite intact, and so they crossed the Niemen and got safely out of Russia. They were 500 men in all.

The *Cossacks* did not leave them as yet. At one point, where the road mounted a little, they came to a standstill once more, and lost all that they had kept together. The *Cossacks* scattered the four or five hundred men in the darkness, and Ney and Gerard found only a few officers with them. General Marchand escaped by a different route. In the end they reached Königsberg. From this point there was no part of the army under arms. They continued the retreat in small bands, flying over the plains of Poland, and were pursued for some miles beyond the Niemen by the *Cossacks*. Then the Russian cavalry turned back, and the *Tsar's* army, which had lost two-thirds of its strength, came to a halt at last.

The old Guard, which had been least hardly used—partly at the cost of the other troops—during the whole campaign, and which had originally been 7,000 strong, was represented only by 500 men at Königsberg. This was the sole armed remnant. The young Guard had been completely broken, and all the other corps had disappeared. There were at Königsberg 10,000 sick and wounded, and an epidemic broke out amongst them, which the physicians of the time called 'frost fever.' The leading physician himself, the heroic Larrey, caught it and died; so did Generals Lariboisière and Eblé. Of their 100 picked bridge-builders there were not more than twelve left after the fights on the Beresina.

In all, 300,000 soldiers perished during Napoleon's campaign in Russia, besides a number of women and civilians that has never been determined. The generals gathered at Königsberg without troops. There was general indignation against the Emperor, but most of them were for a long time half stupefied with their misfortunes and exertions.

It was at this period that the foreign auxiliaries began to fall off, and they continued to do so in the new year. Officers and men had indeed taken a kind of oath to Napoleon and the French colours, and it was a pitiful spectacle for the German troops in 1813 to pass over to their own countrymen in the middle of the fight, and begin to fire on the ranks they had just left. Yet according to our ideas of nationality, they were bound to resent the unnatural pressure, to join with their compatriots and shake off the unbearable yoke that Napoleon had so long laid on Europe.

A secret armistice had been concluded between the Russian General Diebitsch and the Prussian General York, whose men formed the main body of Macdonald's corps. On December 31st, General York marched away with his regiments, and Marshal Macdonald was no longer able to keep the Russians in check. He had to retreat with the 7,000 Poles under Grandjean that were left in his corps. It gradually became impossible to hold the Niemen as a line of defence, and soon afterwards the Weichsel also had to be abandoned. Königsberg was evacuated; it was Ney again who had to cover the retreat with the remains of Heudelet and Loison's divisions.

All of them suffered from the cold, and provisions had to be bought at a high price or taken by force. The next place of refuge was Dantzig, where General Rapp was governor. He shut himself up in the town, and prepared to defend it. Napoleon had destined this position for Rapp long before. During one of the battles in Russia the Emperor had given the general an order to attack, but suddenly changed his mind and sent another cavalry-general. They heard him mutter at the time: 'I need Rapp at Dantzig.'

Murat's headquarters were first at Thorn, and then in Poland. On January 16th, 1813, he could endure it no longer. He abandoned the army and the posts that the Emperor had entrusted to him, and fled to Naples. The chief command now fell to Eugene, the Viceroy of Italy, and he exercised it with his customary firmness. He had led his men throughout the campaign with coolness and bravery, and it was he who put a stop to the retreat. He remained for a month at Posen, restored order and discipline, let his men rest, and gave them time to gather under the colours once more. On February 21st he withdrew to Berlin, after burning the bridges at Krossen and Frankfort on the Oder.

Prince Schwartzenberg had been making a fool of Napoleon the whole time and was in collusion with the Russians. He now openly seceded from the French. General Grenier had been in Italy in 1811, and had been directed by Napoleon at that time to keep an eye on Murat, whose weakness of character was well known to the Emperor. Now, in the early days of 1813, Grenier brought his corps to Berlin, and gave Augereau a reinforcement of 28,000 men. To these we must add 25,000 men under Rapp at Dantzig, and the garrisons of a few fortresses on the Weichsel and at Warschau. These were the only fighting forces left to Napoleon in that part of Europe.

CHAPTER 7

Decline

There was a great difference in appearance between the army that marched singing into Italy—half in their old Republican rags, half in Bonaparte's new uniforms—and the model soldiers, equipped down to the smallest detail, that were called out to face the army of Frederick the Great in 1806. There was a difference again between the latter and the *grande armée* that had marched into Russia. This was certainly the finest army that has ever been seen. Its whole equipment and material was new and modern, and the number of foreign troops helped to give it the appearance of a comprehensive power, as it defiled over the plains of Poland. Its march was like a colossal parade.

It has been regarded as a proof of Napoleon's infatuated ambition that he made such imperfect preparation for this campaign, and had so little knowledge of the geography and climatic conditions of the country. But it was rather the great blunder of his life that led him to do this; namely, the notion that there was a place for him and his family amongst the legitimate princes of Europe. After what he had experienced and attained he saw no impossibility in that. He knew that there was no such thing as memory in the false intercourse of courts. His army must be so powerful and his attack so decisive that the *Tsar* must be compelled out of fear to reach out his hand. But it is possible that Napoleon and his officers did not on this occasion devote the same care to minute details that they had done at the commencement of other campaigns.

All the high officers went more or less reluctantly. The soldiers were too confident in the invincibility of their idol. Hence they had not heeded all the warnings and suggestions before beginning the Russian war. The rough ways had not been smoothed by spies and bribes. The Emperor himself and his whole machinery were a little worn. There was not the absolute reliability in small details of the earlier wars. At Austerlitz in 1806, he had said of General Ordener, the officer who arrested the Duke of Enghien:

Ordener is worn out. We need only a short time for the war.
I myself can only go on for five or six years more, and then I.
must cease.

It was just seven years afterwards that he was ill and fatigued at Borodino.

Thus the Russian campaign differed from all the others in many points besides its failure. From the first march one missed the wonderful order and precision that had been inseparable from him ever since the morning in 1796 when all the corps of the republican army marched together in perfect unison beside the sunlit Bormida. In 1812 orders were misunderstood from the outset. Distances were miscalculated and time wasted; and when there was a victory—as there still was sometimes—there were no men to follow up the advantage as in the old days. The whole plan of the campaign was political rather than strategical. The Emperor thoughtess of beating the Russians than of winning the *Tsar*. Hence there was something of a parade in the great gathering of princes at Dresden, the distribution of the enormous fighting forces, and the advance on the Niemen. It was all done with unusual slowness, and before the eyes of Russia, in order to give the *Tsar* time to reach out a friendly hand.

Napoleon did not understand what any one of us who have come into the world a hundred years afterwards could have told him. He imagined that the descendants of the Corsican bandit could meet and exchange kisses with the Hapsburgs, the Hohenzollerns, and the Romanows, and that the telegraph would spread it over Europe. Assuredly, he came very near it. In 1806, when he was returning from Tilsit to Paris, he was met at Marienwerder by an adjutant of the King of Saxony with a letter of this tenour:

The Emperor Francis seeks my daughter Augusta. What shall
I do?

Napoleon went to Dresden, and prevented the match. 'And I was utterly wrong,' he said afterwards at St. Helena. 'I was afraid that a connection with the Emperor Francis would alienate the King of Saxony from me, whereas Augusta would have won the Emperor for me—and then I would not be here!'

He had come so close to them that they asked his advice on such

151

intimate points. A few years afterwards the Emperor Francis gave him, his daughter in marriage, yet Napoleon did not understand until all was lost what a gulf there was between him and them. It is almost painful to find Napoleon complaining to Prince Metternich on August 25th, 1805, that the Emperor and the new Empress of Austria never ask the French ambassador at Vienna about Napoleon's health and such things.

'They know very well,' he said, 'that I myself do not ask you such questions to learn what I already know. No, it is done for the world to know that the relations between us are those of two sovereigns. Don't you see what a different footing I am on with the Emperor Alexander? We send each other presents, not because they have any importance in themselves, but because they keep up our connexion. I should have sent your Empress a wedding present, but she has never even mentioned my name. There has not been the slightest notice taken of me on your side! My ambassador is not treated with as much consideration as the envoys of Bavaria or Würtemberg, to say nothing of the Russian. These little matters are of great importance.'

'I took the thing humorously,' Metternich writes, 'and answered: "Sire, I will at once see that some valuable objects in porcelain are sent from Vienna, if it will serve to strengthen the good relations between us."'

In the year 1813, before the Saxon campaign. Napoleon said:

> The war I am now entering upon is a political one. I would willingly have spared Russia all the trouble it has brought on itself. If I liked, I could have stirred up the mass of the people against the *Tsar* by proclaiming the emancipation of the serfs. But I avoided this weapon, as it would have brought misery to countless families and have caused endless massacres.

And, finally, at St. Helena, the Emperor once said in conversation:

> People may explain it as they like, but I swear that I had no direct or personal hatred of any of the princes I fought against. For me the whole thing was a political struggle—so free, so light, I might even say, so benevolent was my disposition. It is true that Louis XVIII and the other princes had outlawed me, and put a price on my head. In my opinion that was merely diplomatic rhetoric

All this is very *naïve*, but the fault is not that Napoleon over-estimated the importance for himself and his descendants of penetrating the royal circle. He was quite right. In those days and in ours the power is with the princes, the fate of the nations is in the hands of a few old families. When he thought he had any chance of penetrating this circle, he, having come through the fires of the Revolution, was more convinced of this than we who are so far removed from the great reckoning with kings, and who have so far been cooled by a century of reaction as to entertain once more the old folly that it needs royal blood to lead States; just as we thought when we were boys at school that there must be cat's blood in real licorice.

After his return to Paris the Emperor resumed his normal life as the indefatigable head of the State. He maintained an icy calmness, to show that he was a man lifted above all the vicissitudes of fate. But he saw in every face the effect of the defeat and of the 29th bulletin, in which he had confessed the whole misery so openly. He still made no effort to mince matters with phrases or subterfuges; but he threw himself with exaggerated zeal into the Malet affair.

With great ostentation he had the Prefect of the Seine, Frochot, arrested, and an inquiry opened. He certainly did this in part to divert the attention of the Parisians from his unfortunate campaign, but also because he saw with concern and bitterness from the police-information how many of his faithful servants had been ready to take part in a revolution at the mere rumour of his death, and not one of them had thought of running to the assistance of the Empress and the heir to the throne.

Then he threw himself with unprecedented energy into the work of raising fresh levies. He filled up the attenuated regiments, and brought troops from all the camps in Europe. If he had not such a number of his best soldiers engaged in the Spanish Peninsula, he would have had 500,000 at his disposal once more. Meantime he wanted fresh levies in the four last age-classes up to 1814—a hundred thousand men altogether. It was all given willingly. Every man deemed it a point of honour to maintain the honour of France and its twenty years' supremacy in face of this first blow at their invincible leader. Yet there was something wanting. The nation was not called out in the name of liberty; the Emperor would not venture to put the safety of France in the hands of the people. He was determined to be as before—the Emperor and his army.

It was different in Prussia and Germany. There it was the people's business to throw off the French yoke. Whatever concern the governments had in regard to the people, they had to let the great beast loose for a time, intending to chain it up all the more securely when the danger was over. The whole suppressed youth of Germany broke out into songs of fatherland and freedom. While the old diplomatists lent their ears, and mixed their fine drinks, vast crowds of German youths rushed to the colours, ready to die for the freedom that bore in sight.

That there would be more fighting, they all knew. That Napoleon could not leave his half -shattered empire exposed on the east was as clear as that the other princes were his enemies, and would be until he was destroyed. At the bottom, therefore, not much importance was attached to the amenities of diplomatists, or to what Metternich said to Napoleon. They knew that he knew more than all of them together. It must be war; and war it was—for three more years, and worse than ever.

His destiny fell from stage to stage after the Russian campaign as fatally as a vast waterfall, and with almost equal grandeur. All his enemies gathered like a storm in the east. Far away, in the extreme west General Moreau began to stir. He had lived in peace on his estate at Delaware since the great conspiracy of 1804. But as soon as he heard of the issue of the Russian campaign, he left America and came to Europe. All his ambitious dreams were revived. Napoleon Bonaparte was now ripe for the fall, and it was time for Moreau to take his place.

After an interview with the other traitor, Bernadotte, at Göteborg, Moreau, the great general of the glorious republican wars, the victor of Hohenlinden, went over to the enemies of France in the moment of danger like a common deserter. He went to Prague, and was greeted by the Allies there with jubilation. They gave him a kind of supreme command, together with Prince Schwartzenberg, over the combined armies, when things were sufficiently advanced for Austria to throw off the mask altogether.

Bernadotte also had allowed himself to be bought by the most shameless intrigues to take his place amongst the enemies of his country, in hostility to the man to whom he owed everything.

After settling the regency on Marie Louise, which he did with a certain amount of relief, the Emperor left Paris on April 15th, 1813, at one in the morning, and took the road to Mayence, Never did he astonish the world and his enemies so much as then, when he deployed in the vicinity of Jena, where he had conquered six years before, the new fighting forces he had conjured up out of the earth. The Allies, who were well aware that there were between two and three hundred thousand of his old soldiers in Spain, had expected to see no more than the attenuated remains of the Russian disaster.

They found themselves instead facing the old invincible name and the familiar solid columns of the best infantry in the world. Ney, Oudinot, Eugene, and the other survivors from Russia were now augmented by Marmont, Macdonald, Kellermann, and Bertrand. The cavalry was poor; and on looking closely one would find a disquieting amount of raw recruits in the army. Yet it was precisely these who brought off the remarkable victory at Lützen, with which the war of 1813 opened.

On the day before the battle they met with a great misfortune. Marshal Bessières was killed by a cannon-ball during a slight skirmish at rather long range. It was a painful blow to Napoleon and all his staff, and a great loss to the army, especially the cavalry, to which the marshal had always devoted special care, and which he had led with such distinction. The Duke of Istria was a brave and honourable soldier, but singular in being one of the very few in the army who continued to appear with powdered wig, tail, and curls about his ears.

The Emperor had made himself personally acquainted with the new troops before the great battle. He directed Marshals Ney, Oudinot, and Marmont, and the Viceroy Eugene to draw up in such a way that he could pass continuously along them. He rode slowly down the long lines, stopped here and there to say a friendly word, spoke to the officers or to some old non-commissioned officer that he knew, and all the while ran his eye over the young men in the characteristic way that made each one feel he had been individually noticed. They all, old and young, had time to see him, and he brought them all together in a common confidence of victory. He wanted to begin with a striking victory, that would daunt his enemies and open the way to Dresden. From there he proposed to carry the war into Schleswig and toward the frontier of Bohemia.

The Emperor had left Lützen with Ney's army-corps about nine o'clock in the morning of May 2nd, and he had just dismounted to look over some maps with the marshal, when they heard a strong cannonade in their rear, from the quarter where Ney's troops had spent the night. They could tell at once that it must be Macdonald who was engaged with the enemy. In a moment the Emperor entirely changed his dispositions, and sent adjutants to all the generals with an order to march straight across the country towards the thunder of Macdonald's guns.

It took three hours to execute this manoeuvre, and so those who first reached the field fought for some hours against an overwhelming force. However, the artillery of the various corps gradually came into action, and when the divisions of Bonnet, Morand, Compans, and Bertrand appeared on the field, the battle was already won at all points. The Emperor was under fire the whole day long.

General Mouton, Count of Lobau, led the 16th battalion of the young Guard in a fearful struggle round the village of Kaja. When the young men were nearly overpowered by the heavy pressure, the old generals had only to say a word and they stood like walls. If they heard the Emperor's own voice above the din, they broke into the cry of 'Long live the Emperor,' and swept on with their bayonets like a storm. But it was a lamentable spectacle to see the fine young men on both sides, slim French youths, and pale German students with long hair, falling upon each other like wild beasts. When the sun went down there were 25,000 men lying on the field, and the plain was lit by the flames of four large villages.

It was with great satisfaction that Napoleon redacted the bulletin recording his incredible victory. He had beaten with infantry-divisions full of raw recruits, two combined armies of veteran soldiers, the Russians and Prussians, with 25,000 of the best cavalry in Europe and an enormous artillery. No prisoners were made after the battle, as the French cavalry was still weak. But the moral effect of it was incalculable. The Emperor Napoleon was himself again. The confidence of his generals was restored. The disaster in Russia fell away like a nightmare from which they had at length awakened. The army, nay, the whole of France, returned to its firm belief in Napoleon's invincibility.

The chief feeling amongst the Allies was one of disillusion, and their armies retreated on Dresden. At their head rode the Emperor of Russia and the King of Prussia—just as before; also Generals Barclay de Tolly, Wittgenstein, Miloradowitsch, Blücher, and Kleist, all with their tails between their legs—just as before. Napoleon soon drove them out of Dresden, and rested there for a week. The aged King of Saxony was not at home. Under pressure from Austria he had gone to Prague, and he was now strongly influenced by the other German princes.

But Napoleon invited him to return, and on the 12th of May Friedrich August was back in his capital. The Emperor rode out from Dresden to meet him, and received him with great ceremony amidst his brilliant Guard. The old friendship was renewed, and Saxony remained a faithful ally of his to the end—Saxony and steadfast Denmark. The attitude of Austria became more and more ambiguous; that is to say, all their circumlocution could not conceal the fact that Austria was prepared to join the Allies as soon as the moment arrived.

During the eight days that he spent at Dresden the Emperor received from the King of Saxony some cavalry, which he badly needed. 'If it were a month later,' he said, 'and I had more cavalry, it would be a splendid opportunity to close the whole affair with arms in our hands, and I would certainly not grant them an armistice. They do not know what they are in for.' He was alluding to Marshal Ney's march on Bautzen. At Bautzen and Wurschen again the French army won a brilliant and bloody victory over the Allies on May 20th and 21st. The next day it was on the march to Schleswig, driving the allied troops before it. The French pressed on along three routes. Marshal Victor and General Sébastiani were on the left wing; Macdonald, Marmont, and Bertrand followed Wittgenstein along the road to Schweidnitz; Marshal Ney advanced along the road to Breslau.

The Emperor himself joined in the pursuit with the cavalry of the Guard, Latour-Maubourg's dragoons, and some infantry. He rode the whole day at the head of the Guard, and reached Weissenberg without meeting any resistance. General Miloradowitsch had taken up a position a little farther on, on the heights of Reichenbach, to protect the flying sovereigns. The French cavalry—reduced, it is true, to a mere shadow of its former glory—was still led by its old officers, Bruyères, Lefebvre-Desnouettes, Colbert, and Latour-Maubourg, and after a hard fight the Russians were thrown into retreat. But in this comparatively unimportant battle. General Bruyères, one of the Italian veterans, was killed. Napoleon himself was under fire, and one of the horsemen in his personal escort was killed so close to him that the man fell right at the feet of his horse,

'The luck is with us today, Duroc!' the Emperor cried to his Master of the Court.

They were riding through a crooked village street to reach an elevation from which they would get a better view. The next moment a stray cannon-shot came along, struck a tree, killed General Kirchner, and tore open the body of Marshal Duroc, who was riding beside him. Marshal Mortier, who was quite close, was uninjured. Meantime the Emperor had set his horse at a gallop to reach the hill, and had seen nothing. It was not till he reached it that he learned from one of Oudinot's adjutants that the Duke of Friaul had been killed, 'Impossible!' he exclaimed. 'I have only just been speaking to him,'

As he was speaking Colonel Gourgaud came with a message from Ney, but Napoleon rode back and did not listen to him. He went with Mortier and Caulaincourt into the house in which they had placed Duroc, They exchanged a few words, and Napoleon sat for a long time by the side of the wounded man. He had been his most trusted friend from youth, and was an irreplaceable servant.

The day before he fell Duroc had said to Marmont: 'The Emperor has an insatiable zeal for war. We shall all come to an end on the field. That is our fate.'

The victory and the hot pursuit had broken the courage of the Allies, and they came with a civil request for an armistice. And although the proposal was brought to Napoleon by one of his worst enemies, the Austrian Count Stadion, he accepted the unfortunate armistice. By this means he lost all that he had gained. At that moment—a moment that the younger Bonaparte would have seized as swiftly as lightning—he should have forced them to yield an honourable peace. But he had once more sent the Duke of Vicenza secretly to the *Tsar*, and preferred to engage in a diplomatic struggle in which he was bound to lose. In the eyes of his opponents he was a noxious animal against whom any device could be used.

First the armistice was properly executed, and then it was settled to hold a congress at Prague. In this way the whole of June was wasted without anything being done. Meantime the Allies were besieging Stettin, which was defended by General Dufresne. The Crown-Prince of Sweden acted as if he were merely reviewing the besieging troops during the armistice; but he deliberately rode as near as possible to the fortifications so that his former soldiers, whom he still fancied to be attached to him, could see him. Suddenly a cannon-shot was fired from the fortress and the ball whizzed past Bernadotte's ears. The Allies at once raised a protest against this breach of the armistice. But the commander at Stettin answered: 'A French deserter was said to be in sight, and the guard shot at him. That was all.'

On June 27th Prince Metternich came as a sort of intermediary to Dresden, and had a heated altercation with the Emperor in the Marcolini palace. Austria's demands for a general peace were so unreasonable that the Emperor exclaimed: 'How much is England giving you to spur Austria into war with me.'

The Congress at Prague was conducted on the principle of saying a great deal and deciding nothing. The Allies made various arrangements with each other, but Napoleon's envoys could learn nothing of them. They were either kept at a distance or duped. King Murat returned, and offered his services. After abandoning the army and returning home, he had made a secret arrangement with Austria. He was so foolish, and knew so little of the real value of princely promises, that he imagined he could retain his crown after the fall of the man who alone had the art of making kings out of waiters. At the same time he ventured to offer his services to Napoleon; and Napoleon accepted them, although he knew everything. But he had some feeling for his first cavalry-general, and he expected from Murat nothing more than stupidity and ingratitude.

During the long diplomatic negotiations Napoleon again ruled the world from Dresden. A stream of generals and ambassadors poured about him once more; but there were less kings than in 1812. Under his control things went on their normal way. The regiments found quarters and provisions, the recruits were drilled, and all that the army needed was brought up from the depots. Horses alone were lacking.

The small but brave Polish army under Poniatowski had now no fatherland except under the French colours which they had followed so long. Napoleon gave them the same pay and conditions as to his French soldiers. All the millions he had accumulated in the shape of spoil or war-indemnities during the good years, and which had lain well guarded in the Marsan room at the Louvre, now served to lighten the burdens of the poor Saxons, whose country had become the theatre of war. Suddenly Metternich announced to Caulaincourt and Narbonne that the Congress of Prague was dissolved. The preparations of the Allies were completed, and Blücher attacked the French in Schleswig two days before the termination of the armistice. One did not need to be too scrupulous with the hereditary enemy. The armistice was to run out on the 15th, but on the 12th Blücher attacked Ney, Marmont, and Macdonald, who lay between Bober and Katzbach. Napoleon hurried up, and drove Blücher back step by step.

On the 22nd of August, however, a courier came from Marshal St. Cyr with the news that the enemy was near Dresden—a little to the west of it, as if preparing to move between Leipzig and Dresden. It had been suggested that they should advance in the direction of Leipzig, but Generals Jomini and Moreau had pointed out how dangerous it was to have the Emperor in their rear. Schwartzenberg therefore advanced with all speed on Dresden, while Napoleon was occupied in driving Blücher out of Schleswig.

Prince Schwartzenberg had already collected 200,000 men, but he wanted to wait for General Klenau. Moreau was quite nervous with their delays and precautions, and spoke rather sharply about making good use of their time. The Prince gave him a heated reply; and Moreau, slipping off the mask of a courtier and becoming the old republican once more, flung his hat on the ground and exclaimed, 'Do you know what, sir, the devil knows that I am no longer astonished that you have done nothing but be beaten for the last seventeen years.'

On hearing of the enemy's advance on Dresden, Napoleon wheeled round immediately with his Guard, and the corps of Mortier and Ney, and left Marshal Macdonald alone with Generals Lauriston and Souham to face Blücher. He reached Stolpen with incredible speed, and worked out a great plan of carrying out a manoeuvre over the bridges at Lilienstein and Königstein. But Marshal St. Cyr began to be anxious at Dresden. Napoleon had sent General Gourgaud to him to ask if he could not hold the city two days longer. The general came back at full speed on the evening of the 25th of August, and so much alarmed the Emperor that he gave up his plan and sent his troops by forced marches to Dresden. At the same time he sent General Vandamme with the engineer Haxo and a number of good officers into Bohemia, where, according to Napoleon's calculation, they should catch the Allied armies in flight and take them prisoners if he beat them. But it fell out quite otherwise with Vandamme and his army.

On the morning of August 26th the Emperor himself rode into the Saxon capital, to the astonishment of all; and it was quite time that he came. That very afternoon Schwartzenberg brought the whole of his fighting forces against the town, and his troops gradually advanced as far as the large garden, where they were received by a part of the Imperial Guard. Meantime Napoleon had collected his troops in the town, and suddenly the young Guard, with Marshals Mortier and Ney at their head, poured out of the gates Like two roaring torrents, and swept back the Austrians, Russians and Prussians.

It was a short but vigorous fight, and five generals of the Guard were wounded. The King of Naples drove back the enemy in the direction of Wilsdruff with the cavalry of the Guard and Latour-Maubourg's *curassiers*. The French reoccupied all their positions, and the Allies, who now knew that the Emperor himself was in Dresden, retired at all points. In the evening, after making his preparations for a great battle on the following day. Napoleon joined the King of Saxony at table, and was in what was for him a most brilliant mood.

In the camp of the Allies the night was spent in mutual recrimination. There was a thick mist on the following day, August 27th. It had been raining all night, and continued to do so with great violence during the day. The flint-lock weapons of the infantry, with their open pans, were almost unusable. Thus the great battle was fought with artillery, and with sabre and bayonet. The cannons opened fire at seven in the morning, and thundered the whole day long. Murat and Marshal Victor threw themselves on the Austrian left wing on the Plauen estate. General Mitzko was taken prisoner with his cavalry-division.

The centre of the Allies was gradually pierced, and on the right wing, where Napoleon opposed the Russians, Wittgenstein was forced to retreat after a stubborn resistance. On the heights of Räcknitz, where the Allied princes were with their generals, staffs, and bodyguards, great masses of troops were concentrated, and these could only be reached by the artillery. The cannons of the Guard were directed to drive the enemy from this position, and the Emperor himself commanded the advancing batteries.

At that time the distances were so slight—even for the artillery—that from the French batteries one could see the brilliant group around the Allied sovereigns, and all at once an unusual excitement was noticed amongst these horsemen. It was supposed that some important personage or at least a high officer, had been wounded or killed. And when in the evening a stray dog ran into the line of the French advanced posts, with the name 'General Moreau' round its neck, it was thought possible that it was he who had fallen. Such was really the case. Moreau was sitting on his horse, quite close to Alexander, when a ball from the French batteries struck him. It shattered his thigh, passed through his horse, and tore his other leg. Both had to be amputated, but he did not survive the operation. It is said that the aged hero smoked a cigar while the surgeons were busy on him.

In the evening and during the night Schwartzenberg retreated along the Teplitz road in the direction of Bohemia. All the other roads were closed. He left 30,000 dead, and 12,000 prisoners under the walls of Dresden. Napoleon had been twelve hours on horseback in the pouring rain when he rode back into Dresden. He entered it over the old bridge from Neustadt. The bodyguard, wet through, rode before him at walking pace. Then came the Emperor himself, carelessly holding to the wet saddle, his military coat soaked through with rain, and his famous hat so saturated and softened that the wide brims, usually turned up, hung down to his shoulders. But the soldiers and the

161

whole of Dresden were wild with joy.

The Saxon court gave him a great ovation as he strode into the well-lit room after his bath and toilet. Friedrich August, who had been torn with anxiety the whole year, and could never be quite sure whether he had been betrayed or bought, began to think it was all right this time.

But all this was of no avail. Too much time had been lost, and the resources of the Allied princes in men, horses, and material, were overwhelming. In the weeks following the battle of Dresden, Napoleon let his armies scatter under marshals and generals, and operate on their own account, far more than he had been accustomed to do. It is true that his vast plans embraced all their manoeuvres, but without taking account of possible failures; or, to put it more correctly, without that gift of preventing failures or at least being independent of them that General Bonaparte had had in earlier years.

His record from May to September is as follows: On May 2nd he won the great battle of Lützen. On May 20th and 21st he again conquered at Bautzen and Wurschen. Then came the armistice and the Congress of Prague. On June 21st Marshal Jourdan and King Joseph lost the decisive battle of Vittoria, and with it Spain. On August 21st Napoleon said: 'Today the Duke of Reggio advances on Berlin.' In reality Oudinot was still far from Berlin, partly owing to floods, and partly to the pressure of Bernadotte, who at last beat him at Grossbeeren. On August 26th Macdonald lost the battle on the Katzbach against Blücher. On August 26th and 27th the Emperor won the great Battle of Dresden. On August 30th Vandamme was beaten by General Ostermann at Kulm in Bohemia, and was taken prisoner with 7,000 men. Finally, on September 26th, Ney lost the Battle of Dennewitz against the Crown-prince of Sweden.

It will be readily understood that this record encouraged the Allies. The whole of Germany was heaving under them, and a rising of the entire German nation was very convenient for its generals and diplomatists; while Napoleon's allies fell off one by one, voluntarily or involuntarily. Bavaria declared war; Würtemberg followed suit; the grand-duke of Baden joined them. The King of Saxony alone remained firm against all temptations and promises, and marched with Napoleon as far as the last town in his kingdom. The secession of Bavaria was particularly dangerous, as they had guarded the French frontier to the north of Mayence.

The only thing for Napoleon to do now was to reach Leipzig before the Allies so that his connections with France might not be cut. He had, therefore, to leave Dresden, which he had begun to convert into a great armed centre from which he might hasten to the help of any of his army-corps with his invincible Guard. He left, however, two of his best generals, Marshal St. Cyr and General Mouton, Count of Lobau, in the city with 30,000 fine soldiers. He was never to see them again.

He made these fateful dispositions because he was still deceiving himself with his great plan for routing the Allies. But they were now so astute that his plan very soon proved incapable of being carried out, and his 30,000 men at Dresden were swept away. He had all the more need of these troops since he had now to fight on the open plains of Leipzig with 155,000 men against an enemy that was 300,000 strong, and had twice the force of cavalry that he had. On October 15th the position of the two armies round Leipzig was such that a great battle was inevitable on the following day. The advanced posts approached each other within range of a flint-lock musket.

On the following morning about nine o'clock, three cannon-shots were fired as a signal to the Allies, and at once three strong columns, supported by 200 cannons, advanced from the army-corps of Wittgenstein and General Kleist. On this first day of the battle the fight raged along the line of Markkleeberg, Wachau, and Liebertwolkwitz, far outside the range of the town at that time. The two latter villages were taken and retaken several times in the course of the morning. Marshal Victor defended Wachau against General Kleist, and Lauriston defended Liebertwolkwitz against General Gortschakow. With them were Latour-Maubourg, Sébastiani, and Milhaud of the French cavalry. Meantime the Austrians under Klenau attempted to surround the French to the east of the town. It was known that an army, either that of Blücher or of Bernadotte, was approaching from the north.

The fight was so vigorous from the early morning onwards that by mid-day about 18,000 men had already fallen on both sides. At this moment Napoleon was informed that the enemy was also surrounding his positions on the west side. General Margaron having been attacked by the Austrian General Gyulai. To the north of Leipzig Blücher had already made his appearance. He had heard the guns. Marmont fought him all day long, with the support of Ney, who brought up the divisions of Souham and Dombrowski.

After twelve o'clock the Emperor determined to go on from defending his positions to a strong attack on Schwartzenberg's centre.

Mortier advanced with Lauriston, Victor, and Oudinot. Between them was Drouot's artillery of the Guard, and with them also were the cavalry of the Guard under Latour-Maubourg, Kellermann, and Nansouty, and the divisions of Curial, Friant, and Gerard. There was no question now of sparing any bodies of troops. On the extreme left Macdonald began to force Klenau back, and the Prince of Würtemberg was equally unable to retain his position. But Rajewski's 10,000 grenadiers stood like walls before Drouot's guns, and let themselves be shot. Behind them Schwartzenberg gathered large masses of reserves, and these he sent on and arrested the first attack.

About four o'clock Napoleon decided to venture everything in order to convert the battle into a complete victory. He took the whole of the cavalry at his disposal, and flung them against the village of Wachau. Twelve thousand horse, with King Joachim at their head, flew to the attack. Murat scattered the enemy's cavalry and the ranks of the Russian grenadiers, drove back the whole corps of the Prince of Würtemberg, and took 26 guns.

But before there was any decisive victory, General Pajol, a veteran of the republican days, was blown up by a shell that exploded under his horse. Generals Maison and Latour-Maubourg were wounded and fell from their horses, and in the confusion that followed the *Cossacks* succeeded in recovering the 26 guns from Murat. Then large masses of troops came over from the right, where the Prince of Hesse-Homburg had tried to rout Poniatowski and Augereau. General Nostitz's Austrian *curassiers* forced back Kellermann and Lefort. Murat himself had to stop at the village of Güldengossa. He had retaken the guns; but Latour-Maubourg had lost a leg, and General Pajol was severely injured.

The *Tsar* had agreed to let all the troops advance, including the *Cossacks* and hussars. But Napoleon, who now saw that even his great cavalry attack had not decided the battle, resolved to make a third attempt, and gave a fresh order for the concentration of his whole forces on Wachau. The Allies were receiving constant reinforcements from the right, led by General Meerfeldt. The Emperor sent the old Guard itself under General Curial against him, and the general and his men went to work with such energy that they took Meerfeldt and 2,000 men prisoners. The battle came to a standstill. Neither party could claim a victory, and the darkness was setting in.

Prince Poniatowski had resisted the Austrians who wanted to force the passage over the Pleisse throughout the whole day, and Napoleon made him a Marshal of France. It was now evening, but the Emperor determined on one more attack on the unfortunate village of Güldengossa. Mortier and Maison advanced in their customary way. But Barclay de Tolly sent in the Russian Guard, and it was found impossible to dislodge the Russians from the village, though General Maison stood there in the dark and roared like a lion. He had received a number of wounds, and had had three horses shot under him.

That morning he had said to his soldiers: 'This is the last day for France. We shall all have closed our eyes by tonight.' And neither he nor his men had spared themselves. Hardly a thousand men were left of his division. But the brave general lived to see his prophecy falsified. General Count Maison was made a Marshal of France after the campaign in Morea in 1828. He was afterwards an ambassador under Louis Philippe, and lived until 1840.

The fight at Wachau was the chief one of the day, and cost 50,000 men. There was also fighting to the west of the town, where General Margaron kept off Gyulai, and to the north, where Marmont had to sustain a heavy struggle with Blücher. Marmont and Compans were under fire all day long. The marshal received several bullets in his uniform, a wound in. the hand, and another in the shoulder. Unfortunately a shell fell in Compans' powder waggon, and in the confusion that followed the explosion the enemy succeeded in taking the battery and forcing Marmont to retreat. He had fought with 24,000 men against 60,000 and killed 10,000 of them.

That was the first day of the Battle of Leipzig. On the next day, October 17th, there was no fighting. They had enough to do on both sides to restore order in their armies after the great battle and the long marches in the incessant rain. Napoleon rode, as usual, over the field. It was a ghastly sight. There was blank despair around him on every side. No one could fail to see now that it was all over with the Emperor and his power, or would be in a very short time. He spoke of a retreat by way of Lindenau in the direction of Lützen, but he was unwilling to acknowledge that the battle had been lost, as in reality it had not. However, his army was surrounded in such a way that it could hardly expect any reinforcements, while every fight weakened its strength. On the other hand the allies were so distributed that fresh reinforcements were constantly pouring in at their outer ring.

It was hard for him to have to abandon all the gains of France in these parts and see the new frontiers he had given his empire collapse, while he still had good garrisons in Dresden, Torgau, Wittenberg, Magdeburg, Glogau, Küstrin, Stettin, Dantzig, and Hamburg—altogether 170,000 men. And they were expecting every day General Reynier with 30,000 men, though these were Saxons. The Emperor hesitated all day long, and made no serious preparations for retreat. He sent a marshal's staff to Poniatowski, and had the captured General Meerfeldt summoned to his tent. They talked together for some time, and the Emperor gave him back his sword and his liberty.

Meerfeldt had been one of the Austrian negotiators before the peace of Campo Formio in 1797, when the young General Bonaparte had terrified Count Cobentzl by breaking his tea-service. He was now sent by Napoleon to treat with the Allies. He was to say that the Emperor was prepared, as he had been two months before, to make great sacrifices in the interest of peace; but Napoleon was thinking only of an armistice to get him out of his present fix. He received no answer, of course, to his proposals.

At last, when the evening was already far advanced. Napoleon began to make some preparations for the retreat; but it was to be an imposing retreat—it was to look like a manoeuvre. The Allies had been quiet on the 17th, partly for the purpose of resting and partly because they were expecting Generals Colloredo and Bennigsen from the east and Bernadotte from the north. The latter had to be urged on by Blücher and by the English envoy, and was so careful and anxious that the Allies had doubts both as to his courage and his reliability. In the course of the day the Austrians came up under Colloredo and the Russians under Bennigsen; and at last Bernadotte arrived. People could see the reinforcements from the towers of Leipzig, as they poured in continuously and completed Schwartzenberg's fines. In the evening the whole horizon round the town was marked by an uninterrupted ring of camp fires.

Count Rochechouart, a French emigrant in the service of Russia, rode with an order from the Emperor Alexander to Bernadotte, who was at Paunsdorf. He found the Crown-prince of Sweden sitting on a big white horse, dressed in a velvet mantle covered with violet and gold cords, a hat with white feathers, and above these again a high tuft of feathers in the Swedish colours. In his hand he had a marshal's staff covered with purple velvet with a golden crown at each end. At the end of the battle Bernadotte cried out: 'A few more shells for these French; I love them above everything.'

It was in these days, while the Swedish Crown-prince was firing on the French troops at Leipzig, that there was a great outburst of indignation against him in France. The *Moniteur* contained addresses every day from the provinces and the large towns in some such terms as: 'Let us disown this ungrateful Frenchman, this traitor to his country,' etc.

On October 18th Napoleon began at two in the morning to dispose his troops in a smaller circle round Leipzig. His plan was gradually and with steady fighting to withdraw his army on to the high road at Lindenau, and march westwards from there by the road at Lützen. Colonel Montfort, of the engineers, turned to Berthier and asked for orders to throw several bridges over the smaller streams and watercourses round the town. But Berthier was obtuse as usual, and would not speak to the Emperor about such details.

The struggle on the 18th centred chiefly about the village of Probstheida, to the south-east of the town, where Napoleon was with Marshal Victor's corps. But fighting went on all day also at Dölitz, where Marshals Poniatowski and Augereau resisted the Prince of Hesse-Homburg, who was wounded and replaced by General Bianchi. Marmont again was engaged with Blücher and Bernadotte to the north of the town, as on the preceding day; and finally, the Austrians were again endeavouring to rout Bertrand in the west, who was ordered to prepare the way for the march, and begin with the removal of the great transport-train and the heavier waggons.

Round Probstheida the fight went on furiously all day long. At two there was a grand attack on the village, which the French had had to evacuate twice. The Emperor considered the position so important that he led a final attack in person and drove out the Prussians. Generals Vial and Rochambeau fell in this struggle. Vial was one of the great leaders. He received his command when Kléber was wounded at Alexandria, shortly after they landed in Egypt; and it was Rochambeau who conducted the expedition in Hayti after the death of Leclerc. In the course of the afternoon Schwartzenberg ordered a heavy artillery-fire in the hope of driving the French army into Leipzig and keeping them there. In this he succeeded.

One position after another had to be evacuated, and the French were gradually driven back into the suburbs of the town. Meantime Ney, Marmont, Souham, and Reynier (who had now come up with his Saxons), were fighting with equal energy to the north-east of the town, at Paunsdorf, against Blücher and Bernadotte and the Russians, who were now advancing from the east.

It was at this point that a division of the Saxon cavalry, which was

167

sent against the Russians, turned round instead of attacking, and took up a position in the Russian line of battle. This was only the beginning of the desertions. The moment the enemy appeared at Paunsdorf the rest of the Saxon troops, with 40 guns and the Würtemberg cavalry under General Normann, went over to the Russians, and all their commander's efforts to stop them were of no avail.

This commander was the Bavarian General von Zeschau. He remained with the French like a man of honour, with five or six hundred of his soldiers. It was not enough for these troops to desert in the progress of a battle. As soon as they got some distance away, they turned their guns, and fired into the midst of Durutte's division, which had been drawn up expressly to cover the Saxons and serve as their reserve. General Delmas, another of the old stock, fell under this fire.

There were 200 cannons in action as long as the light lasted. The French understood that now the work begun in Russia was to be consummated, and they fought more heroically than ever. The Allies on their side had enough to avenge. Both Austrians and Russians had an account of many years' standing to settle. But the enthusiasm and fighting spirit were greatest of all amongst the Germans—the youth of Germany that had arisen and flown to the great battle of the peoples, to win freedom for their fatherland, and shatter the tyrants forever.

The French army had to begin its retreat at once, as they had only powder and balls for two hours more, and the next arsenals were at Erfurt and Magdeburg. During the last five days the French had fired 250,000 rounds from their guns, an enormous figure for the guns of that period. All night long trains and waggons were passing over the Lindenau bridge; they were followed by the cavalry, the Guard, and part of the infantry. The greatest obstacle to the march was found in the many watercourses, over which there were not enough bridges.

With the first streaks of dawn there began a furious struggle in the streets of Leipzig, and it became fiercer and fiercer as the light grew. It was worst in the neighbourhood of the large bridge over the Elster, leading to the high road from Frankfort to Lindenau, which was about two miles long in its elevated part. If the Emperor had given the obvious order to fire the suburbs and defend the retreat step by step, destroying everything behind him, the whole army would have had plenty of time to get over the bridge; but he would not ruin Leipzig, out of regard for the aged king. He bade a heartfelt farewell to his one true ally, the only prince for whom he had ever had a personal feeling.

In their delight at the retreat, which they had hardly expected, the Allies rushed impetuously into the suburbs of Leipzig, but the gates were obstinately held by Marmont, Reynier, Ney, Poniatowski, and Lauriston. If they had kept their position for two hours more—and there was every appearance that they could do so—the whole army could have crossed the bridge at Lindenau and reached the road to Lützen. But just then occurred one of those unfortunate episodes that could never have happened to the Emperor in his best days—to say nothing of General Bonaparte—but which abound in the Russian and Saxon campaigns. The Elster bridge was undermined and ready to be blown up. The Emperor had personally supervised the carrying out of this work, and he had left behind orders that the mine was not to be fired until the last moment, when the army was across and the enemy close at hand. He then rode across with his staff.

The crush now became frightful, and the situation was not easy to survey. There were still numbers of foreign troops amongst the French, in spite of the desertions of the previous day. Men in all sorts of uniforms were crossing the bridge in the greatest disorder and under different commands, and the noise of the guns and small arms came nearer and nearer. There ought to have been a general of engineers with his staff on the bridge, but in point of fact it was merely a high officer who had charge of the mines, and he seems to have lost his head. It is said that he thought of crossing the bridge to get more precise instructions from the Emperor. It turned out as he might have expected. Once he got into the torrent of men that swept over the bridge, no power in the world could have brought him back to his place at the mines. There was now only a non-commissioned officer with the burning fuse in his hand.

No one will be surprised that the poor man, with no explicit order or indication of the right moment, fired the mine prematurely. The fearful noise it made, rising above the thunder of the guns and all other sounds, awakened Napoleon, who had dropped off to sleep while he was dictating orders for Macdonald. Murat and Augereau rushed to him and told him that the big bridge over the Elster had been blown up. It meant that 20,000 men were cut off from him and from France, and devoted to destruction. It was almost like the tragedy on the Beresina. Many of them preferred to die rather than surrender. They threw themselves into the river, but only a few good swimmers and the officers who rode sound horses got across.

Marshal Poniatowski heard the explosion, like the others, and knew what it meant. He gave up the fight as useless, and flung himself in the river with a few other officers. But he was exhausted with wounds and with his exertions, and could not drive the animal up the opposite bank. It fell back into the river, and the prince was drowned. The brave Pole only carried for three days the marshal's staff he had so well deserved. General Dumoussier also was drowned. The tall powerful Scot, Macdonald, tore off his marshal's uniform and all his clothes, leaped into the water, and swam across the Elster. He crawled up the opposite bank, and raced across the field. He fortunately discovered a few soldiers of his own corps, and at once resumed command, stark naked at he was. He had to cover the retreat.

Napoleon left the flower of the youth of France and the core of his old invincible army on the plains of Leipzig. Seventeen generals were taken prisoners, including General Lauriston. And Napoleon lost here also the confidence of his officers and the whole of his influence in Europe, yet he kept his saddle and fought from Leipzig to Erfurt against the force, four times as great as his own, that was pursuing him. The enemy never ceased to look on him as the dreadful soldier whom it was dangerous to approach.

On October 22nd he reached Oppenheim, with French troops only about him; not a man was left of his foreign auxiliaries. And now the unreliability of his own men began to be apparent. Murat, who had returned to his old brilliance in the three days at Leipzig, had a secret conversation during the night with the Austrian, Count de Meer, who had stolen into the camp. The count promised Murat, in the name of Austria and England, that he should retain the crown of Naples if he abandoned Napoleon.

Two days later Napoleon and Murat parted. There was only one serious obstacle to the march on Mayence. The Bavarian General Wrede, who had served so long under Napoleon, opposed the French in a strong position at Hanau, with such a strong force that the Emperor seemed to be lost. But the Guard bitterly attacked them, and opened out a way for the army. General Wrede was severely wounded.

They reached Mayence at length on October 31st. It was the last time that Napoleon halted in this town with his troops, as he had so often done on the march out or on the return to Paris. He remained there six days, reorganised his army as far as possible, and selected the troops that were to defend the Rhine and the frontiers of France as the Republic had determined them. Macdonald was to hold the river at Cologne, Marmont at Mayence, and Victor at Strassburg. The Duke of Valmy, the aged Marshal Kellermann, was sent to Metz to drill the recruits. The rest of the army was distributed within these limits.

On November 9th, the Emperor was back at St. Cloud. It was a much worse return than that from Russia in the previous year, and now the time was shorter; his enemies were not far away. He worked as he had never done before, and was on his feet night and day. But Paris was now the goal of the Allied princes. They carried on a pretence of negotiations in order to deceive Napoleon, but they had a complete understanding with each other. They would have nothing more to do with him. He was to be exterminated.

Field-marshal Schwartzenberg was to advance from Switzerland, and General Bubna to follow him. Blücher was to wait for their invasion, and then cross the Rhine at Mannheim. Bernadotte was to invade Holland. There was nothing left of Napoleon behind this line; except that Rapp held Dantzig, and Davoust Hamburg.

On November 11th, Marshal St. Cyr capitulated with the 30,000 men that Napoleon had left at Dresden, on the condition that he should be free to draw off. He has been a good deal blamed for his capitulation. But Schwartzenberg, contrary to all law and precedent, refused to recognise it, and led the whole corps to Austria as prisoners of war. On November 21st Stettin had to surrender after an eight months' siege. On November 24th General Bülow entered Amsterdam, and proclaimed the House of Orange. On December 2nd Utrecht fell. On the 4th the Swedes were in Lübeck. In the end everything had been taken back from France, and it had not a single ally amongst the Powers. Even faithful Denmark was forced to sign peace with Russia.

Davoust alone stubbornly held Hamburg and kept the gates closed.

CHAPTER 8

Fall

All the experts on war are agreed that Napoleon never showed himself a greater leader than in the struggles that he conducted between Paris and the eastern frontier in the three months of 1814. That he continued to oppose his last troops to a hopelessly overwhelming force, despite all sound reason, is a proof of the inflexible self-confidence of this unique man. But that the others should cling to him after all that had happened, and spend their last energies as brave and honourable men, only shows that their whole life and thought were full of the man. There was scarcely one of them who did not understand that every day of fighting now was a loss to France and a criminal waste of human lives. But one man held them all in his hand, and they fought and fought, day after day, without hope, but so bravely, in pure devotion to their leader, that the Allies were often in serious trouble.

On January 23rd the Emperor signed a document conveying the regency to the Empress. He entrusted the protection of the capital to his brother. King Joseph. Embracing Marie Louise and the little King of Rome for the last time, he went to his headquarters at Chalons-sur-Marne. Battles now followed each other in quick succession. They were nearly always victories where the Emperor was, but there were also failures. Indeed, one was as little use as the other, because they all reduced the strength of his shrunken army.

Meantime the Allies held a congress at Châtillon, and Napoleon's envoy, the Duke of Vicenza, did his best to secure tolerable terms. But Napoleon had not learned prudence from misfortune; after a victory he would put up his claims so high that they only laughed at him. When he did badly, he was for continuing the struggle. It was impossible for him to acknowledge defeat. There was a fight at Brienne on

172

January 29th, at La Rothière on February 2nd, and at Champaubert on the 10th. On February 17th Napoleon had instructed Marshal Victor to occupy the village of Montereau near Fontainebleau. But the Marshal did not carry out the order with his customary precision, and when he arrived there, on February 18th, the opportunity was gone, and the Würtembergers were in occupation.

Napoleon was beside himself. He took away the Marshal's command, and gave it to Girard, swearing that he would dismiss Victor from the army. The Marshal, who had lost his son-in-law in the battle, replied with tears in his eyes that he would not leave the army. He would rather take a musket and fight in the ranks. The Emperor's anger died away at once. He gave the Duke the command over a part of the Guard, and invited him to his table. General Gouyot, who had survived Vandamme's defeat at Kulm, was also scolded by the Emperor, because his men had lost two guns. Napoleon angrily flung his hat on the ground, and ordered General Exelmans to take over the command. A little later, however, when the fight over Montereau developed into a pitched battle, he gave General Gouyot the command over the four squadrons that formed his bodyguard.

It was at Montereau that Napoleon, in the thick of the fire, said to the gunners who begged him to go away: 'Be quiet. The ball is not made yet that will hit me.' In the end the Würtembergers suffered a decisive defeat, as they deserved. General Chateau, Victor's son-in-law, was fatally wounded owing to an accident in the blowing up of a bridge, and General Pajol had another mishap; he fell under his horse.

On the same day, February 18th, Macdonald and Oudinot drove Generals Wrede and Wittgenstein before them at such an extraordinary pace that the French marshals were able to sit at the tables prepared for their opponents. They found the hot dishes still smoking and the table decorated with laurel. This victory at Montereau inspirited Napoleon to such an extent that when Adjutant Rumigny came for the fourth time with dispatches from the Congress at Châtillon, he merely told him to take his compliments to the Bourbons.

The Allied princes were in full retreat for a moment after the Battle of Montereau, and Paris again received a gift of captured flags. But the net was drawn close once more. Blücher, especially, dragged along the Austrians and Russians, and inexorably sought his revenge for Jena and Auerstädt. The town of Soissons, an extremely important point in the fight over the retreat, was shamelessly surrendered by a French general of the name of Moreau. Marshal Augereau, always worthless, now completely deserted Napoleon's interests, and kept his army corps in idleness at Lyons. Even Napoleon's faithful friend Savary, Duke of Rovigo, lost courage. Talleyrand had his treacherous plans ready, and waited quietly for the inevitable end.

On March 5th there was a vigorous fight at Craonne. Ney and Victor with the infantry. Grouchy and Nansouty with the cavalry, all more or less wounded, and General Belliard, who had succeeded Murat in the command of the cavalry, drove the enemy out of Craonne, with the help of Drouot's guns. But it was a sombre victory. Everybody about Napoleon knew that the end was near. Soldiers and statesmen alike looked to Châtillon, where, they all felt, the fate of France and their own fate were to be decided.

Amongst the Allies, however, there was a feverish anxiety to reach Paris. The Emperor Francis, King Frederic William, and the Tsar Alexander, in whose capitals Napoleon had so often resided, wanted to enjoy their revenge. Many wanted to see once more the city in which they had spent a part of their gay youth at one of the finest courts in Europe. But the fortune of war swung to and fro. They were seized with a sudden panic when the dreadful man once came right upon them. The *Tsar* said that half his hair had turned white in one night.

On March 20th, in the course of a battle at Arcis, the Emperor made his horse step over a shell that had just fallen. Exelmans wanted to warn him, but Sébastiani prevented him.

'Don't you see that he is doing it on purpose,' he said. 'He wants to make an end of it.' But when the shower of soil and stones had settled down, the Emperor was sitting unhurt on his horse.

After a masterly retreat from Arcis, the Emperor did not think that the Allies would dare to slip past him toward Paris. This time, however, they plucked up courage, and marched after Marmont and Mortier, who were attacked by an overwhelming force at Fère-Champenoise. Generals Pacthod and Amey had a disproportionately large number of transport waggons in their divisions, which they were to protect. This long train of waggons led the Allied generals greatly to overrate the strength of the enemy, and, anxious as they always were, they resolved to attack in full strength.

The whole of the combined cavalry was therefore sent into action, and so suddenly that the princes with their general staffs had not time to get out of the way. They had to put their horses to the gallop, and join in the onslaught or else be ridden down. In two minutes the Emperor Alexander and the King of Prussia were in the midst of the French columns, surrounded on all sides by the swarm of 16,000 horse—Russians, Prussians and Austrians, dragoons, *uhlans*, hussars and *Cossacks*.

'Never in my life,' says Count Rochechouart, 'shall I see such a medley again. I was hardly able to tell what was going on, and in a moment it was all passed.' The small French army that was routed at Fère-Champenoise consisted mainly of young recruits, still wearing their blouses and peasant's dress. Generals Pacthod, Amey, Jamin, and Thevenot were taken prisoners.

On March 28th, the Emperor learned at St. Didier that the Allies were before Paris. He mounted his horse and set off at full gallop. He still believed he could defend Paris; certainly he did not think for a moment of surrendering or losing courage. The remains of the French armies concentrated on Paris, the Allies following closely in their steps. They fought many a good battle, and kept the enemy off, and on March 29th, they found themselves under Montmartre and the outer walls. The last battle was round Paris, and Marshals Mortier and Marmont carried the desperate struggle to its conclusion on March 29th and 30th. They had only 30,000 men, with the reinforcements they found at Paris. Neither King Joseph nor the Minister of War, Clarke, had done anything for the defence of the city, though they had had plenty of time and opportunity to do so. The Minister had even hesitated to distribute 20,000 new weapons that were in the arsenal. He was preparing to desert.

At twelve o'clock on March 29th one could see the foreign troops from the hill of Montmartre, and King Joseph sent orders to the marshals to surrender Paris. Marmont, who received the order, put it in his pocket. There had been a council at the Tuileries. The dignitaries of the Empire, the ministers, King Joseph, and the Empress Marie Louise, were all agreed that the Regent ought to leave Paris with the young heir to the throne. Talleyrand alone held to the last that the Empress ought to remain in the capital and continue the regency which the Emperor had settled on her with full powers. He had long made his own plans as to the Allies and the Bourbons, and it would have been a triumph for him if he had been able to present at once to the Emperor Francis his daughter and the young prince. The others, however, had not provided for themselves so prudently, and they accompanied the Empress to Blois.

Talleyrand went home and packed up. But he took so much time to do it that, when he at last reached the barrier in the evening in his carriage, the guards prevented him from leaving the city. He was taken back to his palace under a sort of arrest. His rooms became the centre for all that was left of Paris. The *Tsar* took up his residence in the Hotel Talleyrand. The old spider sat in the middle of his fine, strong web, and held all its threads,

Marmont had said nothing to Mortier about King Joseph's order, which he kept in his pocket, but he concluded an armistice, and Mortier joined him. After an heroic defence, the marshals withdrew to Fontainebleau, and left Paris open to the enemy. Compans, Arrighi, Ricard, Christiani, Curial and Lagrange were the last generals to lead divisions against the whole of armed Europe.

The Emperor had sent on General Dejean to announce that he was coming to Paris. He had marched forty-five miles that day with the Guard, and arrived at Troyes. On the morning of March 3rd he was again in the saddle, and by ten in the evening he was close to the city. He was changing horses on the road for the last time when General Belliard told him that Paris had capitulated, and he himself was engaged in removing the cavalry from the capital.

The Emperor listened to him in silence.

'Well,' he said at last, 'we must get on to Paris.'

'But, sire, there are no troops in Paris.'

'That doesn't matter. I shall find the National Guard. My army will concentrate tomorrow. Follow me with the whole of your cavalry.'

'Your Majesty,' Belliard answered, 'will only succeed in being taken prisoner and witnessing the looting of the city. It is surrounded by 130,000 men. In order to get away from it, I have myself had to engage not to return to it.'

'Six hours too late and everything lost!' cried the Emperor. He went inside, and sat in a small chair in the little post-house on the road, and at last fell into a deep sleep.

During the advance of the Allies into France the Crown-Prince of Sweden had led the army corps in the extreme north. The princes had not much confidence in him, and preferred to keep him at a distance. He himself felt all along how weak his position was. While he was pushing westwards through the north of Germany, he annexed all the estates that had been given by Napoleon to his former comrades in arms. But he was still so unsafe, and so used to keeping every road open, that he continued to intrigue on all sides, and was ready to betray anybody or anything to retain his kingly dignity. When he had to invade Flanders, which was defended by his old comrade.

General Maison, he gave a written promise to disarm the Prussians under him and go over to the French with his Swedish troops, if the Emperor Napoleon would give him a written guarantee of his royal dignity in Sweden or some other kingdom. Napoleon agreed, but on condition that King Joseph signed the declaration, and the negotiations fell through. However, Napoleon had taken Bernadotte's letter from General Maison, and he afterwards put it in the hands of the Emperor Alexander. That was the source of the ill-feeling against the Crown Prince and later King of Sweden, and the conspicuous coldness of the other European courts to the house of Bernadotte. Still, there were plenty of other reasons.

Bernadotte also tried to enter into correspondence with Carnot, but the honourable soldier, then holding Antwerp, said to the intermediary: 'I was a friend of the French General Bernadotte, but I am no friend of the foreign prince who bears arms against his country.' But the worst of all is, perhaps, the proclamation that the Crown Prince of Sweden sent over the French frontier, when the Allied armies were approaching. In this it is threatened, in the name of a French hero who had once fought for the honour of France, that the whole population will be sacrificed to the vengeance of the Cossacks if there is any resistance.

On April 1st Napoleon was still thinking of marching on Paris. He rode from Fontainebleau to Essonne and inspected Marmont's corps, which was quartered there, and consisted of fine, effective troops. He spoke to Marmont for the last time.

On April 2nd he mustered his own Guard in the large courtyard in front of the palace of Fontainebleau, as cool and quiet as ever. The Duke of Vicenza came with bad news from Paris, yet the Emperor continued to talk of fresh battles. In reality he now had, if he collected all the divisions that were faithful to him, the following troops: Soult and Suchet in Spain, General Grenier in Italy, and all the fortresses in France and Italy. These were forces enough for a frightful civil war, and it might have ended in putting him on the throne once more. He collected his Guard and made them swear that the enemy should be driven out of Paris. In the course of the night, in fact, they marched some distance toward the capital.

April 3rd was the day of his fall. The troops at Yvonne, under Marshals Oudinot and Macdonald, declared that in the circumstances they would refuse to advance on Paris. Macdonald offered to take the news to the Emperor, and rode to Fontainebleau. Meantime, the highest officers about Napoleon held a deliberation, and, with the Prince of Moskwa at their head, they went to the Emperor's room and asked him to abdicate. At the same time Marmont's unfortunate treachery was taking place at another spot.

The following morning his dispirited officers once more assembled in Napoleon's room. There were Berthier, Caulaincourt, Moncey, Maret, Lefebvre and Ney. The Emperor tried several times to draw up a deed of abdication, and in the meantime Marshal Macdonald came with his news. The Emperor then turned to the circle of officers, and asked them if they would support his son. They all answered in the affirmative, Macdonald doing so with particular warmth. He selected Caulaincourt, Ney and Marmont to convey his abdication and treat for him with the Allied princes at Paris. But shortly afterwards he replaced Marmont with Macdonald, although at that time he could know nothing of Marmont's defection.

Napoleon's first abdication ran thus:

As the Allied Powers have announced in their proclamation that the Emperor Napoleon is the sole obstacle to the re-establishment of peace in Europe, the Emperor Napoleon—true to the oath he has taken—declares himself ready to give up the throne, France, and even life, for the good of his country, without any prejudice, however, to the rights of his son, the regency of the Empress, or the laws of the Empire.

The Duke of Vicenza and the two marshals were dispatched with this document. But at the last moment Napoleon said half-aside to Macdonald: 'Come, and let us attack them tomorrow. We shall beat them!' The marshal pretended not to hear him.

Marmont was born in 1774, and died in 1852. He lived longest of all Napoleon's marshals. He had been with General Bonaparte from Toulon onwards. He had won distinction everywhere—in Italy, Malta, Egypt, at the crossing of the Alps in 1799, at Marengo, and in Dalmatia, where he took Ragusa, from which he had his ducal title. He came to Wagram the day before the battle, and beat the Austrians on his own account at Znaim. He was then made marshal and governor of Illyria, and Napoleon honoured and rewarded him above all the others. If there could be any question at all of favourites with Napoleon, it would certainly be Junot and Marmont.

But while Napoleon showed his favouring of Junot by always—

or at least for a long time—being indulgent to him, his relation to Marmont was very different. He appreciated the great military- gifts of the young officer, and regarded them with gratification. Marmont matured under the Emperor's own eyes and leadership more than any of the others. Hence we can understand that the Emperor had a certain tenderness for him.

This did not prevent him from being just as hard and cold towards Marmont in the service as toward any of the others. After the battle of Montebello, Bonaparte sent his brother Joseph to offer Marmont the hand of Pauline. When the family began to rise, she was always offered when any man was to be honoured. But it seems that several declined her, and at all events Marmont did so. When Napoleon was at a safe distance, he married a wealthy lady at Paris, Mlle. Peregeaux. His wife was much attached to him at first, but she was foolish and perverse. The long separations, which were fatal to so many marriages at that time, led her to be unfaithful, and she eventually gave him a very unhappy time. When Marmont had to go to Portugal in 1810 to relieve Masséna, the Emperor said to him:

When the Spanish Peninsula is taken it will be divided into five kingdoms, each with a viceroy at its head. They will have courts and the honours of royalty. One of these kingdoms is for you, so go and take it.

When Napoleon was speaking in 1813 of the foreign officers who went over to the enemy in the field with their troops in the Saxon campaign, he drew a distinction between a conscientious man and a man of honour, and said, turning to Marmont:

If, for instance, the enemy had taken France and were in possession of the heights of Montmartre, and you thought—perhaps rightly—that the good of the country demanded that you should abandon me, you might be a good Frenchman, and a brave and conscientious man, if you did it, but you would not be a man of honour.

Marshal Marmont, who relates this himself in his memoirs, adds quite coolly: 'I was destined to recall these words afterwards at Essonne.' He had been one of the best fighters in the Saxon campaign— at Lützen, Bautzen, Wurschen, Dresden and Leipzig—and at the very end he had defended Paris heroically with Mortier. Then he suddenly changed, and became one of the most ungrateful to Napoleon. While his corps was marching round the city from Montmartre to Essonne, which was on the way to Fontainebleau, Marmont rode to his palace in Paris. Covered with blood and dirt as he was after several days fighting, he would very well need a wash and the barber, and a little rest. But he was at once visited by envoys from Talleyrand, who was working assiduously for the overthrow of Napoleon, and who would like to be able to offer the Allies a marshal like Marmont, commanding an army corps in the immediate vicinity of Paris.

Talleyrand had chosen Bourienne, the former private secretary of Napoleon, and an intimate friend of Marmont's, as his agent. Marmont refused all appeals, declaring that he would die by the side of his Emperor. In this mood he left Paris and rejoined his corps at Essonne. But on the following day, April 3rd, the secessionists sent messenger after messenger to him, and at last he began to move, and entered into negotiations with Prince Schwartzenberg's agents. It was agreed that his corps should march through the lines of the Allies.

As Caulaincourt and the two marshals passed by Essonne on their way to Paris with Napoleon's abdication, Marmont confessed what he had done to his three old comrades, and seemed to be in great perplexity. He had brought his generals together early that morning (April 4th), and found them nearly all willing to join in his defection. But now that he met the Emperor's envoys he was ashamed, and asked that he might be allowed to accompany them to Paris; he hid himself in the carriage. He left word to his officers to do nothing until they had explicit orders from him.

Meantime, Napoleon, who had no suspicion of what was going on, sent a messenger to Essonne asking Marmont to come to Fontainebleau, as he wished to speak to him. Marmont's generals took this as an indication that they had been betrayed. They became anxious, and, without waiting for further orders, they marched during the night through the lines of the Allies, which were opened to them as had been agreed. General Souham led them. He had never been a friend of Napoleon; but the brave Compans and his splendid division were also in the march. Colonel Fabrier rode with all speed to Paris to inform Marmont, and he promised to come in an hour; but before the hour was up another officer came from Essonne to say that all the rest of Marmont's corps was on the march.

The Poles alone remained faithful to the Emperor. They rode to Versailles under General Ordener, to join the regiments at Rambouillet that had not gone over to the enemy. But Marmont had now fallen so far into the power of the tempters that he galloped to Versailles and forced his men to leave General Ordener and the Emperor's party and go over to the Allies.

Marmont's defection is not merely noteworthy for the ingratitude it evinces; ingratitude is not so rare. But it shows how insecure the men felt themselves who accompanied Napoleon in his adventurous rise. As soon as the old society appeared, in the old forms and names and places, the life of the last twenty years melted away like a dream; like children awakening from a dream, men grasped the familiar hand that was stretched out to them.

Meantime, the three envoys were admitted to the King of Prussia, who was rude, and to the Tsar Alexander, who was charming and hollow. But while they were still dallying over the abdication, a messenger came with the news of the defection of Marmont's whole corps. As the news was communicated in a loud whisper to the *Tsar*, who was rather deaf, he repeated: '*Totus corpus!*' and all who were in the room knew that it was Marmont's corps. They must have spoken elegant Latin in Russian imperial circles. The intermediaries then received the abdication back again with the assurance that it could not be entertained unless it included Napoleon's family and descendants.

For two days Napoleon fought against the determination. He kept to his room, and spoke alternately of retiring to Elba and of marching to destroy the Allies and free Paris. At last, on April 5th, he entirely renounced the throne of France and Italy for himself and his descendants. A treaty was drawn up by the Allies in this sense on the 11th, and brought to Napoleon by Caulaincourt, Schuvaloff and Macdonald. Napoleon would not sign it that day (the 12th). Those about Napoleon at Fontainebleau now began to realize what was passing.

The soldiers would have remained faithful to their great leader if they had been left to themselves, but the officers began to look about for a means of saving themselves and their property in case the wreck sank; and the more they had, the more anxious they became. Marshal Berthier, Prince of Wagram and of Neuchatel, loaded with riches, honours, glory, and distinctions of all sorts—and all from the same hand—came to the Emperor's room and asked permission for a short run to Paris. He obtained it, bowed, and departed. As the door closed behind him, the Emperor said quietly and coldly: 'He will not come back.' He was quite right. Berthier went to Paris to submit, and to offer his services to the provisional government.

On April 12th Napoleon's appearance was such that all those about him were greatly concerned. The official in charge of his cabinet, Turenne, unloaded the pistols in his bedroom. During the night Napoleon awakened his servant and told him to make a fire. He heard the Emperor write letters and tear them up again. At last he took a small black pouch out of a secret cavity in his dressing-case, emptied it into a glass of water, and went to bed! We do not know for certain whether he then took a strong poison that he had had in Russia—in a signet, I believe; at all events this and the pouch were empty the next morning. But he did not die; either he was too strong, or the poison was too old. He awakened his Egyptian servant Ivan, who came and assisted him. Ivan then went into the stall, saddled a horse and rode off, and never came back again.

The Emperor was up at eleven the next morning, and summoned Marshal Macdonald. It was in these days of trouble that Napoleon first learned to appreciate the solid qualities and fine character of this man. He had spent a bad night; his face was pale and drawn, like that of a corpse, and his eyes sunk back deep in their sockets. But he mastered himself, and signed the treatise in his usual hand. He then thanked Macdonald in fine, manly words, and regretted that he had only just learned to appreciate him. He sent the marshal, as a memento, Murad Bey's splendid Turkish sabre, which he had himself taken in the Battle of Tabor,

By the treaty the Emperor, Empress, and imperial family retained their rank and title. Elba was to be an independent kingdom with a revenue of two millions—one million being for the Empress, Marie Louise. She also received Parma, Piacenza, and Guastalla, the Italian duchies that Napoleon's sisters had held. A million was settled on Josephine, and many other settlements were made on Napoleon's friends and the army; but it is sad to read of these things, as no one received the money that was promised. On April 10th the court that Marie Louise kept at Blois was dispersed, and she and her son were sent to Vienna. All the Bonapartes fled to Switzerland.

At last, on April 20th, Napoleon had to part from the army, and from the Guard. They were drawn up in the great courtyard at Fontainebleau, and he came down the steps and walked slowly through the ranks. There were still faces he had seen at Arcole, Aboukir, Marengo, Austerlitz, Jena, Friedland, Somo-Sierra, Wagram and Moscow. The whole brilliant history of his career was unfolded about him. With some difficulty he spoke his short and admirable speech:

> I have to bid you farewell, soldiers. We have been together for
> twenty years, and I am proud of you. I have always seen you on

the path of honour. Europe has turned against me, and some of my generals have been untrue to their duty and their country. France itself would have a new future. I might have fought a civil war with you and the other brave men who have been loyal to me; but France would have suffered. Be true to your new king, listen to your new chiefs. Let our dear country never lack your arms. Bemoan not my fate. I shall be happy if I hear that you are. I might have chosen death. If I have chosen life, it is to enhance your great fame. I will write of the great deeds we have done together. I cannot embrace all of you, but I will embrace your general. Come, General Pelet, and let me press you to my breast. Then hand me the eagle, and let me kiss it. May that kiss resound in the days to come. Farewell, my children. My good wishes will ever follow you. Bear me in your memories.

It is not surprising that the hardened soldiers and the man of marble wept as they stood there to take farewell in the old courtyard that had so often rung with their band and their '*Vive l'Empereur*.'

During the journey through France to the south there was danger more than once of the excited people laying hands on the fallen Emperor. But on May 3rd he reached Porto Ferrajo, on the island of Elba, in an English frigate. His suite consisted of Generals Bertrand, Drouot and Cambronne, and 400 men of the Guard. His mother and Pauline afterwards joined him. His faithful lover, Countess Walewska, was also in Elba. His servants, too, were there, with the exception of his chamber-servant Constant, who had been with him many years; an unfortunate misunderstanding kept him away.

Constant tells the story himself as follows. On one of the last days at Fontainebleau the Emperor gave him a draft for 100,000 *francs*, and told him to convert it into gold and hide it. He did so, and hid the gold in his garden in the belief that the money was a parting gift from the Emperor; and in view of the freedom with which money circulated about Napoleon the idea was not very improbable. Hence, when Constant put his accounts before General Bertrand on the last day and handed over all monies belonging to the Emperor that he had, he made no mention of the 100,000 *francs*. Napoleon told Bertrand that there were 100,000 *francs* short in Constant's accounts, and that he did not remember having made him a present of the sum.

Pained that the Emperor had put him in a questionable light to Bertrand, Constant dug up the money, and handed it over; but in his agitation he also begged General Bertrand to tell the Emperor that he had left his service and was not going to Elba.

It is difficult to say what was passing in Napoleon's mind at the time. It is unlike him to be unjust or inconsiderate to his servants. They all loved him, and remained with him. He afterwards made some attempt at reconciliation, but Constant remained obdurate.

CHAPTER 9

Encore

It was clear that the fall of Napoleon was equivalent to the rein-statement of the legitimate royal house. Hence, although the Allies came into Paris as enemies and conquerors, there was a certain air of festivity about their entry. In spite of the Revolution and Napoleon there were still many who were loyal to the old house; and ladies, old and young, came out with flowers, and court was paid to the foreign princes, the *Tsar* especially being honoured in certain circles at Paris. He was not unwilling to receive their homage, though his wild sol-diers were doing more than all the other foreign troops to ravage Paris and the north of France.

Meantime, the foreign princes had to return to their countries and restore order everywhere. Some of them pondered with alarm on all they had endured in the way of songs and speeches during the so-called 'wars of freedom.' It was quite time to put a stop to all this. Moreover, the boundary-stones of Europe had to be shifted back to their old positions. They were all mixed up after the doings of this ter-rible man. A great congress was fixed for June 20th at Vienna.

As soon as all danger was over the Bourbons swarmed in with their hungry flocks of emigrants, stout King Louis XVIII at their head. The times were changed at a stroke. The Tuileries was filled with new faces, the faces of old families that had not been seen there for twenty or thirty years. Instead of the noisy officers with swords and spurs echo-ing through the rooms, one now saw discreet, bewigged courtiers in ancient dress, or young dandies who had had nothing to do with the banishment.

Instead of the Emperor walking into the rooms with short, firm step, with close silk hose and shoes, or glittering cavalry boots with a slight jingle of spurs, one now saw the adipose Bourbon moving ponderously about with huge purple velvet slippers on his gouty feet.

If we would understand the attitude in 1814 of the men who had worked with Napoleon, we must—knowing what happened afterwards—forget the Hundred Days, and imagine that the first return of the Bourbons was the definitive close of Napoleon's career. On this supposition it seemed quite natural to numbers of officers to remain in their positions and take the oath to the new head of the State. One was in the service of France just as before, and was ready to fight its enemies under the generals appointed by the government In this way Marshals Macdonald, Oudinot and Lefebvre could retain their commands under the King without any scruple. So also Victor, St. Cyr, Kellermann, Maison and Lauriston, and a large number of officers, went over to the Bourbons while Napoleon was in Elba.

But there were some who had been in such close personal touch with Napoleon that they found it impossible to serve under another prince. Amongst these were the Viceroy Eugene, Napoleon's cousin Arrighi, and Sébastiani, Generals Mouton, Savary, Cambronne, Grouchy, and many others. The Bourbons were ready to receive the distinguished men, especially Napoleon's less loyal friends. They needed them for several reasons. But however eager they were to attach a man who had won European fame, they were just as merciless to the lower officers and the common soldiers.

Wherever they found it possible to disturb and displace what had been respected in France for the last twenty years, they set to work with the petty malice that was characteristic of the family. The army was flooded with elderly generals who knew nothing, and did not want to know anything, about its new organization, its glory, and its traditions. The young nobles had grown up abroad in a disdainful contempt of Napoleon, his army, and everything he did.

They at once chose as Minister of War the man who had the worst reputation in the army—General Dupont, who had capitulated at Baylen. An immense number of subordinate officers were dismissed, and were replaced by lackeys and other useless people. Three thousand veterans of the republican and imperial wars were driven out of the Hôtel des Invalides, where they had found refuge, and were forced to wander over the country as crippled mendicants. Their place was occupied by old royal servants from La Vendée, who had opposed the Revolution and Napoleon as long as possible.

In the course of a few months a deep, silent anger spread amongst the people. Though the infatuated Bourbons and their men had no suspicion of it, there was a temper throughout the whole of France that was extremely dangerous, seeing that the man who had led them a short time before to unexampled power and glory was still alive and not far away. The Emperor was well aware of all this. He knew the country so well that he could read between the lines of the journals he received and see the awful blunders of King Louis; how not only the army, but the whole people, just as in the revolutionary times, was enraged at the stupid and unfair treatment.

It is true that he had few visitors in Elba. The English saw to that. But King Joachim had veered round once more and drawn close to Napoleon. He had from Italy the best opportunity of communicating with Elba, and when he sent word in the beginning of 1815 that the Vienna Congress was disposed to follow Talleyrand's advice and send him to St. Helena, the Emperor's resolution was made. Ammunition was secretly brought from Naples, a few arms from Algiers, and a few small boats from Genoa, Suddenly, at a pre-arranged signal, his men embarked at Porto Ferrajo at eight o'clock in the evening on February 26th, 1815. There were 1,000 men altogether: the 400 grenadiers went with the Emperor on board a small brig with twenty-six guns. The others were distributed amongst the smaller boats.

In order to divert attention the Emperor gave a feast that evening, at which his mother and sister did the honours. He then slipped on board in the darkness, and sailed with six other small craft for France. He had the same wonderful luck that he always had on the Mediterranean. He reached a French harbour with his flotilla on March 1st, without being discovered by the English. The only incident during the voyage was that he was hailed by a French frigate, and asked how the Emperor was doing at Elba. Napoleon himself replied that the Emperor was doing very well. Otherwise the whole time was taken up with working, dictating and writing proclamations.

A modern author has pointed out that the man who came from Elba was no longer the General Bonaparte who leaped to land after the return from Egypt. The little officer of 1799, thin, inflexible in will, had become the stout head of a state, irresolute and sensuous. Everything depends on the bodily frame. It is the thin men who succeed, and to whom the future belongs. Those who become stout have to struggle against irresoluteness, or, rather, their qualities change and degenerate. Nevertheless, in stout men the original characters continue to predominate. The thinker remains a thinker; the man of action retains his power to bend and lead men. But the salient features are modified in both types of men. The thinker becomes coarse-grained and cynical; the man of energy becomes egoistic.

In the case of Napoleon there were other reasons that contributed to his change and downfall. He was accustomed to see the most scandalous advances on the part of all the women he came in contact with. The imprudent Pauline wrote from Elba letters that were stolen and read by others. In letters to two colonels who were intimate friends of hers she told one that he must not come because Napoleon was so jealous, and the other to come as quickly as possible because she had so much time left.

But that he was by no means so greatly altered as to entertain anything strange or new, or that he had lost anything of himself, was soon to be made quite clear. Apart from the renewal of trouble and the fresh outrages that his return brought upon France, the deed itself is one of the most splendid that any man ever achieved. The man who had barely escaped being torn to pieces by his embittered people ten months before, now returned to the very same spots, and no sooner did the armies that were sent against him catch sight of his grey coat but they broke out into wild cries of 'Long live the Emperor!' No sooner did they hear his voice but they faced about, and were ready to follow him to death once more.

It began at Grenoble. The road was blocked, and the king's soldiers were ready to fire on Napoleon and his little troop. He walked on foot up to his grenadiers, drew aside his old military coat, and said quietly:

'Is there any one here who will shoot his Emperor?'

Their whole attitude changed at once. The ranks broke out into a unanimous cry of 'Long live the Emperor!' A single shot from either side would have given the whole thing a different turn. The brave Colonel Labedoyère led the seventh regiment over to him. He entered the fortress of Grenoble, the townsmen themselves tearing down the gates. The rejoicing was indescribable. In one moment the Emperor had become again the idol of the French army.

When it was known in Paris—news did not travel fast a hundred years ago—a royal resolution appeared in the *Moniteur*, declaring General Bonaparte an outlaw. The journal announced at the same time that the venture was a failure, and that Bonaparte was hiding in the mountains, without any supporters, from the vengeance of the people. The king's nephew, the Duke of Angoulême, was waiting to receive the Emperor at Lyons, together with Marshals Masséna and Macdonald and Generals Marchand and Duvernet. The troops deserted. The

Duke and Macdonald had to fly from the town, and it received the Emperor as Grenoble had done. He had spoken words at Grenoble that awakened the highest hopes: 'From this time forward I shall not be the despot of France, but its best citizen.' But before he left Lyons the despot appeared in him, even worse than ever. He published a decree dissolving the Chambers and ordering a fresh extraordinary assembly of the elective colleges of the kingdom. They were to revise the constitution, and crown the Empress and the King of Rome.

But at the same time he published another decree, in which a number of deserters were impeached and their property confiscated. Amongst these were Talleyrand, Marmont and Bourienne. Augereau's name was struck off the list at the request of the generals. Even General Bertrand and Maret hesitated to sign these decrees. 'I won't sign,' said Bertrand. 'This is not what the Emperor promised.' And when the Emperor asked his companion at a banquet at Lyons, Mme. Duchatel, if her husband, who had control of the State property, had confiscated Talleyrand's property yet, she drily answered: 'There is no hurry. Your Majesty.' The Emperor turned away, and changed the subject.

The unfortunate Marshal Ney, whose head was very much out of proportion to his courage, had promised Louis XVIII that he would bring him Napoleon in an iron cage. But when he approached his old master, he went over to him. Napoleon received him well and embraced him. However, they both felt that this iron cage had come between them. The relations between them never became like what they had been, and Ney was no longer the same man.

At four o'clock in the morning on March 20th Napoleon rode once more into the courtyard at Fontainebleau, where he had parted from his Guard a year before. He now had his whole army back again. That night Louis XVIII left the palace of his fathers, surrounded by a nervous group of people anxious to get away from Paris. The Vienna Congress, where dissension had begun to set in, now joined in a strong alliance against the common enemies.

On the evening of March 20th the Emperor entered Paris. In front of the Tuileries he was seized by the crowd, which could contain itself no longer. They lifted him out of the carriage, and carried him up the steps into the brightly lit rooms, where he found his old ministers and marshals, and the officers, servants and ladies of the Court. All the Bonapartes were there, even Lucien. An improvised guard, consisting of generals alone, kept watch in his antechambers, and the rejoicing was universal. The next morning it was announced in the *Moniteur*: 'His

Majesty the Emperor returned to Fontainebleau last night.'

With incredible swiftness Paris and the greater part of the country accepted the situation. Once more, for a hundred days, France became an empire fighting the whole of Europe. Many of his faithful supporters were ready to take up at once the positions they had formerly filled, so that a great deal of the vast administration went on almost without interruption. The Postmaster-General, Lavalette, whom the King had dismissed, returned to his bureau at the first news of Napoleon's landing. But there were hard times for a good many. Thousands of officers had sworn fidelity to King Louis, and now the Emperor was there, inviting them to return. It was difficult to resist, and difficult to know how the whole thing would end. His return and the way in which the country received him seemed to prove that the future was with him once more.

When they had recovered somewhat from their astonishment the people looked to Napoleon to make good the promise he had made repeatedly since he landed, of giving France a free constitution and ruling in constitutional form. In spite of the advice and resistance of all his old friends and servants, the Emperor published a supplementary Act to the imperial constitution, maintaining the absolutism of former days. France at once understood that Napoleon had come back unchanged, without any appreciation of the popular demand for freedom such as one might have expected from so great a man after such trials.

All the friends of legal conditions under a free constitution, who had gladly hailed him as the dictator who would rid the land of the stupid and malicious regimentalism of the Bourbons, were bitterly disappointed, and withdrew in despondency. From this day forward there was nothing to face the fresh humiliation that Europe was preparing to inflict on France except an army under the control of one man, and a nation that silently and despondently waited for the inevitable.

The Emperor named 118 new members of the House of Peers. This time he did not choose his men chiefly from the old nobility, for whom he had formerly a weakness. There were five or six who refused the honour. To the Emperor's distress, Macdonald was one of these. Afterwards all the emigrants ran about boasting that they had refused to accept the peerage from Napoleon.

He then held the great assembly that he had projected. It was called the Champ de Mai, and was to recall the ceremonious oath that Louis XVI had sworn in 1790 on the same spot. An immense altar was erected in the Champ de Mars. Napoleon appeared in a fantastic imperial garb with huge feathers in his hat that covered the stout little man. The ceremony, which he had arranged himself, was very pompous. Oaths and promises were made in flamboyant language, and the army was jubilant. Otherwise, however, the general attitude was tame, and nothing came of it. This was on the 1st of June.

At last war broke out, and Napoleon left Paris in the night between June 11th and 12th. The campaign was short, and was only conducted in the north, on the Belgian frontier, against the English under Wellington and the Prussians under Blücher. Murat was never restored to his real self, though he had returned to Napoleon's side. On May 3rd he attacked the Austrians prematurely, and against Napoleon's orders, at Tolentino, and his Neapolitans were badly beaten. He threw himself time after time on the enemy, but proved to be still invulnerable. After aimlessly wandering about he was taken prisoner and shot.

The great names now made their last appearance in the last army, though many of the Emperor's best generals were missing. Davoust had met Napoleon at Paris and accepted the position of Minister of War. Marshal Soult came from Spain, and took a command, as did also Generals Clausel, Decaen and Labord. A comparatively large number of officers came from Spain, where the troops had not shared the Russian and Saxon campaigns and Napoleon's defeat. With them were Ney, Exelmans, Gerard, Girard, Milhaud, Morand, Friant, Lefebvre-Desnouettes, Pajol and Vandamme. General Grouchy had been made a marshal.

Napoleon's plan was that Marshal Ney with the left wing should— as soon as possible— take the position of Quatre-Bras in the direction of Brussels, where Wellington had his headquarters. At the same time Marshal Grouchy was to occupy the village of Fleurus, and thus Wellington and Blücher would be kept apart. The plan was good, and it looked as if all was going to be done according to their calculations. On the evening of June 14th there was perfect confidence and quietness at Brussels, Charleroi and Namur. No one had any suspicion of the Emperor's plan, and the army began to march. But on the evening of June 16th a French general deserted, and went over with two colonels to the Prussians, and in this way Napoleon's plan was made known to Blücher.

The traitor was General Bourmont. He was a brave officer, and had fought with unflinching courage down to the Battle of Montereau in 1814, at which he was wounded. He was one of the officers that Na-

191

poleon did not particularly trust, but Ney and Girard had so warmly recommended him that he received a command. There were not now so many officers to choose from, and Napoleon no longer acted on his own ideas. The same General Bourmont who deserted from Napoleon the night before the battle gained honours and dignities under the Bourbons, and was at length made a marshal after the war in Algiers in 1830.

It was even worse for Napoleon that Ney by no means led his corps as he used to do. Instead of advancing rapidly on Frasnes with the whole of the second corps, which would have enabled the first corps to take up a position at Gosselies, and from there easily occupy Quatre-Bras, which was not far from Frasnes, the Marshal sent only a small division on Frasnes, and as a result the left wing remained too far behind.

On June 16th the Emperor beat Blücher in a pitched battle at Ligny. Here General Girard, one of the heroes of Lützen, met his fate. Both before and during the battle the Emperor sent message after message to tell Marshal Ney to march as quickly as possible eastwards from Quatre Bras, and drive the Prussians into the arms of Grouchy who was at Sombreuf. In this way Blücher's army would have been completely surrounded. 'The fate of France is in your hand,' the Emperor said to Ney. 'The war can be decided within three hours.'

Now, however, General Drouot, Count of Erlon—not the artillery-general Drouot—made a false move, in consequence of a misunderstanding, and the opportunity of surrounding the Prussians was lost. Napoleon then broke clean through the enemy. Blücher, who believed he was on the point of winning, was kept off by the French cavalry under Milhaud and Gerard. The aged Field-Marshal himself fell under his horse, and the French cavalry swept over him without knowing it. The Prussians lost 20,000 men, 40 guns, and 8 flags at Ligny. It was a complete victory; but it was nothing in comparison with what it might have been but for Count d'Erlon's misunderstanding, and if Ney had advanced at the proper time with the left wing.

After the battle Napoleon sent his adjutant Flahaut to Marshal Ney with orders to occupy Quatre-Bras at once and keep off Wellington until the Emperor could come up. In order to ward off Blücher and General Bülow while he finished the English, the Emperor sent Marshal Grouchy eastwards with a strong force of 50,000 men, and told him to watch the movements of the Prussian generals. This led to disaster. Blücher, who had found Bülow, gained so much time and marched so rapidly that he passed Grouchy to the north and hurried westwards to Waterloo, and reached the field in the afternoon.

The battle had begun at one o'clock, and the whole plan was based on the fact of Grouchy opposing the Germans with 50,000 men. In the afternoon the battle was as good as lost for the English. Ney had completely recovered on the field and performed marvels of bravery. At last he advanced on foot at the head of his battalions of the guard, together with Friant, Cambronne, and Duhesme.

But Grouchy was marching away from the field in a totally unintelligible fashion. He took no notice of the orders he received from Exelmans and Gerard, and ignored Napoleon's old general order to march always towards the thunder of the guns. And while he failed to come up in time to take part in the battle, Bülow did so, and Blücher shortly after him, and the battle was irretrievably lost to the French. The whole army was destroyed. Only a few stubborn fragments of the guard remained on the field, and were eventually saved by Morand and Colbert.

It is very striking to see how often In these two battles, Ligny and Waterloo, everything hung on a single thread. If Ney had made haste he might have caught Wellington at the ball at Brussels. If D'Erlon had not made a false move, the Prussians would have been surrounded at Ligny. Blücher might have been taken prisoner if anyone had recognized him; and Napoleon might have won the Battle of Waterloo if Grouchy had done his duty. All this means, of course, that the whole apparatus which had once worked so accurately and flawlessly, as well as the chief himself, were somewhat worn. His generals had lost their blind faith in his invincibility in Russia. It was now plain that this belief was the real cause of his invincibility.

In the indescribable confusion that followed the battle Napoleon rode alone and unrecognized in the stream of fugitives. After the battle the general staff, with the Duke of Bassano and the Emperor's secretaries, had lost sight of him. They looked for him for a long time, and at last heard that he had been seen riding on the road to Laon. They then hurried after him through the turmoil and the enemy's cavalry, which was at work everywhere. They happened to come across Napoleon's own horses, and took one each. Maret was so impregnated with reverence that they had the greatest difficulty in persuading him to mount one of the Emperor's own horses, although the Prussians were close on their heels. They found the Emperor in a frightful condition at Philippeville—in a wretched house, without carriage or anything.

His officers were covered with wounds and blood and dirt, and almost unrecognizable. Their eyes were swollen with weeping, and they were quite undone.

Luckily Marshal Soult's carriages came along, and the Emperor mounted one of them with Bertrand. In the next were Maret, Drouot, and a couple of generals, and in the third were the younger officers, Fleury, Labedoyère, Flahaut, and Corbineau. The officers spent the time in talking. Labedoyère thought the disaster would bring the whole of France together. Fleury was of opinion that the Chambers would fall on the Emperor as the man who had ruined the country. 'If they do,' said Labedoyère, 'we shall have the Allies at Paris again in a week, and then the Bourbons, and I shall be the first to be shot.'

Flahaut believed the Emperor was lost if he went to Paris. It was only at the head of an army that he would be able to treat with the Allies in favour of his son. 'But,' he added, 'perhaps most of our generals are at this moment making their submission to the king.' 'I agree with Flahaut that he is lost if he goes to Paris,' said Fleury. 'They will never forgive the Emperor for leaving the army four times—in Egypt, Spain, at Smorgoni, and now here in the middle of France.'

At Laon there were about 3,000 men with King Jerome, who behaved like a man now that the disaster had come. There were also Marshal Soult and Generals Morand, Colbert and Petit. It was the general feeling of the higher officers that the Emperor ought to go at once to Paris, and they made every effort to persuade him. He resisted them for a long time, and when he yielded at length to their pressure he said: 'Very good, I will go to Paris. But I am quite sure that you are inducing me to do something foolish.' General Bonaparte could never have spoken those words.

He left it to Marshal Soult, who took Berthier's place as head of the general staff, to collect and organize the remains of the army, and he began to dictate the bulletin on the Battle of Waterloo, which he submitted to his generals. He was just as candid in describing his defeat as he had been at Smorgoni in the 29th bulletin. Curiously enough, however, the generals could not induce him to say in the bulletin that all the imperial carriages had fallen into the hands of the enemy. They contained his clothes, his money, his papers, and a number of small private matters, as well as a very valuable diamond necklace that Pauline had given him to be used in emergency.

On his arrival at Paris the Emperor descended at the Elysée Palace, not the Tuileries, which he never again entered. If he had gone into the Chamber of Deputies just as he came from the field—as he had thought of doing—and had described in his irresistible language what great resources he still had, thanks to his vast preparations, it might have been possible to carry the assembly with him and obtain fresh sacrifices from the exhausted country. But his powerful frame had at length succumbed to the terrible fatigue. He had been in the saddle almost continuously from June 16th, and in great pain part of the time. He had fought two battles in three days, and had gone through the awful night after Waterloo. He was quite unfit to speak in a large assembly.

Meantime, Fouché contrived to set feeling against the Emperor in the Chamber. The Chamber of Peers followed suit, and Napoleon was forced to abdicate the crown a second time. He did so in favour of his son, Napoleon II. A provisional government was formed by Fouché, Carnot and General Grenier, and was to treat with the Allied princes, who now approached Paris for the second time.

On June 22 the Emperor asked for two frigates, which lay at Rochefort, to be put at his disposal, to take him and his family to America. He decided to wait at Malmaison for the answer to this request, as a large crowd of inquisitive folk had gradually formed round the Elysée Palace. If he had obtained the ships when he asked for them he would easily have escaped, as the English were not yet watching the coast. But Fouché, who was very anxious that one or the other Napoleon should be done away with, wasted time and made a great parade of getting the frigates ready; and at the same time wrote to Wellington for passes for Napoleon and his suite. It hardly needed so much as that to put England on the alert, and from that moment it was impossible to leave the French coast.

While the Emperor was at Malmaison, where he had spent a happy time as First Consul, Count Flahaut rode one day to Paris to ask for the passes they were to receive. In the Tuileries he met the Prince of Eckmühl. 'Your Bonaparte is taking his time,' said Davoust. 'Tell him from me that he had better make haste. If he does not start at once I shall have to have him arrested. I will come myself, in fact, and arrest him.'

'I did not expect to hear such language as that from a man who was at Napoleon's feet a week ago,' said Flahaut.

Davoust adopted a lofty tone, and wanted the adjutant arrested, but Flahaut fulfilled his mission. When he came back to Malmaison and told of his meeting with Davoust, the Emperor said resignedly: 'Let him come. I am ready to offer him my neck.'

The indecision and confusion amongst Napoleon's officers were now at their height. A large number of them had compromised themselves in the Hundred Days, and they all knew that the Bourbons would take serious measures with them on their return. Savary and many others went abroad. Masséna had gone over to the King at the first restoration, and Napoleon had failed to bring him back when he returned from Elba, The marshal was given command of the National Guard at Paris in succession to General Durosnel, the man who had saved his wife at Prince Schwartzenberg's ball.

During the Russian campaign the news reached Paris that General Durosnel had been killed. His wife put on deep mourning, and made the whole family do the same. But it was announced shortly afterwards that the general was only wounded, and she tore off her mourning. She told the servants to bring their black clothes into the courtyard, and they made a bonfire of them with great rejoicing.

Marshal Jourdan and General Rapp were with the army on the Rhine, and they retained their commands. Napoleon asked General Drouot, who had been with him in Elba, to follow him to America. But Drouot would not abandon his command of the Imperial Guard, fearing to expose them to the vengeance of the Bourbons. The Emperor then turned to Savary, the Duke of Rovigo, who promised to accompany him. Meantime the Allied armies were approaching, and the Prussians seemed to be advancing on Malmaison. The Emperor, therefore, took leave of Queen Hortense and the few faithful friends and servants who were still with him, and reached Rochefort with Savary and Bertrand on July 3rd.

On that very day Paris was surrendered to Field Marshal Blücher at St. Cloud, where he had fixed his headquarters. The French army was sent across the Loire to be disarmed. The *Moniteur* at the same time published a declaration from the King, in which he said: 'I hear that a gate is open to my kingdom, and I hasten to return by it.' It is a very different style from Napoleon's. The declaration, which had been prepared by Talleyrand, as chief of the ministry, also promised the royal pardon to all except those who had taken part in the revolt of the Hundred Days.

At Rochefort and on the west coast of France there was still a strong feeling in favour of the Emperor. General Clausel had a few ships ready at Bordeaux, but it was obviously impossible to elude the English, and Napoleon went of his own accord on board the English frigate *Bellerophon*, and said to Captain Maitland: 'I surrender to the generosity of the English nation.' In point of fact it was the best, if not the only, thing he could do. If he had been captured, his life might have been in some danger.

It is true that Napoleon cared little about life at the time, but it is an intolerable thing for an officer to be taken prisoner, disarmed, and perhaps shot by a file of soldiers. His relations to all the foreign princes were such that he would have found it a torture worse than death to see them again in his present position. They were the King of Prussia, whom he had pitilessly robbed and humiliated, the Emperor of Austria, his own father-in-law, whose armies he had fought for twenty years; and lastly, the Emperor Alexander, who had cynically duped him and brought about his downfall.

Of the English he was only acquainted with subjects of the King, They also were enemies, but he had no others to turn to. And he was quite right in trusting to the generosity of the English people. He was destined to be disappointed, but it was a disappointment for the whole world as well. People had then, and have still, a better opinion of the English; and I believe Great Britain's gentlemen are ashamed to this day of what was done. Exaggerated as some of the accounts are, it is certain that Napoleon was treated with a deliberate pettiness and made to suffer in the most tasteless manner. If there had been a single great man amongst his enemies he might have prevented them all from passing down to posterity with the disgrace of their vindictiveness.

Napoleon wrote a letter to the Prince Regent, the most powerful, dignified and noble of his enemies. But his letter met with a worse fate than any other of his autograph letters to sovereigns. Gourgaud, who took it, was not even allowed to land in England. The *Bellerophon* spent an interminable time cruising between the coasts of England and France, and at last the news came that Napoleon had to be taken to St. Helena. He and his companions were disarmed and searched. Diamonds, money, and objects of value were taken from them to be 'used in paying for their maintenance.' All letters to or from them were to be read by the governor.

Generals Bertrand, Montholon and Gourgaud, and the Lord of the Chamber, Las Cases, were allowed to accompany him. But Generals Savary and Lallemand, who had already been condemned to death by King Louis, had to leave the ship. On August 7th the Emperor and his suite were transferred to the frigate *Northumberland*, and on October 17th he was landed on the island of St. Helena.

CHAPTER 10

Finis

Napoleon was a changed man when he came from Elba, but the Allied princes also were very different beings when they entered Paris in triumph for the second time. They were full of confidence, and restored to high spirits after their recent anxiety. They had a cordial reception, as there was now much more ill-feeling against the Emperor. The *Tsar* took up his residence at Talleyrand's once more and received general homage. And when they had once more gone thoroughly through the collections at the Louvre and elsewhere, to make sure that there was not a single bit of canvas or marble left that the Emperor had brought to Paris, they departed for their various countries, and left the adipose Bourbon to restore peace and order in his rescued country, on which the *Cossacks* had again made their violent impression.

The German princes returned home chiefly with the intention of stifling as quickly as possible the rising of the people that had been so useful to them when their thrones were in danger, but which was of no further use to them now. They went back with the stupid and ungrateful determination to suppress or break the forces from below, which seemed to them to spell nothing but revolt and danger. All the light that the movement in young Germany would have spread over Europe, if the outbreak had been understood and appreciated, was now rigorously put out by the arch-extinguisher Metternich. Germany settled down again, in apparent content, in the semi-darkness. It is there still; and a colossal amount of beer has flowed in the meantime.

It is this reaction that I had chiefly intended to study. At first it was almost worse in France than in Germany. The arrogance and the stupidity of the Bourbons were boundless. What they did to Ney was not the worst. Ney had boasted of his iron cage, and it had been hard for the legitimate King to see how the majority of his magnates and the whole army had gone over to the hated enemy. They had to show some rigour, and make an example somewhere; and Ney's case seemed a very bad one. Several attempts were made, however, to prevent an execution that every Frenchman felt as a knife in his heart. The marshal was almost afforded an opportunity to escape. But he was completely dazed and incapable of decisive action. He would not move, and so he was arrested, to the general regret.

His legal defenders did all they could. The marshals refused to condemn him; some because they were his friends, some because they were his enemies. The Chamber of Peers had to intervene to pass the verdict, and he was condemned to death, as was to be expected. His wife begged in vain for a pardon. The King was inexorable. The mean, miserable being to whom France owed nothing thought fit, in virtue of his legitimate royal blood, to put to death the greatest soldier of the country. Ney was shot by twelve poor soldiers, who were commanded to do it.

When the marshal had dropped—it was in the garden of the Luxembourg Palace—an Englishman rode up at full gallop, leaped over the fallen hero, and disappeared. This was supposed to symbolize the triumph of the conquerors. It was as tasteless as everything that England did to Napoleon and his men. There was also a Russian general in full uniform on horseback amongst the spectators; but the Emperor Alexander drove him out of the army when he heard of it.

The brave Colonel Labedoyère also met his fate, as he had predicted in the carriage when they were flying from Waterloo. He was executed, to the general regret. Lavalette, who had taken over the Postal department, was arrested, and only escaped execution by his wife changing clothes with him in his cell, and sending him out disguised while she remained in his clothes. She was a cousin of the Empress Josephine.

The Bourbons inaugurated a reign of terror, known as the White Terror to distinguish it from that during the Revolution. Men were tried, transported, or executed, and there was no limit to the abasement of the army. The emigrants—the five thousand that Talleyrand had spoken of—swarmed like grubs, and heaped ridicule and scorn on Napoleon's armies and generals. The way in which the Bourbons maltreated the non-commissioned officers and the soldiers soon led the French troops to lose the fine form of the 'grand army.' And the deterioration was completed when Napoleon III brought in his rabble of *zouaves*, who even in the wars in Algiers made fun of the old uniforms of Bonaparte's time.

The Prussians, on the other hand, pursued the opposite tactics after Jena. When the armies faced each other again in 1870, the great Napoleon would certainly have led the Prussian army with far more satisfaction than his own old regiments, as they then were.

For the military nobility that Napoleon had founded the new rulers found some use, especially in view of the great wealth that many of these families had accumulated. Hence it is that many of Napoleon's great dignitaries came through the fire unscathed. In the first place, they had gone over to the Bourbons at the first restoration; then they returned to Napoleon in the Hundred Days; and then they came back to the King in 1815. A considerable number of them did this. Marshal Soult mounted the white cockade and became Minister of War under Louis XVIII, although he had been with Napoleon at Waterloo. He was a peer of France in 1827 and minister in 1830. He lived until his eighty-second year as Duke of Dalmatia, and left great wealth and a famous gallery of Spanish paintings that he had 'collected.'

It was much the same with Davoust. When he had returned half dead, like the others, from the Russian campaign, he reorganized the army in North Germany, blew up the old bridge at Dresden in 1813, and shut himself up in Hamburg. For ten months he had the unfortunate town in his power; its older inhabitants still shiver when his name is mentioned. It was not until May, 1814, that he would believe in Napoleon's fall and mount the white flag of the Bourbons.

The Prince of Eckmühl retired for a time to his large estates in France, but on March 21st, in spite of all that lay between them, he became the Emperor's Minister of War. The preparations he made for the war are famous. After Waterloo the King accepted his submission. He had married a sister of General Leclerc, Pauline's first husband; and his youngest daughter or granddaughter had a large lighthouse built in 1897 in the north of France, which she christened the Phare d'Eckmühl. Thus the peaceful name of a little German mill became the title of a great French leader, and shines out over the sea today in memory of him.

Marshal St. Cyr entered the ministry. Macdonald became Commander-in-Chief of the army. Mortier, who had blown up the *Kremlin* in 1812, was himself blown up in 1835 by the infernal machine that Fieschi set for Louis Philippe. The Count of Lobau, General Mouton, became one of Louis Philippe's marshals. He was a hard but able officer. Napoleon married him to a distinguished lady of the Bavarian

Court. She was in her twentieth year, and very charming; he was in his fortieth, and very ugly. He made a short speech to his officers on the occasion of his wedding. 'I desire, gentlemen, that you will look on my wife as a marble statue—a statue of *black* marble,' he said, with a stern glance at the young adjutants.

General Sébastiani was distantly related to the Bonapartes. He never abandoned Napoleon, yet he lived in high position at Paris until 1851, and became a marshal. Many of Napoleon's officers, who had worked their way up through the service, retained their wealth and founded families of which members are still found in the highest French aristocracy: such are Ney's descendants, the Prince of Moskwa and Duke of Elchingen, Lannes' family, and the Dukes of Montebello, Caulaincourt and Vicenza. Many other names, however, sank into poverty and disappeared. Some thought it lowering to go over to the royalists.

That was the case with Las Cases. After his return from St. Helena he was urged to accept a position at Court in consonance with his rank, but he refused. 'We have served the great lord of the earth,' he said. 'When he sent us to foreign courts we were treated as the equals of princes because we wore his uniform, and we felt ourselves to be their equals. We have seen seven kings waiting in his antechambers like ourselves.'

At the same time there were many men of a very different type about Napoleon; men who never came really close to him because they never wholly appreciated him, out of a feeling that they took to be pride. General Thiebault was one of this category. He was a brave man, but he would not push himself forward, and so he let every opportunity of advancement slip by. He therefore very soon joined Masséna and the other malcontents, and maintained a very foolish attitude toward the First Consul and his friends. His criticism was always directed against the men who rose, and he was one of the party of grumblers.

He says, for instance, that it was the younger General Kellermann who won the battle at Marengo; that it was not Rampon, but an unknown officer, who took the redoubt at Montenotte; that it was not Davoust who earned the honour of the Battle of Auerstädt, but his generals of divisions, Morand and Gudin; that Bonaparte's manoeuvres before the battle of Marengo were conducted on a plan that he, Thiebault, had sent some time before to the Ministry of War. In everything he betrays the jealous man's inability to appreciate. Otherwise he was courageous and brave and generous. He severely criticizes Bonaparte for not observing the quarantine regulations when he returned from Egypt. However, at another place in his memoirs he tells how when he and his comrades came half-starved out of Masséna's defence of Genoa, they threw the quarantine officials in the sea, made for Nice, and fell upon the available food, some of them eating for seven hours continuously.

The figure of Napoleon stands out amongst a crowd of men like these and a thousand others. Their devotion and their hatred, their discontent and their flattery, their loyalty and their treachery, cast light and shade alternately about him, but from his own unique superiority a light is ever cast over all of them, gives them their character, and guides their development with almost the same force with which he controlled their destinies and their external conditions. Although his ideal did not go beyond himself, his personality was so strong that the others felt they were fighting and suffering for a greater ideal. His judgment on those who fell was always a measure of the individual and his value.

After the Battle of Waterloo the whole of Europe breathed freely once more. The misery and devastation that the man had brought in great waves wherever he went had spread all over the Continent. And the farther men were from the centre, the less they saw of the glamour of war. They only felt an intolerable pressure and an uneasy dislocation of trade, commerce, shipping, and industry. In Great Britain, and along the coast of the North Sea as far as Hamburg and even Norway, it was difficult to follow Napoleon's career of victory with any kind of satisfaction. Everything was held up in consequence of the infatuated blockade of the Continent.

It was, directly, England who nearly exhausted the life of Norway, but it was France that was responsible. Between 1807 and 1811 the English took nineteen ships belonging to my great-grandfather. The fate of one of my great-uncles was also caught in the meshes of the Napoleonic net; he was appointed head chamberlain to Bernadotte, when he became king. He found so much favour with the king that he was included amongst the envoys sent to attend the coronation of Nicolas I in 1826. At St. Petersburg he visited General Jomini, who had taken part in the deliberations as to the crossing of the Beresina.

He abandoned Napoleon in 1813, and went over to the enemy. My uncle found him adjutant-general to the *Tsar*, and thought him a man 'of striking features, but crafty.' At Moscow he often attended great festivals given by Marshal Marmont, Duke of Ragusa, who was the French ambassador. I should have liked something better than to find my great-uncle dispatched as envoy by one traitor, visiting a second and dancing at the house of a third. However, these are political features of his mission that deserved some mention.

The embassy consisted of the old Field-Marshal, Count von Stedingk, and one or two other counts on the part of Sweden, and only Major Jens Bull Kielland on the part of Norway. It is interesting to see how careful Sweden was from the very beginning of the union to give expression to the equal dignity of the two realms, especially when there was question of representation abroad. On the Norwegian coast there was always a good deal of feeling for England, our big brother in the North Sea, in spite of all the hostilities and the injury done to us by the arrogant English naval officers. I do not remember ever to have seen a picture of Napoleon in the old houses in my earliest years, or heard a song about him, or any mention of his name. He does not seem to have occupied the place that we should expect in the literature and the correspondence of the time in Norway.

Napoleon's attitude to women was somewhat similar to his attitude towards men in this respect: he took everything that *was* offered him, and nearly everything was offered him. In many other respects he was a considerate and almost affectionate husband. His feeling for Josephine was maintained long after the divorce. One day her accounts were not in order, as usual; she never managed to live within the generous allowance he made her. 'Go to Josephine,' he said sharply to a minister, 'and tell her that this sort of thing must stop. She must give up this folly.' The minister went, and returned the next day.

'Well, what does she say?' Napoleon asked.

'Oh, your Majesty, the Empress wept and——'

'What,' cried Napoleon, 'she wept? It was certainly not my intention that you should make Josephine weep. Go back to her at once and say that we will put her money-matters right—she must shed no tears. Say the Emperor has commanded that she must not.'

Josephine herself had a few straight lines in her not over-straight character. She had been the friend of the great man, and she never forgot it. At the time when the whole of Paris forgot the ruling Empress and the heir to the throne, during Malet's brief revolt in 1812, Josephine said:

If there had been any real danger for the Empress and for Napoleon's son, I should have gone to her and taken my place beside her, no matter what people said. Hortense would have done the same.

Marie Louise was made of very different stuff. She never cherished the memory of having been the wife of the great man. She said as early as 1815: 'Lord Wellington does not know how much he did for me when he won the battle of Waterloo.' Wellington did know, however. He has himself said:

It is a fact that she was already expecting a child by the Austrian Baron Neippberg, whom she afterwards married. If Napoleon had won at Waterloo, the Empress would have been compelled to return to him in that condition.

When he did not care to be amiable Napoleon could be terrible in regard to ladies. We can readily believe that it was a genuine pleasure to him to reply to Mme. de Staël, when she asked him what kind of woman he thought most of: 'The one who brings most children into the world.' He knew well how rude he was, but this fishing for compliments was too much for him. At the same time he spoke the truth. He did not like intellectual women. Nor had he much more esteem for virtuous ones.

He could not endure Queen Louisa of Prussia, though she was very beautiful. When, in her great sorrow at the misfortunes of her country she went so far as to give the conqueror a rose with the words, 'This rose for Magdeburg,' Napoleon coldly ignored the opportunity of being gallant to a noble lady. He took the rose and kept Magdeburg. It was no wonder that he was called a 'a lout' in all the courts of Europe.

The truth was he never allowed himself to be overruled by a woman. Josephine might succeed in influencing him in small matters or persuading him to do something that was not quite right, but that went to the account of friendship rather than love. The success of Countess Hatzfeldt in obtaining forgiveness for her husband at Berlin in 1807, and the Mmes. Polignac for their husbands after the Cadoudal conspiracy, had nothing to do with the sex of the petitioners. No one ever knew him to be drawn into a bad deed or a political crime for the sake of a woman. However strong his amorous passion became, Napoleon never had about him the scandalous troop of mistresses that is so often found about the courts of kings, beginning with King David, whom we were compelled to admire when we were young.

Religion and the clergy were equally powerless to influence him.

There was never any element of mysticism about Napoleon Bonaparte. He did not spend his youth in morbid dreams about the mystery of his future. He knew very well who he was. He was a great man, a man to whom greatness came naturally; not in the same way as other pretenders to the crown, who go about talking of kingly ideas and saying they feel the presence of royal blood in their veins. Napoleon's ambition was healthy and strong. He knew nothing of supernatural powers. He trusted to no help beyond himself, but relied on his own genius and the defects of others.

Some have represented him as having a superstition about certain days, and pretended that he believed he had a star. Napoleon knew what power there is in remembrance, especially for soldiers. As he knew well the art of concentrating his force on a given point at a given moment in a battle, he kept fresh the memory of the days of victory; and this intensified the courage and zeal of his soldiers, so that he had only to mention a number of dates and names to set the whole army aflame. In that sense he used to choose certain days, but there was no superstition in it. It was the same in regard to his star.

One night at the Tuileries Cardinal Fesch had said a good deal in a moderate tone of all that had been done. He spoke of the arch that is strained, the vessel that goes so often to the water, and so on. Napoleon listened attentively to him, and when the cardinal had finished, he led him to one of the high windows, and pointed to the clouded sky above.

'Do you see the star up there, uncle?' he asked.

The cardinal looked and looked. 'No;' he could see no star.

'Well, I see it,' said Napoleon seriously, and walked away.

Was there a star? No one can say; but it is at all events certain that prudent cardinals never see it. There was no superstition in the matter.

To be quite candid, I have never understood the affair of the Concordat and the whole of his relations to the papacy and the Church. I can only see that, though Napoleon had to deal with a pope who was an honourable and noble man, yet there was not the slightest fear of the clergy—or any hypocrisy—in himself or any of those about him. His proclamations and pronouncements never spoke of anything but France, honour, and himself; and in this he was quite right. He had great princes of the Church in all their pomp at his gorgeous church ceremonies, but otherwise he had no use for the apparatus of religion.

Money he treated with cold indifference. He never suffered cheating, and could never be imposed on by the big financiers. If he thought any one had accumulated too much, he did not hesitate to tap him to the extent of several millions. The kind of thing that we have seen so often—kings mixing with speculators and becoming so dependent on them that it is doubtful whether the country is really ruled by the men with golden crowns on their heads or the men with silver crowns in their banks—was inconceivable in relation to Napoleon.

He was moderate in eating and drinking. He could not unbend over a glass with his higher officials, as some kings do; and, on the other hand, he could not stoop to the potations and the senseless abuse of power that so many kings have been guilty of since the days of Alexander the Great.

He knew very little about the fine arts. He liked order, splendour and symmetry, and so he was best disposed to architecture and decoration. His taste in regard to paintings was poor, and he failed to appreciate the advance made in his time. In literature he liked best a well-arranged drama, with great, simple passions described in verses that hung solidly together like his own soldiers. In musical matters he was hardly any better than the usual French officer. Beautiful singing was the highest musical achievement in his esteem. The Italian *aria* with the most difficult trills and cadences sent him into raptures. He would hardly have been pleased with more elaborate music, in which pure melody is expressed in its finest shades by the voice and the harmony of voice and instrument. From head to heel he was full of admiration of C major. There was no sharp for him and no b flat, and the minor key was far out of his range.

It is needless to point out the vast difference between Napoleon and the great religious founders who had also caused great movements in their respective ages. In their case the movement increased, and only became a veritable power after their death. When Napoleon died, the Napoleonic movement was over. He had had no idea to give to the world. His thoughts did not go beyond his own life; throughout his whole career he never thought of anything but himself. He shrinks at once in comparison with a modest man of science who expends his life to create a thought that will nourish and elevate posterity. But amongst his kind—amongst those in whose circle his great gifts fated him to penetrate, namely, the princes—the Emperor Napoleon stands out high above all. He, if any man, was the ideal 'tyrant,' in the old sense of the word.

Napoleon had to play with the figures that were on the stage, and he did not succeed. In his mind peace could only mean a pause between two wars. The idea that peace could be the normal relation of the nations never entered his head, or the head of any man about him. If there were any head that harboured such an idea, it was on the shoulders of some unknown man in some obscure attic, writing of his Utopia in the dim light.

If Napoleon reached the highest summit as a prince and a commander, he was also the last who succeeded in gathering about his person all the glamour that had been wont to accompany and adorn the bloody business of war. There was no more of it after his fall. War became afterwards an academic study. Military affairs came to resemble industrial interests, in which it is the best machines that gain the victory. We now strip our armies of their gold cords and waving plumes. The admiral, who used to stand on the bridge in his gala uniform, with his decorations and sash, now sits in a steel box and presses buttons like a telephone girl. When the glamour goes from a thing, it is near its end. It is possible that one day the glittering form of Napoleon in the remote past will be contemplated with equanimity by the idealists he so much despised; on that day when we shall have won the greatest of all victories—peace between nations.

All the languages of the world have used their strongest adjectives at the top and the bottom of the scale in regard to this man. Many writers have even speculated as to what a remarkable animal the tiger would have been—if he had also had the qualities of the lamb. Nothing is perfect this side of eternity. Neither in the kitchen nor in life do we get perfection by taking a little bit of everything, and putting it all in one pot. Perfection is only found in a thing that has all that pertains to it, and not a trace of anything else. For my part I am glad that I need not run my adjectives, either the worst or the best, to death. For me. Napoleon is above all things a man—a male through and through, a being compounded solely of masculine qualities.

The social circle at Longwood, the Emperor's residence at St. Helena, lived for six years with the great man as its centre. There was General Montholon with his wife and family. His wife presided over the domestic establishment. General Bertrand and his family lived at a short distance from Longwood. Then there were: Las Cases with his young son. General Gourgaud, the Irish physician O'Meara, and a number of faithful servants. These few men, who all depended on the person of the Emperor in one or other way, were strangers to each other. During the long and painful solitude—as great as if they were on a ship at the North Pole—they often distressed the Emperor by their petty quarrels and jealousies, the remains of their earlier ambitions. There was very nearly a duel between Generals Montholon and Gourgaud.

The bitterness was increased, and the Emperor's last years were made more painful by the pettiness and refined malice with which the English treated him. The sort of life that was led about Napoleon would have proved intolerable if he had not himself arranged their daily doings and work with his characteristic good sense. Each one had his place and his regulations, just as at a court; and this pitiful discipline, which was maintained to the end, never took on any tincture of absurdity. The Emperor was just as aloof from them as he had been at the Tuileries, but the irresistible magic that always surrounded him delivered them from the tediousness that would otherwise have killed them.

The Emperor arranged the daily round for himself and the others with fixed hours for work. He dictated an account of his campaigns to the generals, the Italian to one and the German to the other. At night the little circle sat together in conversation, and listened to the sea breaking hopelessly on the island. The Emperor walked to and fro, or sat down to tell of some old experience or talk of his men. But his maladies gradually got the upper hand, and his iron frame slowly yielded. He saw the end draw near with his wonted calmness. He was ill during the whole of 1820. In 1821 he became rapidly worse.

On April 21st, he wrote his will; no one, from his son to his servants, was forgotten in it.

I should like my ashes to rest by the Seine, in the midst of the French people whom I loved so much.

It was one of the few wishes of his that were fulfilled. I fear little care was taken in the distribution of the millions of *francs* that made up his private fortune. That does not detract from the man; his intention was good.

I leave to my son my decorations, snuff-boxes, silver, etc; and my arms, saddles, spurs, uniforms, and clothes, the grey coat and the blue cloak of Marengo. I give Count Montholon two million *francs*, for accompanying me here.

There was a small remembrance of his mother and all his sisters. They had at the bottom been strongly bound together. He even spoke in fine terms of Marie Louise; although the English had assuredly not spared him an account of the way she was behaving.

On May 2nd, in the delirium of high fever, he called out the names of the generals of his youth:

'Steingel, Desaix, Masséna!' He saw the sun of Italy flashing on the bayonets. On May 4th there was a great storm on the island, and it tore up the last tree at Longwood. The Emperor lay still while the storm raged without. But as long as there was a spark of life in him, they heard him muttering words of command.

Years afterwards, until 1838, when the curtain had long since dropped and the darkness; had settled over Europe once more, Talleyrand dragged his lame foot to the green tables, and sat amongst the clinking piles of gold, and played with other gold-seekers, new and old.

LEONAUR

ALSO FROM LEONAUR
AVAILABLE IN SOFTCOVER OR HARDCOVER WITH DUST JACKET

THE 9TH—THE KING'S (LIVERPOOL REGIMENT) IN THE GREAT WAR 1914 - 1918 *by Enos H. G. Roberts*—Mersey to mud—war and Liverpool men.

THE GAMBARDIER *by Mark Severn*—The experiences of a battery of Heavy artillery on the Western Front during the First World War.

FROM MESSINES TO THIRD YPRES *by Thomas Floyd*—A personal account of the First World War on the Western front by a 2/5th Lancashire Fusilier.

THE IRISH GUARDS IN THE GREAT WAR - VOLUME 1 *by Rudyard Kipling*—Edited and Compiled from Their Diaries and Papers—The First Battalion.

THE IRISH GUARDS IN THE GREAT WAR - VOLUME 1 *by Rudyard Kipling*—Edited and Compiled from Their Diaries and Papers—The Second Battalion.

ARMOURED CARS IN EDEN *by K. Roosevelt*—An American President's son serving in Rolls Royce armoured cars with the British in Mesopatamia & with the American Artillery in France during the First World War.

CHASSEUR OF 1914 *by Marcel Dupont*—Experiences of the twilight of the French Light Cavalry by a young officer during the early battles of the great war in Europe.

TROOP HORSE & TRENCH *by R.A. Lloyd*—The experiences of a British Lifeguardsman of the household cavalry fighting on the western front during the First World War 1914-18.

THE EAST AFRICAN MOUNTED RIFLES *by C.J. Wilson*—Experiences of the campaign in the East African bush during the First World War.

THE LONG PATROL *by George Berrie*—A Novel of Light Horsemen from Gallipoli to the Palestine campaign of the First World War.

THE FIGHTING CAMELIERS *by Frank Reid*—The exploits of the Imperial Camel Corps in the desert and Palestine campaigns of the First World War.

STEEL CHARIOTS IN THE DESERT *by S. C. Rolls*—The first world war experiences of a Rolls Royce armoured car driver with the Duke of Westminster in Libya and in Arabia with T.E. Lawrence.

WITH THE IMPERIAL CAMEL CORPS IN THE GREAT WAR *by Geoffrey Inchbald*—The story of a serving officer with the British 2nd battalion against the Senussi and during the Palestine campaign.

www.ingramcontent.com/pod-product-compliance
Lightning Source LLC
Chambersburg PA
CBHW032056080426
42733CB00006B/300